739.27 Y

6-12
BD

Gemstone Settings

Gemstone Settings

THE JEWELRY MAKER'S GUIDE TO STYLES & TECHNIQUES

ANASTASIA YOUNG

INTERWEAVE.
interweave.com

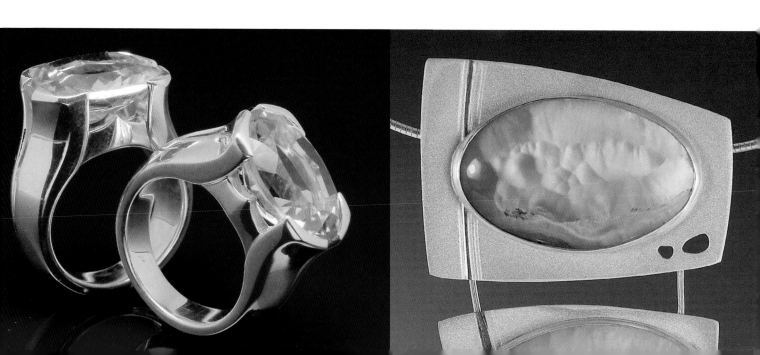

A QUARTO BOOK

interweavestore.com

Copyright © 2012 Quarto Inc.

Published in North America by

Interweave Press LLC
201 East Fourth Street
Loveland, CO 80537-5655
www.interweave.com
All rights reserved.

Conceived, designed, and produced by
Quarto Publishing plc
The Old Brewery
6 Blundell Street
London N7 9BH

QUAR.SGS

ISBN: 978-1-59668-636-6

Senior Editor: Ruth Patrick
Art Editor: Jacqueline Palmer
Designer: Julie Francis
Art Director: Caroline Guest
Copy Editors: Lindsay Kaubi and Ruth Patrick
Proofreader: Liz Jones
Indexer: Helen Snaith
Photographer: Phil Wilkins
Illustrator: John Woodcock
Picture Researcher: Sarah Bell
Creative Director: Moira Clinch
Publisher: Paul Carslake

Color separation in Singapore by Pica Digital
Pte Ltd
Printed in Singapore by Star Standard Industries
(PTE) Ltd

Library of Congress Cataloging-in-Publication Data
not available at time of printing.

10 9 8 7 6 5 4 3 2 1

Contents

Foreword

It must be something of a cliché to start a book of this nature with "I have enjoyed making things since I was a child," however true—and it is. I ended up as a jeweler as the result of serendipity rather than any kind of planning, having abandoned studies in science before deciding to go to art college. It was a fascination with the miniature and a desire to know how to make things from scratch, particularly in metal, that made jewelry rather than any other art form most appealing, as well as being able to wear what I had made.

I am still fascinated by the processes involved in making jewelry, and always eager to learn more—either from the long history of metalwork or more recent technological developments, although I tend not to use the latter much in my own work. The challenge of designing a piece of jewelry and then figuring out how to make it is like no other, and engages both analytical and imaginative mental processes. I prefer to make by hand, and do my own stone setting and engraving because it gives me complete control over the outcome of a piece and the sequence of its construction. I started to include gemstones within my work as soon as I was able, and must admit a particular fondness for garnets.

So, I approach this book from the perspective of a contemporary artist-jeweler, rather than an apprentice-trained craftsperson who has specialized in a particular aspect of mounting or setting stones. This means that for some techniques that are perhaps a bit more mired in "tradition," I have applied a more experimental approach. I strongly believe in a good craft skills-base, even if this is eventually rejected. My appreciation of an object or piece of jewelry is weighed against not just how it looks or functions, but also how it was made—I believe that

sensitivity to materials, attention to detail, and some kind of technical ingenuity are what makes a piece of jewelry special. I hope that this book encourages you to try new approaches, to push your personal boundaries, and to embellish your jewelry with gemstones in a way that is both meaningful and considered.

I have included techniques and methods which I think will be most useful to students, aspiring early-career jewelers, and practicing professionals, and hope that as well as providing useful information on as many stone-setting techniques as I could think of, this book serves as an overview of current contemporary practice, which is why the sections on computer-aided design and manufacture have been included. The importance of technology in designing and manufacturing jewelry cannot be ignored, and while many designer-makers choose to stick to traditional bench skills, it should not be denied that CAD/CAM has its place alongside them, allowing much time to be saved in the manner of any mechanized process, as well as offering design solutions that would not otherwise be possible.

For many, the future lies in CAD/CAM, and therefore design innovations will become the currency. As technology improves, can be provided at a lower cost, and is more accessible, the distinctions between pieces will be fought out through design more than quality of production. It is not that the physical piece and its quality becomes less important, but that the ways in which it is judged will change. There are some artist jewelers who have already embraced the technology, and many who never will, but thankfully this will only help to maintain the diversity of jewelry as an art form.

Anastasia Young

CHAIN DENTATA
This handmade chain by Anastasia Young is set with rose-cut and cabochon garnets in scalloped open-backed bezels, and porcelain crowns, which are rub-over set on one side and secured by a prong on the other.

About this Book

The book is organized into four chapters covering all you need to know about gemstones and settings, introduced by a section on the jewelry design process.

Chapter 1: Introduction to Design (pages 10–29)

The first chapter explores the jewelry design process, beginning with a section on historical and contemporary gem-set jewelry. It examines gem cutting before discussing methods of getting inspiration for a piece and working up a design through research, sketches, and prototypes. Some pieces of jewelry are designed around a particular stone so this process is detailed, before a section on commissioning—with an example of an actual commission. There is also a look at outsourcing complicated or specialist processes.

Chapter 2: Gemstone Directory (pages 30–51)

The Gemstone Directory is a comprehensive listing of the most popular precious and semiprecious gemstones, and organic and man-made gems, ordered in terms of value with the most expensive appearing first within each category. Information is given on the properties, availability, qualities, treatments, and care of each, so you can make an informed decision when selecting a stone for a piece.

Detailed descriptions of each stone

Beautiful photographs of a wide selection of examples of each stone

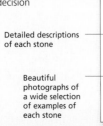

Chapter 3: Techniques Directory (pages 52–189)

This chapter begins with a section on health and safety and a comprehensive tools listing, before moving into the stone-setting techniques. Traditional, contemporary, popular, and more unusual styles are featured, organized in terms of difficulty, each with a description of the setting accompanied by a clear step-by-step guide to the process, photography, and diagrams.

Each grouping of techniques is introduced by a gallery of finished examples, demonstrating the variety of design that can be achieved within each category of setting.

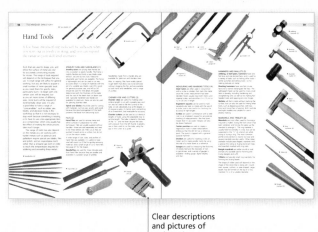

Clear descriptions and pictures of each tool

Each technique is accompanied by one or two inspirational finished pieces by jewelers from around the world.

SKILL LEVEL

Each technique is accompanied by a skill level symbol indicating the level of difficulty.

Basic

Intermediate

Advanced

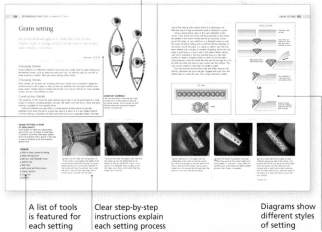

A list of tools is featured for each setting

Clear step-by-step instructions explain each setting process

Diagrams show different styles of setting

Chapter 4: Reference (pages 190–206)

This chapter contains essential measurement conversions, stone hardnesses and weights, and ring size charts; stone cut and settings diagrams; and glossary, suppliers, and gallery listings that you will refer to time and again.

Templates for settings that can be adjusted to fit the gemstone

Comprehensive glossary defining key terms used in the book

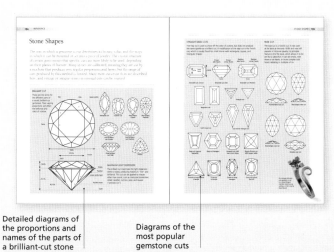

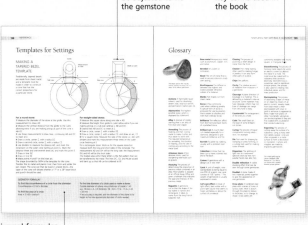

Detailed diagrams of the proportions and names of the parts of a brilliant-cut stone

Diagrams of the most popular gemstone cuts

Universal formulas for calculating measurements of a setting

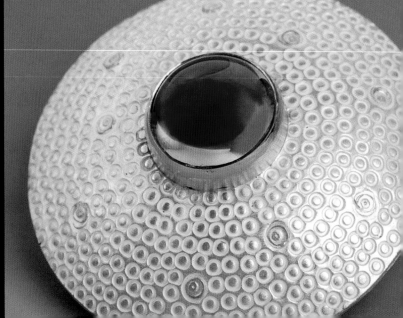

Whatever your approach to making jewelry, some decisions about design will enter the process—whether it's deciding which materials to use, refining the function of a stone setting, or choosing which shape or color of gem will work best in a piece. Learning how to interpret information in a useful way is a very personal process, but it does eventually provide a store of visual and technical stimuli that can be drawn on for a lifetime.

CHAPTER 1
Introduction to Design

History of Gem-set Jewelry

Gemstones have been used in jewelry for thousands of years and have played a vital role not just in the history of body adornment, but also trade, social status, and notions of value. To this day, gemstones have a powerful allure that cannot be explained by their beauty alone—there is a deep cultural significance resonating still.

Gemstones are deeply woven into the fabric of human culture, endowed with magical powers because of their pure colors, internal light, resilience, and scarcity. In practically every world civilization, gemstones permeate myths and religions, specifically ideas of heaven and paradise. The otherworldliness of these mysterious objects led to beliefs that they hold healing, protective, and restorative properties. Historically, jewelry and the gems set in it were also an important and easily recognizable signifier of status within society.

Geographical Factors

The history of gemstones used in jewelry is long and fascinating and is influenced not only by design and technology, but also by which stones could be found in a particular location and when they became part of the global trade—and therefore, often fashionable. The abundance of particular stones has also had an effect on their popularity, with a sizable resource needed to spark demand. Many mines historically renowned for particular stones are exhausted, but more recent developments in treatment technology allow the colors of less desirable stones to be altered to match the accepted ideal. Tastes for particular shades of stones have changed over time—in the nineteenth and early twentieth centuries, sea-green aquamarine was the most popular, but now sky and dark blue are the most desirable.

Although pearls have been used in jewelry and precious objects for many centuries, overfishing eventually led to a decline in the sources of both salt and freshwater natural pearls, and it wasn't until the early twentieth century that a reliable method of creating cultured pearls was developed by Japanese pearl jewelry house Mikimoto. Cultured pearls have sustained the supply of pearls for jewelry, while natural pearls are still rare and therefore expensive.

ROMAN INTAGLIO
A Roman intaglio in carnelian, depicting two figures, dating from 200–50 BC. Stone carving and engraving can be traced back to ancient Greece; the scenes are often figurative and have narrative or symbolic meaning with the intaglios often used in devotional objects. The mount for this ring is nineteenth-century but sympathetic to the stone, in keeping with the fashion of the time for the "archaeological" style, because it copies a Roman bezel setting.

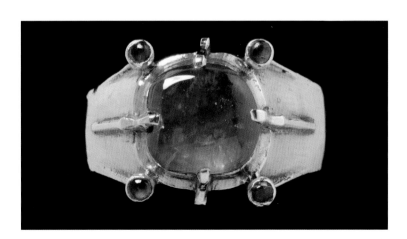

MEDIEVAL RING
An English medieval gold and sapphire ring, c. 1250–1300. The small purple sapphires are tube set and the large, irregular blue sapphire, although supported by a short bezel, is held by four prongs. The prongs have been elegantly shaped and partly extend around the ring shank; the geometric arrangement is reminiscent of architectural features of the time.

REGARD RING

In sentimental jewelry, stones are often chosen for their symbolic meaning. This acrostic ring from c.1810 uses the first letter of each stone to spell out "regard" with the paste equivalents of ruby, emerald, garnet, and diamond. The use of designs made from locks of hair held under bezel-set rock crystal was also popular in nineteenth-century sentimental jewelry, often combined with seed pearls and enamel.

IRON WIRE NECKLACE

The Art Nouveau and Arts and Crafts movements at the turn of the nineteenth century saw a renewed enthusiasm for cabochon-cut stones; the exploration of materials characterized by jewelry of these styles included the use of semiprecious stones combined with horn, steel, and vitreous enamel. This iron wire necklace (c. 1890–1910) by Albert Gilbert, known more for his sculpture, is experimental in its use of glass and ferrous metal, but is nonetheless typical of the fluid lines used in Art Nouveau jewelry.

Development of Stone Settings

Styles of setting developed alongside the means to cut and polish the stones in new and interesting ways, as well as the use of synthetics—from ancient Egyptian faience that imitated turquoise, to eighteenth-century "paste," or cut lead crystal, which imitated faceted precious stones. These developments allowed stone-set jewelry to become more available to those who were not part of the nobility, religious establishment, or royalty.

The rose cut started being widely used in jewelry from around 1600—previously, most cuts were beads, cabochons, and flat slabs that were either used for inlay in metal recesses or carved as intaglio or cameo designs, and polished uncut crystals such as diamonds. Rose cuts, slabs, and intaglios were most commonly held in bezels, but examples of prong- and grain-set stones in historical jewelry can be found. One notable style of setting is the sixteenth-century quatrefoil bezel, having four sides that may extend up to modified prongs, and is perfect for holding octahedral diamond crystals or table-cut stones.

The availability of paste stones in the eighteenth century gave rise to large, bold Rococo jewels such as bodice ornaments; the fashion was for naturalism and many examples of jewel-encrusted floral bouquets exist. Prong setting was used for these pieces to set the brittle imitation gems.

Technology and the Jewelry Industry

The effects that changes and improvements in technology had on both cut stones and the ways in which they were incorporated into jewelry have had significant impact on the industry—cutting wheels were not used until the late 1400s, allowing diamonds to be cut with a rounded outline, and it wasn't until the end of the seventeenth century that the "old cut"—a forerunner to the modern brilliant cut—was developed.

Industrialization had its effect on the nineteenth-century jewelry industry, with smaller jewelry workshops giving way to larger mechanized operations, as well as the gold rushes in America and Australia that led many European goldsmiths to resettle.

The means to work platinum was not effectively developed until the early twentieth century—until then diamond-set yellow gold jewelry was often fronted with silver to give the stones a reflective white-metal ground. Diamond-set platinum or high-karat gold jewelry is now part of the standard vocabulary of commercial jewelry, and often used in high-end designer pieces, too. The twenty-first century has seen an increase in the range of metals used for jewelry making, with palladium now having its own assay mark.

The significance of gemstones as indicators of status and wealth has not diminished over time, nor has the demand for valuable gem-set jewelry.

Contemporary Gem-set Jewelry

It is difficult to offer one coherent picture of contemporary stone-set jewelry because it is so varied. Traditions remain—the diamond engagement ring is still a staple of the jewelry industry. And yet there are vibrant art- and studio-jewelry contingencies pushing farther forward from the studio jewelers of the late-twentieth century, continuing to challenge notions of form, function, and the ways in which materials can be used.

Designer-makers

The area in which a jeweler works has a major influence on the materials and processes that are used. Designer-makers, as the name suggests, take responsibility for the design and manufacture of their jewelry, and many produce work that supplies galleries and craft or design fairs. The work will range from the very accessible, both in terms of price and wearability, to expensive fine jewelry aimed at a much smaller market. Many designer-makers will make several types of work, from one-offs and exhibition pieces to small batch production, as well as taking on private commissions.

Designer-makers can also be described as studio jewelers, and although there is some overlap into the area of art jewelry, artist jewelers have a less commercially minded approach to their work, which tends to be design or concept led.

Unusual and nonprecious materials are often used, sometimes combined with precious metals or stones in experimental ways. Each artist-jeweler lends a uniquely distinctive voice to their work.

Luxury Brands

Independent luxury brands range in size from independent "bespoke" jewelers who use outworkers to manufacture their designs, to companies that may have one or more retail premises—design and production is often the result of a highly skilled in-house team, with some skills outsourced when necessary. This jewelry is very often stone set, with a signature style reinforced by the use of particular types of stones.

GLUE RING
Philip Sajet cuts his own stones, which allows a certain symbiosis between metal and stone in his work because both elements are designed and made with each other in mind. This ring displays a classic role reversal with the shank cut from rock crystal and the "stone" made in gold; the two parts are joined with adhesive.

ECLECTIC NECKLACE
Characteristic of Dauvit Alexander's work, this piece, entitled "Are You Washed in the Blood?" contains many types and cuts of stones in many styles of settings. The piece was fabricated from constructed elements and combined with found objects; garnets and blue topaz are set upside down in a modified channel around the crown, quartz brilliants punctuate the handmade chain, and a ruby briolette dangles from the press-formed steel heart.

Fashion Jewelry

The scope of fashion jewelry runs from very commercial mass-market pieces, through costume jewelry, to runway pieces. Inexpensive or synthetic gems are most commonly used for this type of jewelry, in combination with plated metal mounts and other materials such as leather, plastics, or textiles.

Large-scale and flamboyant runway jewelry needs to be reasonably lightweight and bold so that it stands out from a distance. Fashion and jewelry designers will collaborate closely when designing pieces for a collection so that the pieces complement each other; sometimes the line between the clothes and the jewelry is indistinct, with the jewelry being an integral part or extension of the clothes.

Commercial jewelry is often mass produced, with economies of scale allowing for lower sale prices. The design of these pieces closely follows seasonal fashion trends, which will dictate not only style and form, but also colors, textures, and how the pieces may be worn.

Featured Contemporary Jewelry

The images used throughout this book to illustrate techniques and ideas reflect the diversity of creators across the professional field of designing and making jewelry. The range of influences is as broad in jewelry as in any other art form, and comes from culture, experiences, and aspirations.

Some of the forms the jewelry in this book takes will be recognizable: for example, a large stone surrounded by many smaller ones, or a single stone carefully displayed as the dominant focus of the piece. There will also be many forms that are not familiar, which do not reference historical sources and instead create unexpected juxtapositions of form, color, or theme through a range of skilled techniques.

DOUBLE SPHERE BAROQUE RING
This multifunctional piece by Elizaveta Gnatchenko is formed of two spheres; the outer is attached to the inner by means of screws that can be undone to release the inner ring. The outer shell can be worn as a pendant, and both pieces are richly studded with diamonds. The overall impression of the piece is decorative, but it is a functional ornamentalism—the structure of the pieces themselves consist only of decorative elements, expertly executed in rhodium and rose-gold-plated silver and platinum.

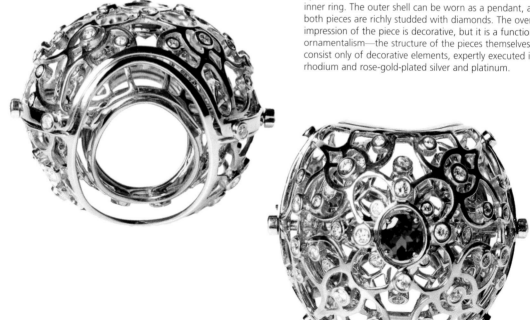

Gem Cutting

To bring a gemstone to its full potential, and to maximize its color, shape, internal light, optical effects, or patterns, it needs to be cut or carved. While many stones are rightly left to the professionals, it is not difficult to carve softer material successfully.

Cutting Softer Gems

You can carve gemstones of 7 or 8 on Moh's scale of hardness and below easily enough by hand, although a large amount of patience is required. The softer the stone, the more quickly you can carve it, but factors such as crystalline structure, porosity, and cleavage can affect the outcome. Jade, agate, and chalcedony are ideal because they have a tightly knit granular structure. Crystalline stones can be more problematic, so choose a stone that is tough, free of internal stresses, and easy to polish, such as heliodor (beryl). When cutting or carving stones with inclusions, try to place them to the best advantage within the design of the stone; this may mean removing a greater amount of material, but will result in a more attractive outcome.

The main obstacle for those without the proper equipment is cutting up rough material into manageable pieces. You can do this with diamond burrs if that is all that is available, but this will take some time. Commercially, diamond-edged rotary saws or lasers are used.

Carving Tips

When carving, it is important to keep the tools and the stone wet. This not only prevents the very fine dust from being released into the air, which is incredibly bad to breathe in, but also lubricates the cutting tool and stops it from getting blunt as quickly. Lubricating the tool also prevents a build-up of heat that could cause sensitive stones or those with inclusions to crack.

Carving a stone follows the same basic rules as carving a form in wax (see page 78)—although obviously it is a much harder material, the steps for creating a form accurately and to a design are very similar. Mark out the outline of the desired shape directly on the stone using pencil or permanent marker pen, and carve the piece with a rough diamond grit pad until the edge matches the line. Then mark the depth of the stone, and carve to that—for a cabochon, the edges will be reduced so that the top forms a domed shape, whatever the profile of the shape. Mount small stones on a wooden stick with adhesive or wax that is heated to receive the stone; this makes

CARVED PENDANT
The surface of this sinuous pendant by Gwyneth Harris has been carved to evoke the texture of snakeskin. The red tourmaline form is suspended on a rose gold chain.

▲ Concave facets cover this emerald-cut "Swiss" blue topaz, creating interesting reflections through the stone.

▲ Fancy-cut aquamarine of 3.25 ct. The greenish tint of this stone indicates it may not have been heat-treated.

▲ This deep reddish-brown garnet has been cut into an unusual star shape.

▲ A very large table on this triangular-shaped white topaz shows off its interesting inclusions.

▲ This cut of this hexagonal amethyst creates interesting linear reflections in the stone.

▲ The flat back on this deep purplish rose-cut garnet means it can be set as if it were a cabochon.

handling and rotating the stone during the carving process much easier.

Once the basic shape has been achieved, move onto a finer Diagrit pad to refine the surface of the stone. Simple shapes can be cleaned up reasonably easily, but you must take time to carefully remove scratches with each successively fine grade of abrasive used. Do the final stages with very fine wet-and-dry paper used with water—work through grades 1200, 1500, 2000, and 2500. This will make polishing the piece much quicker. Rub a felt or suede buffstick with cerium oxide powder mixed with water over the surface of the stone—this will soon cause a shine to appear. You can polish the stone with a soft bob (mop) in a flexshaft motor, but because the polishing compound is in solution, this can be rather messy. Always take care when using water as a lubricant with electrical tools such as flexshaft motors, for the obvious reasons—apply the water little and often, stopping to rinse away residues and check on progress at regular intervals.

Making Faceted Cuts

Faceted cuts are most easily done on a lapidary wheel. These flat wheels come in several grades and have a reservoir of water set above the wheel that lubricates it while it rotates. The stone is applied with a firm, even pressure to create flat areas. The size and proportion of the facets is important in commercial cutting, and for standard cuts the process can be controlled by a computer.

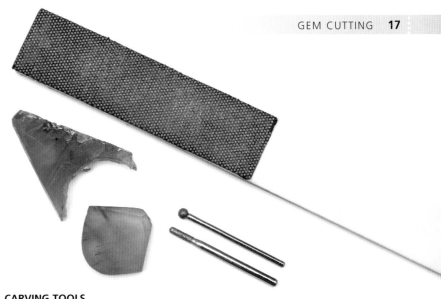

CARVING TOOLS
You can use diamond-coated burrs, drills, and abrasive pads to carve semiprecious gemstones.

HAVING STONES CUT TO ORDER

It is possible to have stones cut to order, and lapidaries will cut stones to a particular design. Ask your local gem dealer if they can recommend someone—many will employ a lapidary to recut stones on site, or they will know one, and should you ever need a chipped or scratched stone recut, this should be your first port of call. It is usual to obtain a quote before agreeing to the work, but the gem cutter will need to see the stone to ascertain how much cutting needs to be done.

▲ It is unusual to see faceted amber such as this checkerboard-top stone because it is very soft.

▲ The checkerboard top of this smoky quartz adds interesting reflections across the stone.

▲ This hexagon-shaped smoky quartz has been cut with so many facets around the crown that the table facet is almost round.

▲ The unusual shape of this Thai ruby would require a bespoke mount.

▲ An unusual, shard-shaped, medium-color aquamarine that would make a striking piece of jewelry.

▲ Care would be needed when making a mount for this 3.19-ct six-sided aquamarine, to accommodate its angles.

Design Inspiration

Inspiration is quite a personal process—from identifying a theme or seeing an object to understanding which aspects provide useful design information. The ways in which a designer interprets and adapts this information within the designs should lead to the creation of unique jewelry that fulfills their unique vision.

DO YOUR RESEARCH
Background research may include looking at other jewelry as market research, providing information on current trends in colors or what kinds of prices are charged. Any aspect of jewelry making, marketing, or history can be researched easily through the Internet.

The best sources of information are often those outside the field of jewelry—architecture, world cultures, historical artifacts, natural forms, mechanisms, and other design disciplines such as textiles, glass, and ceramics are all rich sources of visual information. Visiting museums, collections, galleries, shows, and fairs can also provide a wealth of material, as can collecting interesting images.

Magazines and books, as well as the Internet, are useful research tools, providing information about current trends, how jewelry is represented both on and off the body, as well as reviews of exhibitions and shows.

Sketch Your Ideas

The translation of information is best achieved through observational drawing, often in a sketchbook. Drawing an object from life is the best way to gather and interpret information about it because it can be studied from many angles and understood as a three-dimensional object, helping you to understand how shapes and lines intersect with one another and within space; photography is useful for quickly gathering information but is no substitute for studying an object in real life. Abstract concepts, such as emotions, can be difficult to express on paper unless appropriate visual metaphors can be found to evoke them, and drawing should still play an important role in the development of ideas.

Drawing allows you to build up a personal visual language that will inform your design decisions and it will become second nature, allowing your work to evolve into a recognizable style. This will be partly to do with the subject matters that interest you, and partly to do with the range of skills you use in your work that determine what and how you make your designs.

Analyze Your Research

The visual material you create during research will

DESIGN DEVELOPMENT
The design for this ring was derived from the relationship between the two stones, which dictated the basic form of the ring, and the aesthetic taken from uneven crystalline facets. It is easiest to thoroughly think through a design on paper, refining areas of the piece so that they look right and function correctly.

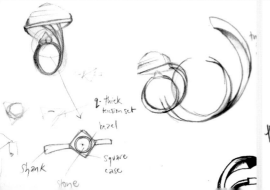

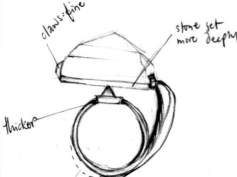

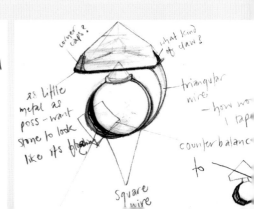

EARTH TREASURES COLLECTION

The translation of information from inspirational objects onto paper is often the starting point of the design process. These designs by Chris and Joy Poupazis were developed using CAD by Gala Creations to produce a realistic rendering of the pieces (above). The information was translated into physical form by a 3D wax printer, allowing the models to be cast into gold. Variations of the piece were made in different colours of gold, with the edges "fishtail" set with diamonds and a peg setting for the pearl.

require analysis to allow you to translate it into forms suitable for jewelry. Spend time drawing out forms and experimenting with the ways they can be abstracted from the original source; take elements or small areas and exaggerate, stretch, shrink, flip, add to them, or interchange parts. Work on large pages so you can clearly see and develop the progression—one idea should lead to another. The abstraction of forms can lead directly to the design of a piece of jewelry, and will be informed by the decisions about what specific form the piece might take, how it might be constructed, and which techniques will be used. More focused technical drawings are useful at this stage, to refine the ideas and work out what is plausible.

You can gather further information about how a design works by making three-dimensional models: to explore form, function, and weight; to explore technical aspects such as mechanisms and moving parts; and to experiment with texture

techniques, or the suitability of a particular material. Sometimes it is necessary to make a model in order to draw a design from several angles, before adapting it further. You may need to explore several models to resolve an idea, and it is often useful to photograph these as a record of the development of the piece.

Make a Prototype

Once the design has been finalized, the next stage is to make up a prototype piece—mistakes made in precious metals can be expensive, so this process gives you the opportunity to work out any remaining design flaws that were not previously apparent. Prototypes also give useful information about the fabrication of a piece—from the metal "cutting list" or the weight of a piece to the order in which it is constructed.

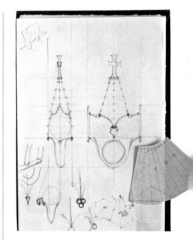

TECHNICAL JOURNAL
Before fabrication, map pieces out in a technical journal to check details and proportions.

▼ When viewed from above, the triangular-tension-set topaz is visible threefold through the large claw-set rutilated quartz.

▲ More detailed drawings will help to define exactly how a piece looks and is constructed.

Starting with the Stone

When designing for stone-set jewelry, the nature of the piece, as well as the style of setting are often determined by the stone itself. The technical considerations, such as the properties of the stone and its method of setting, must be carefully weighed against aesthetic considerations to produce a successful piece.

Inspiration from the Stone

The stone itself is often the source of inspiration for a piece and may suggest the type of piece or form that might be best suited. There is a strong tendency among jewelers to compulsively buy stones, so when designing a piece, the chances are that the stone is already waiting for attention and you have already considered its properties and method of setting to some degree. Approaching the design of a piece with a particular style of setting in mind before you have chosen a stone may require less decision-making, although in some senses it does limit the choice of stone. Research in terms of which cuts suit which stones and in what sizes they can be sourced is a good idea if you require a less common cut or stone.

For example, if you are designing a piece that will be pavé set in areas, it is reasonable to assume it will be possible to source suitable stones in most colors and price ranges because they are standard, round brilliant-cut; for large trillion-cut stones, on the other hand, there will be a lot less choice. When designing sets of jewelry, pairs of earrings, or other pieces with multiple stones, it is often important to color-match the stones because any slight difference in the shade will become apparent when the stones are closely set. Matching pairs or sets of stones are often more highly priced for this reason.

As described on the previous two pages, it is important to have visual input for a design

in order to help justify decisions about colors, materials, form, function, surface finish, or texture. In some ways, having a particular stone in mind for a piece can be a limiting factor, hindering the progression of the design as it dominates proceedings; but the stone can also evoke all sorts of responses, suggesting imagery or cultural references with its color or shape.

Analyze the Work of Others

The jewelry that illustrates the pages of this book covers a wide range of genres and tastes, but each piece was designed with specific consideration to the message it gives, and how that message is communicated through the materials used. When looking at these images, consider not just how the piece was made, but why it was made that way—how the colors work together, what metals are used; if it is an abstract form, how do the parts of the piece relate to one another? What source material or inspiration was the designer working from? It does help to understand your own work if you can analyze that of others.

SUPERMAN RING
The emerald crystals set into the top of this 18-kt gold ring with granulation by Ming make a humorous cultural reference, and were obviously the catalyst for the design.

SIMIENS MOUNTAIN EARRINGS
Ornella Iannuzzi uses not just the stones for inspiration, but also their origin. This pair of earrings is set with two large Wello opals from Ethiopia; the design, and those of the rest of her collection directly reference the landscape, architecture, and wildlife of the area.

The Design Process

The key to a well-designed piece of jewelry is also the key to making an aesthetically successful piece of jewelry—every part of it, from the form and the surface texture to the way the stone is set should look intentional, as if it were meant to be like that. Be informed and know what you are doing, use materials with an understanding of their properties, play and experiment before you commit, and find out the limits of a technique or metal by pushing it as far as it will go. Keep records of the things that didn't work and analyze them so that you can make improvements.

Even the most simple mount on a ring shank has had design time spent on it. The shank may be made from D-section wire so that the ring is comfortable; the way in which the shank intersects with the mount is also telling because there are a number of traditional solutions, and they have evolved over generations as the most metal-efficient, elegant, or simple method of combining the two elements. These solutions are useful for adapting, building upon, or completely rejecting.

Design development of a stone-set piece of jewelry needs to incorporate both the decisions about how the piece looks and functions, together with the very practical considerations of incorporating a functional mount or area on the piece in which stones can be set. There is little point in designing something that would be impossible to set, either because it is too complicated or the settings are too close together or obscured. A basic knowledge of fabrication and setting techniques should provide a reasonable ideas of what is and isn't possible, and you may need to construct the piece in a particular sequence so that certain operations are possible— designs may well need to be tailored after a trial run or prototype. This is not an easy process, but do try to remember to enjoy it as the end results so often justify the struggle to get there.

CHRYSOPRASE AND AMETHYSTS COLLECTION
Stones may be the inspiration behind a range of pieces. This collection by Ben Day contrasts the opulent colors of the chrysoprase, amethysts, and fire opals. Pear, oval, and marquise cabochons are used as blocks of color, set in yellow and rose golds.

REVERSIBLE SPIRAL NECKLACE
Natural diamonds and rubies will fluoresce under UV light, as can be clearly seen in this necklace by Jayce Wong. The stones are pavé set in white gold around a spiral form so that the light effects change as it moves when worn.

Design Considerations

Designs that look fantastic on paper may not be successful jewelry items if you don't take practical considerations into account. The comfort, finish, and durability need to be weighed up against constraints such as time, cost, and function.

The translation of a two-dimensional design into a three-dimensional one is a many-layered process. Throughout, you'll need to address many issues as part of your design methodology. After a time, the points described below will seem a natural part of designing jewelry.

Wearability

How comfortable a piece of jewelry is to wear is often determined by what kind of piece it is, and how wearable it needs to be. Consider how often it might be worn—if it is an everyday piece such as an engagement ring, it needs to be practical, comfortable, and easy to wear. Pieces with protrusions that are liable to snag on clothes or are sharp will be acceptable under certain circumstances. The larger and more rigid a piece is, the less comfortable it will be; articulated forms will flow with the body.

The weight of a piece is also very important—if a piece is too light it may feel flimsy and if it is too heavy it will not be comfortable to wear; earrings should be no heavier than ¼ oz (7 g).

Remember that gold and platinum are much denser than silver, and equivalent-sized pieces of jewelry will weigh more, and cost much more. Some stones are much denser than others and while some stones may be suitable to use for a piece, other similar sized stones of differing gem material may be too heavy.

Finish

The majority of commercial jewelry is polished, because this gives a reasonably durable finish and complements faceted gemstones by helping to reflect more light within them, intensifying their sparkle. Polished surfaces are also the most hygienic, so even on matte pieces it is common

ONYX DRUSY PENDANT
Drusy is a fragile crystalline surface on a stone, which must be set carefully. The onyx has been cut to allow minimal setting to hold it in this pendant by David Fowkes, using a fine scalloped line of gold to set the point of the stone, and secured along the rough top edge by bezel-set diamonds and pink tourmaline.

GOLD AND BERYL RING
This 18-kt yellow-gold ring
by Roger Morris makes
a design feature of the
method of setting the
mirror-cut yellow beryl. The
front frame that holds the
stone has been riveted into
position using structures
that protrude from the ring
shank; the front section
places even pressure around
the edge of the stone,
so there is no risk of the
thinner edges or corners
fracturing during setting.

to find that earring wires or the insides of rings
are polished and therefore easy to clean, as the
surface is not porous and dirt is not so easily
trapped. Scratches aren't as immediately obvious
as they might be on other finishes and the polish
can be easily restored with a cloth or mop to
remove dirt and fine scratches.

A greater range of finishes can be seen in
studio jewelry, from matte, satin, or frosted to
heavily textured, enameled, or reticulated. Matte
surfaces have a tendency to shine up over time,
although they are easily restored and more durable
on harder metals; textured surfaces can be quite
resilient because they hide most marks.

Like any surface finish, electroplating will
eventually wear away. This can be best avoided
through using hard, thick plate. White gold and
platinum are often plated with white rhodium to
make them appear brighter—if the color of the
plate is close to the color of the underlying metal,
the patches of wear will not be so obvious. Pieces
can be replated and polished. Plating takes on
whatever finish the metal already has—matte,
polished, or frosted surfaces will remain so.

Silver is more easily patinated than other
precious metals, although if they are silver plated,
similar effects can be achieved. Patinas are most
durable in recessed areas, which is why pieces
blackened by oxidizing chemicals are often rubbed

back to highlight raised areas—this would happen
anyway. Some jewelers prefer to leave the patina
over the whole surface, allowing wear of the
piece to affect the way it rubs away and changes.
A more durable alternative to black oxidizing
is to electroplate the piece with black rhodium
or ruthenium.

Durability

While it is arguable that handmade jewelry
should always have a degree of longevity, ensured
by virtue of being well made, its lifespan does
depend on the materials and processes used in
its manufacture, as well as how often it is worn.

Certain types of settings will be more secure
than others, however well they are constructed;
the use of harder metals will improve the
durability of a piece, especially as harder stones
are often used. If both materials are harder they
will be much more resistant to scratches, and
are therefore more appropriate materials for
an engagement ring, which needs to last for
decades, than a softer metal such as silver which
will gradually wear away if worn continually
for years.

Pieces for occasional wear can be a bit less
durable in terms of materials, but it is a matter of
personal taste as to whether a piece is perceived
as "everyday" or not.

TANZANITE AND DIAMOND PENDANT
The platinum wire mount for this tanzanite pendant by Cathy Stephens was laser welded together from 142 separate components before being soldered to reinforce the joints.

Practicalities

The practicalities of a piece are most likely to be determined by the design brief. An engagement ring will have quite a different brief to, for example, a stone-set necklace featuring the use of mixed materials. When designing, it is important to consider the practical aspects of how a piece will behave when it is worn as well as the aesthetic considerations.

One of the most basic factors is using a stone with suitable properties for a particular project. Softer stones are relatively unsuitable for rings and other pieces that will receive a lot of wear or be subjected to much movement and possible knocks. There are other factors that may not arise until the three-dimensional object is finished, although with experience these can often be anticipated and resolved through design before the prototype stage. A ring that is weighted more on one side and always wants to swivel around on the finger can be annoying, or perhaps a ring is more comfortable on the right hand rather than the left because of its asymmetric form.

You must also consider the practicalities of the construction of a piece, because the particular sequence of what goes where and when will affect which elements need to be finished first, and to what degree. Some areas may be inaccessible once the piece is assembled, so make sure to clean or polish these while it is still possible. The position of a solder seam on one part may affect how or where it is joined to another. Use the process of making models or prototypes to work through issues of this nature.

Cost

The type of jewelry has a fundamental impact on how and from what materials a piece is made, and therefore how highly it is priced. Weigh up the time it will take to make a piece against the materials it will be made from. Designs that are complicated and will take many hours or days to complete will not be perceived as so valuable if they are executed in silver, and it may not be possible to justify the high price. The material costs of gold or platinum, however, are already high and the proportional cost of the labor in the sale price is therefore much lower. Expensive fine jewelry must be durable, so harder precious metals such as platinum and high-quality stones are used, and as they have a high intrinsic value they will help to justify the cost of such a piece to a customer.

While art pieces may also carry a high price, the emphasis may not be on durability and the pieces may not be designed to be worn very often. In the commercial marketplace, it can be difficult to justify a high price on a piece that is made from base materials, or even from silver. The quality of design also influences the perceived value of a piece, and a recognized brand can charge much more for a piece than an unknown one.

PRONG DETAIL
The prong setting, which includes three groups of smaller prong settings for diamonds, mirrors the shape of the tanzanite, and is tapered so that only the tips of the prongs are visible from the front of the piece.

Using Bought Settings

There are benefits and drawbacks to using manufactured mounts in handmade jewelry; they can be a tempting and easy solution for setting stones, but may look incongruous when combined with fabricated elements.

Disadvantages of Bought Settings

The main disadvantage of manufactured settings is that they will almost always look like bought mounts, which not only reduces the value of the design of a piece as a whole, but means it will be very similar to thousands of other pieces of jewelry. However, the mounts can be adapted or significantly altered while still retaining their primary function, which is to securely hold a stone. Whether a setting is bought or handmade, it should always relate to the piece it is part of, and if possible should be designed to be integral to a piece rather than looking "stuck on."

Although you can source a good range of cast and stamped mounts, from simple stamped bezel cups to complex multiple-stone clusters and gallery strips, the use of a prefabricated setting prescribes a limit on the stones that can be set because the mounts are usually only available in standard sizes, so for unusual sizes or shapes of stones it may be easier to start from scratch.

Advantages of Bought Settings

If you can find a bought setting that is similar to what the design dictates, you will make your life easy! When making a commission, bought settings are one way of bringing the costs down because they can save an immense amount of time; you can adapt basic tapered bezels to specific requirements, whether carved to make a crown prong mount or embellished with other techniques, and because most of these mounts are cast, there is no risk of a solder seam opening up when they are joined to a ring shank.

Manufactured mounts can also be a useful reference, whether how-to, or how-not-to in terms of design and aesthetics, but also for metal thickness or gauge and proportions.

When working in metals such as gold or platinum, bought mounts will keep costs down because there will be no scrap or wastage from the fabrication process, so there is no extra outlay. Try exploring contrasting colors of metal within one piece—the use of a gold mount in a silver ring provides an affordable way of using gold in a piece, and will make a more secure setting for a valuable stone.

PYRITE PENDANT
A simple frame for a hand-cut pyrite cabochon was constructed from stamped gallery strip to make this pendant by Annie Cracknell. The structure of the bezel creates an interesting contrast to the random patterns within the stone, and because the silver is oxidized, the lighter colors of the pyrite are the focal point of the piece.

4/2 RINGS
A prefabricated oval tapered bezel was used to set the 0.5-ct ruby in one of this pair of commissioned wedding rings by Anastasia Young. For standard shapes and sizes of mount, such as this one, the cost of making the setting from sheet metal cannot be justified against the cost of the cast tapered bezel, especially when working to commission.

Commissions

Commissioned jewelry can be quite a different way of working from producing your own designs. You'll still need to draw up a design, but the parameters of the brief are usually defined by the client in terms of the type of jewelry, materials, timescale, and cost.

The Nature of a Commission

Working to commission can be very rewarding because although the brief may be clearly defined, chances are that there will be aspects of the piece that are not part of your usual repertoire as a jeweler, such as the shape of the chosen stone or its method of setting. Also, creating an object that has previously only existed in someone else's imagination is a very special experience for them. A client will want you to make a piece either because they like your style and want something similar but quite specific, or they may have their own design in mind and wish it to be made for them. The most common commissions are wedding and engagement rings—a client may wish to have a wedding ring made to complement an existing engagement ring, or you may be lucky enough to be asked to make a pair of wedding bands and an engagement ring.

The Commissioning Process

For stone-set jewelry, there are usually two forms a commission will take: Either the client already has the stone they wish you to use because it is a family piece that they would like remodeled; or they have a good idea of what they would like— for example, an oval brilliant sapphire. If it is the latter, you need to negotiate the overall budget for the commission to determine how much you can allocate to buy the stone after metal costs, your time, and overheads (which includes workshop rent), any outwork such as CAD/CAM, setting, plating, or hallmarking.

If the client provides their own stone, it is a good idea to have a gemologist look at it; many stones look quite similar to the inexperienced eye and the "heirloom topaz" may turn out to be a much less valuable citrine. It is also important to know the properties of a particular stone because this may affect the way in which it is set. For more information on gemstone properties, see the Gemstone directory on pages 30–51.

THE ORIGINAL RING
The client provided an Art Deco-style emerald ring, from which the 0.75-ct emerald and two diamonds were to be used in the commissioned ring. The ring shank was 18-kt yellow gold, faced with white; the yellow gold was reused and drawn down into wire to make a prong for the emerald, and the mixed-metal portions that could not be used were recycled as scrap.

DAMAGED EMERALD
The emerald was badly chipped and scratched from being loose in its setting, and needed to be repolished professionally. This image was taken on a USB microscope, allowing the damage to be seen at many times the actual size of the stone. The white gold prongs were carefully cut away on two sides with a jeweler's saw to allow the stone to slip out before taking it to the lapidary. In agreement with the client's wishes, the corners were cut to give a more traditional emerald cut, thus removing the minimum possible amount of the stone.

When you have worked out how much there is left to spend on the stone, you will need to do some research. The client will have an idea of the size of stone they want, but this may well be above the budget! It may be possible to find a less expensive stone of the right size, but the quality may not be top—either the color may be a little too pale or too dark, the stone may be slightly cloudy, or it may have small inclusions, none of which is evident to the naked eye. Be honest with your client—they may want to spend more on a high-quality gem and increase the budget, or they may be happy to compromise on size or quality. You can arrange to borrow stones "on spec" for short periods of time from gem dealers in order to allow your client to choose their preferred stone.

Clients are usually well informed and will probably have a good idea of the type of setting they would like, too. You will need to work closely with the client to make sure your design meets their expectations, and that they understand how the piece will look once made. In this respect, CAD is very useful because it allows a high-quality image of a piece to be rendered that can be shown to the client, and changes such as the color of the metal or stone, or the surface qualities can be altered quite easily before the piece is made up in metal.

Once the design has been decided on, draw up a contract agreeing a timeframe for the project and the cost, and ask for half of the fee upfront, which will allow you to pay for the materials. The rest of the fee is payable on delivery.

For this type of work, many jewelers will make the piece and then hand it over to an experienced professional setter to set the stone, because mistakes can be expensive. Stone-setting techniques such as pavé are almost always done by a professional.

THE NEW RING AND SETTING

Once the design was decided on, a silver model of the ring was fabricated. The central mount for the emerald was derived from a cast form and combined with sheet, wire, and tube to make the ring and the combination setting for the emerald. A cold-cure mold was made of the ring—this minimized the shrinkage, meaning that the stone would still fit into its seat; a wax model was made from the mold and this was cast into 18-kt white gold.

THE FINAL PIECE

This cast gold ring was cleaned up, and yellow gold tube settings for the diamonds soldered into place, as well as the upper prong on the left-hand side. The two diamonds were set first, followed by the emerald, which is held quite deeply within the mount to prevent it from being chipped.

Outsourcing

Outsourcing is often the most time- and cost-effective way of achieving certain aspects of jewelry manufacture, making use of service providers who have both the equipment and the skills to perform specialist techniques or processes.

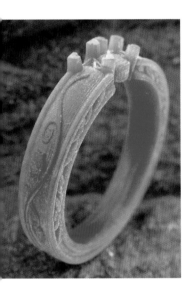

Finding an Outworker

The best recommendations are usually word of mouth, because they allow one to judge many aspects of a service and to weigh quality of work against turnaround. You might be prepared to wait longer for a piece if you are sure a good job will be done, or alternatively the job might need to be completed very quickly, so while quality is still important, it is not always the deciding factor.

When approaching an outworker about a job, it is advisable to have a good idea of what you would like them to do; if you're not sure, do some research first to find out more about the processes involved. There is no harm in calling in advance to discuss the work, but quotes are rarely given unless the work has been seen.

CAD/CAM

Services that offer to build a design for renderings and/or to produce wax models for casting can work from a sketch, which will end up more expensive, or from a detailed spec produced in a program such as Adobe Illustrator. A detailed technical drawing from several angles is always going to be easier to understand and less open to interpretation than a rough sketch.

Casting

Companies that provide a lost-wax casting service usually cast in a range of precious metal alloys. Some casting companies have arrangements with CAD companies, which may be preferable because it means transport of the fragile waxes is taken

WAX CARVING
Jeweler's wax can be carved by a computer-driven milling machine to a very fine degree of detail, as shown above. Complex pieces may be carved in several sections that can be soldered together once cast into metal. Waxes can also be "built" using a 3D printer that deposits the wax in layers to create the form.

WAX CARVING MACHINE
Milling machines such as the one at right are used to cut and carve waxes to a high degree of accuracy. The cutting tools are driven by a computer that uses the vector data created when the virtual representation of a piece is built.

care of. Mold-making to produce multiple pieces is a standard service, and some companies also provide services as wide-ranging as hallmarking, finishing, and stone setting.

Electroforming

Electroforming involves the deposition of metal onto nonmetallic surfaces after an application of conductive paint, and the process results in hollow metal forms. Stones and glass incorporated in a wax model can easily be electroformed into a piece, but natural materials require several coats of varnish to protect them from the harsh chemicals involved. The resulting electroforms are one-off and can be quite fragile.

Stone Setting

For valuable stones, for example in commissioned pieces, you might not want to risk damaging the mount or the stone if you don't have much experience, so taking the piece to a professional to set the stones is a good alternative. Also, a setter will be able to do the work much more quickly. Setters usually charge per stone, but this may depend on the type of setting.

Pieces should be finished and polished and ready to set and you should provide the stones, which should be calibrated for techniques such as pavé, ensuring that all the stones are exactly the right size and so are more easily mounted.

Laser Welding

Laser welding is a useful alternative method for joining metal to metal when soldering is not possible, or impractical. This makes it ideal for resizing rings and retipping prongs if they break off, without the need to remove the stone first, as well as laser welding already-mounted stones into frames or pieces. Some companies offer while-you-wait or drop-in services for laser repairs.

Plating and Polishing

Silver, gold, rhodium, and ruthenium electroplating services are widely available in a range of colors and types—hard plate is more durable than soft plate, and the thicker the plate, the longer it will last. Flash plating is a quick deposition of about 1μm (micron; one-thousandth of a millimeter).

All the work must be complete on pieces prior to plating, including stone setting. However, certain types of stones cannot be plated because they are too sensitive for the solutions, or they are slightly conductive because of the metal content of their mineral structure. Some stones may need to be plated with the plating solution cold. Most platers also offer a polishing service, so do say if you don't want the piece polished, for example if you wish the surface to remain matte.

PROFESSIONAL SETTING
Stereo microscopes, as shown below left, are used by professional setters for techniques such as micro-pavé, but are also useful for checking the progress of other types of setting in minute detail.

POLISHING IN ACTION
A professional polisher at work on a buffing wheel (below).

Choosing the right stone for a project can be essential to its success. This section provides all the technical information—including physical statistics and qualities, and common treatments to improve color or clarity—required to make informed decisions about which stones are suitable for a design before purchase, and what the potential drawbacks may be. It is illustrated with images of the gemstones in different cuts. Stones can easily be selected by color and are arranged according to their hardness, starting with diamonds.

CHAPTER 2

Gemstone Directory

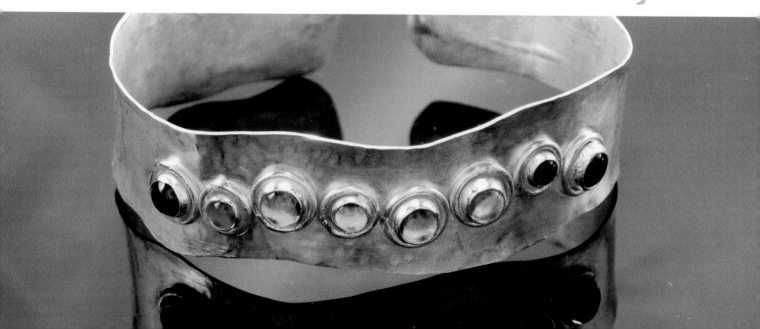

DIAMOND

◀ The straight facets of this 0.74-ct emerald cut emphasize the transparency of this E color VS1 clarity diamond.

▶ Although a 1.07-ct brilliant cut, the low color and black marks mean this stone is of a comparatively low value.

▲ I to J color brilliant-cut diamond of 0.70 ct with I1 clarity.

▶ Possessing a D color and VVS2 clarity, combined with its 0.70 ct size, means this diamond is an expensive stone.

▶ 0.70-ct princess-cut G color and VS1 clarity, this stone has a square outline but the facets are modified from a round brilliant cut.

▲ Natural color brown pear shape of 0.57 ct.

▲ This 5/32 in. (4 mm) princess-cut diamond has been treated to obtain the vibrant yellow color.

▲ 0.50-ct green diamond, this color has been obtained by irradiation treatment.

DIAMOND

To many, diamond is the ultimate gemstone. Produced around 93 miles (150 km) inside the Earth, it is the hardest of all known natural gemstones. Diamonds boast superb luster, transparency, brilliance, fire, and scintillation. Diamonds also occur in a range of tints, usually brown and yellow, through fancy colors. White (transparent) diamonds are graded by the four Cs (see below) but fancy colors have their own set of rules.

CHEMICAL COMPOSITION Carbon
COLORS White (transparent), yellow, brown, green, gray, pink, blue, black, red, and purple.
VARIETIES Diamond is mined for industrial use as well as gem-quality material.
LOCALITIES INCLUDE India, Brazil, South Africa, DRC, Namibia, Tanzania, Angola, Sierra Leone, Russia, Botswana, Australia, and Canada.

AVAILABILITY

CUT A brilliant-cut diamond's proportions have been designed to show a colorless diamond's properties to maximum effect. It reflects all light from the back facets back through the front of the stone and is the most common cut. Stones with straight facets show the supreme transparency of diamond. Other cuts may appear to intensify the color. Stones are available from around 0.7 mm.
COLORS Naturally colored red and purple are the rarest, and pink and blue are also very rare. The setting of a diamond can affect its perceived color. This is why it is necessary to remove a stone from its setting before grading in a laboratory. Diamond has a high dispersion of light, responsible for flashes of spectral colors.
CLARITY Inclusion-free material is the most desirable and is relatively rare. However diamond is extensively mined, so SI material (see right) is reasonably common.

QUALITIES
The Four Cs

The quality of a diamond is judged by four main factors. These are color, clarity, cut, and carat weight. Each of these factors affects the price per carat of a stone. The grading system described here is the GIA grading scale; however, other grading organizations such as CIBJO may use slightly different grading terms. You may also come across old grading descriptions no longer used.
COLOR If a diamond is white and transparent, the most desirable stones are those that are nearest to colorless. Diamonds are color graded by the Gemological Institute of America (GIA) through the alphabet from D to Z—D grade is the nearest to colorless. Between D and H the stone does not have a tint when viewed through the table. It is

very difficult to see a difference between grades D to G. From the color I down to M, a body tint becomes increasingly obvious; the color grade M shows a noticeable body color through the table. As a diamond's body color becomes increasingly saturated, it becomes a fancy color. The body color of a diamond will be more obvious from the back than the front. This is the direction in which diamonds are graded.

Color grading factors for fancy colored diamonds are different than for white. These include purity of color, strength of saturation, and evenness of color.
CLARITY The most desirable clarity for a diamond is to be free from inclusions. This is described as internally flawless and is very rare, especially in larger stones. Grades are judged under a 10x magnifying loupe. The GIA grading system continues to VVS (very very small inclusions), VS (very small inclusions), SI (small inclusions)—inclusions can be seen with a 10x loupe—and I, where inclusions are visible unaided. SI material is known as "eye clean."
CUT A well-cut stone can show off the beauty of a diamond to better effect. Proportions, symmetry, and polish are considered during the grading process of a diamond.
CARAT WEIGHT A heavier stone is more valuable than a lighter one. This is partly because of weight increase, but prices per carat also increase as a stone gets larger. This increase is particularly prominent at major increments. For example, a stone of 1 ct weight is more desirable than that of 0.99 ct, therefore a 1 ct stone usually has a higher price per carat than the 0.99 ct, despite there only being a 0.01 ct difference in weight.

When graded, diamonds in laboratories are judged under controlled conditions, with comparison master stones. Fluorescence may also affect the price of a diamond by interfering with the appearance of its body color.

HARDNESS 10
TOUGHNESS Good, but diamond contains four directions of internal cleavage. Although breakage along these planes is difficult, it is possible.
LUSTER Adamantine
RI 2.42
Diamond should never be placed on a refractometer glass because it may scratch the surface.

TREATMENTS

COATING Carried out to improve the color.
LASER DRILLING Drilling a tiny hole or producing cracks to a dark inclusion. The inclusion is consequently bleached to white and improves the perceived clarity of a stone.
FRACTURE FILLING Fractures are filled to reduce the severity of their appearance. Laser-drilled holes and bleached cavities may also be filled. It is important that coating, laser treatment, and fracture filling are disclosed upon sale.

IRRADIATION WITH HEAT TREATMENT This combination of processes can produce a variety of bright colors such as greenish-yellow, teal blue, magenta, light brown to cognac, blacks, and deep greens. These are usually noticeably different shades than naturally colored diamonds. Some brown diamonds can also be whitened and colors changed in a high-pressure, high-temperature environment.

SYNTHETICS Diamonds can be produced synthetically. They appear exactly the same as natural diamonds and require laboratory equipment for identification. Synthetic diamonds can be treated.

CARE Diamonds can burn because they are carbon based. To avoid this, cover the diamond in flux when using a jeweler's torch. This should protect the stone up to around 3272°F (1800°C).

Diamond is very hard and resists scratches but may be broken by a sharp knock in the wrong direction. Diamonds attract grease that reduces their brilliant appearance, so clean them with washing up liquid, warm water, and a soft toothbrush.

STONES WITH A SIMILAR APPEARANCE
Cubic zirconia (CZ), sapphire, synthetic sapphire and spinel, white zircon, synthetic moissanite, YAG, glass, strontium titanate, and synthetic rutile.

THE KIMBERLEY PROCESS

Some diamond mines have been used to fund conflicts in the countries in which they are based. The Kimberley Process came into effect in 2003 to try to prevent this from occurring again. It is a certification system that is used from the mine to the cutting center. As the rough (uncut) diamond passes each border of a participating country it must have a Kimberley certificate certifying that suitable requirements have been met and the diamonds can be sold as "conflict free." Participating countries can only trade with other participants.

Kimberley certificates are only required for rough shipments of diamonds, but subsequent sellers should show a "system of warranties" declaration on their invoice. This declares that the diamonds sold have been through the certification scheme and are therefore conflict free. For more information see www.kimberleyprocess.com.

EMERALD

The most prominent and desirable property of emerald is its color. This can be an awe-inspiring deep bluish or yellowish green and is spectacular in large, clean stones. Unfortunately emerald is much more prone to inclusions than many other gemstones.

GROUP Beryl
CHEMICAL COMPOSITION Beryllium aluminum silicate
COLOR Green; varies with locality.
LOCALITIES INCLUDE Columbia, India, Brazil, Zimbabwe, Zambia, Siberia, and Pakistan.

AVAILABILITY

CUT The emerald cut was created especially for this stone; corners are removed to protect the brittle material from damage. Large stones with corners still on are difficult to obtain. Straight cuts show off emerald's spectacular color. Large, round stones in particular are unusual.
COLORS A rich green is most highly recognized. Columbian material often has a bluish tint that is popular, while African tends to look more grassy colored.
CLARITY Emerald is naturally a very included material compared to other members of the beryl group. High-clarity examples are rare and expensive, particularly in large stones.

QUALITIES

The most desirable emeralds have a good saturated color and are as free from inclusions as possible. Emerald usually contains a lot of inclusions and fissures, and it is difficult and expensive to find examples with both good color and clarity.
HARDNESS 7½
TOUGHNESS Poor
LUSTER Vitreous
RI 1.56 to 1.60
BIREFRINGENCE 0.003 to .010

TREATMENTS Almost all emeralds are oiled. Inclusions and fractures can also be filled with resin to minimize their appearance. This should be disclosed upon sale.

SYNTHETICS Synthetics can be created by the flux and hydrothermal methods. These can contain identifying inclusions; however, if they do not, the material must be laboratory tested.

CARE Avoid knocks because this is naturally a brittle material. Care must be taken in fashioning, setting, storage, and wear. Do not use in ultrasonic cleaners, and do not soak in chemicals that may remove oils or other fillings from fissures.

EMERALD

▶ This 12.55-ct cabochon emerald contains inclusions but it has a good, strong green color.

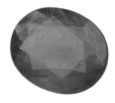

◀ This 1.28-ct oval emerald appears translucent from many inclusions, but still shows a vibrant color.

▶ Cutting this beautiful Columbian 1.64-ct emerald to an emerald cut reduces the risk of chipping the corners of the stone when setting.

◀ A light color makes this oval-cut, 2.26-ct, good-clarity emerald more affordable.

▶ 0.69-ct heart shape, showing a grassy green color typical of African emeralds.

▶ This 1.2-ct emerald is an elegant drop, but care should be taken with the apex when setting.

RUBY

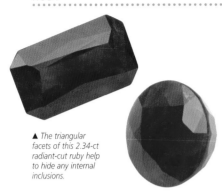

▲ The triangular facets of this 2.34-ct radiant-cut ruby help to hide any internal inclusions.

▲ The low clarity of this round ruby makes it more affordable, while still showing a deep color.

◄ It is common for cabochon rubies like this 1.88-ct stone to have a very deep base, which you need to consider when making your setting.

▲ A marquise-shaped 3.53-ct ruby. This shape may also be called a navette.

▶ Bright, brilliant-cut stones like this 1.75-ct round ruby are often set in prong settings to allow as much light as possible into the stone.

▶ The lively appearance of this 7.3 mm x 6.6 mm ruby pear shape is very pretty but the stone would not fit in a standard setting.

◄ This 2.88-ct oval Burmese ruby shows a very desirable strong red color with a slight pinkish tint.

STONES WITH A SIMILAR APPEARANCE

Fluorite, glass, chrysoprase, dyed green agate, soudé emeralds, green tourmaline, tsavorite, chrome diopside, aventurine quartz.

RUBY

Ruby is the red variety of corundum. Traditionally a highly prized color is a pinkish-red known as "pigeon blood." Their stunning color, luster, and durability make rubies a beautiful and practical choice of gemstone.

GROUP Corundum
CHEMICAL COMPOSITION Aluminum oxide
COLOR Red
VARIETIES Star- usually 6-rayed
LOCALITIES INCLUDE Afghanistan, Australia, India, Kenya, Madagascar, Myanmar (Burma), Pakistan, Russia, Tanzania, Thailand (Siam), Sri Lanka (Ceylon), United States, and Vietnam.

AVAILABILITY

CUT When faceted, a good cut combined with few inclusions can produce beautiful, lively stones. Large round and pear shapes are rarer than oval and cushion shapes. Square and emerald cuts command a premium over oval and round-cut stones because they need larger roughs to produce them. Cabochons and beads are available—often cut from lower-grade material. Star stones must be cut as cabochon.

COLORS A good strong red color through the table without a brown, purple, or orange tint is most desirable. "Pigeon blood" is a popular term to describe a strong red color with a pinkish tint. Most stones on the market are heat treated to improve their color, unless otherwise specified. Unheated stones carry a huge premium.

CLARITY Less included material commands a higher price, although parallel inclusions in star stones are necessary to create the star effect. These inclusions in patches can be a hindrance for clarity but may be dissolved by heat treatment.

Translucent natural star material containing a strong color and a sharp star is rare.

Inclusions are helpful features for discerning a stone's origin.

Rubies are comparatively more included than sapphires for a similar price per carat.

QUALITIES

Color and clarity are the main factors when valuing a stone. Apart from at the highest prices, at least one of these factors will be compromised. Quality of cut is important to ensure a stone appears bright. When large stones are certified, an opinion of origin and level of heat treatment is also given. Certain localities (e.g. Myanmar) and lack of evidence of heat treatment can increase the value of a material.

The level of treatment carried out on a stone affects its relative value.

HARDNESS 9
TOUGHNESS Very good if few inclusions.
LUSTER Bright vitreous
RI 1.76 to 1.78
BIREFRINGENCE 0.008 to 0.009

TREATMENTS It is very common to heat ruby to improve the color.

Other elements may be added to improve color and/or clarity such as beryllium, glass, or resin. Added elements should be disclosed upon sale. These additions may be identified using standard gemological equipment; however, a laboratory may need to be consulted.

Oil or wax can also be used to improve clarity. A combination of natural, treated, and poor-quality corundum may be used to produce composite stones.

SYNTHETICS Synthetic rubies created by the Verneuil technique are common. They are effective, giving the appearance of top-quality material for little money. Internal zoning and bubbles may give away their origin. Commercial material produced by this method usually has a width of less than ¾ in (20 mm).

Synthetics can also be grown by the hydrothermal methods and flux that are much harder to identify.

Synthetic star stones are also fairly common. Synthetic stones may be additionally heated to induce more realistic-appearing inclusions.

CARE If any internal fractures have been filled, avoid heat and acids. If the material is heavily included, take particular care.

Ruby is thermally expansive so can be heated safely, however, beware of inclusions, which may be damaged. If a treatment does not penetrate the whole stone, the effects may disappear if the stone is repolished.

STONES WITH A SIMILAR APPEARANCE

Glass, red beryl, tourmaline, garnet, composites, and spinel.

SAPPHIRE

Sapphire encompasses all other colors of corundum. If the term "sapphire" is used alone, it is assumed the material is blue; otherwise the color is used as a prefix. Their color range, luster, and durability make sapphires an excellent gemstone choice.

GROUP Corundum
CHEMICAL COMPOSITION Aluminum oxide
COLORS Blue, pink, yellow, green, purple, and black.
VARIETIES Padparadscha—a pinkish orange color
LOCALITIES INCLUDE Africa (Nigeria, Kenya, Mozambique, Madagascar, South Africa, Tanzania) Australia, Myanmar (Burma), Kashmir (India), Sri Lanka (Ceylon), Thailand (Siam), and United States (Montana).

AVAILABILITY

CUT When faceted, a good cut combined with few inclusions can produce beautiful, lively stones. Large rounds and pear shapes are rarer than oval or cushion. Square and emerald cuts command a premium because they need proportionally larger roughs to produce them.

Cabochons and beads are available—these tend to be cut from lower-grade material.

Star stones must be cut as cabochon. Natural star stones often are left with a deep, uncut base.
COLORS A good strong blue color is most desired, without grayish or greenish tints. The popular term "cornflower" blue describes blue material with a hint of violet, particularly from Sri Lanka. Cornflower blue sapphires may be dark or light material. A padparadscha's color is very desirable and very rare. It is common for blue sapphires to contain straight internal color zoning. The position and noticeability of this affects the value. Most stones on the market are heat treated to improve their color unless otherwise specified. Unheated stones carry a huge premium.
CLARITY Less included material commands a higher price, though parallel inclusions in star stones are necessary. These inclusions in patches can be a hindrance for clarity but may be dissolved by heat treatment.

Translucent natural star material containing a mid- to dark color and with a sharp star is rare. Inclusions are helpful features for discerning a stone's origin.

QUALITIES

Color and clarity are the main factors when valuing a stone. Below the highest prices, at least one factor will be compromised. Quality of cut is important to ensure a stone appears bright. When large stones are certified, an opinion of origin and level of heat treatment is also given. Certain localities (e.g. Kashmir) and lack of evidence of heat treatment can increase the value.

The level of treatment carried out on a stone affects its relative value.
HARDNESS 9
TOUGHNESS Very good if not too included
LUSTER Bright vitreous
RI 1.76 to 1.78
BIREFRINGENCE 0.008 to 0.009

TREATMENTS It is very common to heat sapphire to improve or alter its color.

Other elements may be added to improve the color, clarity, or quality of a star. These can be beryllium, titanium, glass, or resin. Added elements should be disclosed upon sale. These additions may be identified using gemological equipment; however, a laboratory may need to be consulted.

Oil or wax can also be used to improve clarity. Sapphire can be irradiated to alter its color. A combination of natural, treated, and poor-quality corundum may be used to produce composite stones.

SYNTHETICS Synthetic sapphires created by the Verneuil technique are common. They are effective, showing the appearance of top-quality material for little money. Internal zoning and bubbles may give away their origin. Blue is the most common color but other colors are available.

Synthetics can also be grown by the hydrothermal methods and flux that are much harder to identify. Synthetic star stones are also fairly common. Synthetic stones may be additionally heated to induce more realistic-appearing features.

CARE If any internal fractures have been filled, avoid heat and acids, and take care if the material is heavily included.

Sapphire is thermally expansive so can be heated safely, but beware of inclusions, which may be damaged.

If a treatment does not penetrate the whole stone, the effects may disappear if the stone is repolished.

STONES WITH A SIMILAR APPEARANCE

Glass, iolite, tourmaline, tanzanite, spinel, synthetic spinel, composite stones, and kyanite.

SPINEL

Spinel is a much underrated gemstone, often historically confused with ruby. The "Black Prince's Ruby" set into the front of Britain's Imperial State crown is actually a spinel. Spinels can be lively, durable and beautiful.

CHEMICAL COMPOSITION Magnesium aluminum oxide
COLORS Pinks to orange to red, blues to purplish, greenish, and black.
LOCALITIES INCLUDE Afghanistan, Brazil, Myanmar (Burma), Nigeria, Sri Lanka, and United States.

AVAILABILITY

CUT Spinel is mainly faceted. Large stones are rare.
COLORS Bright, pleasing colors are the most valuable, particularly red; soft red is the most common.

SAPPHIRE

◀ Color zoning across this oval 5.64-ct sapphire is visible, but should be less apparent once set.

▶ This lively pear-shaped 3.35-ct sapphire would benefit from an open setting to allow maximum light into the stone.

◀ Cabochon cut and a deep blue color, this 3.77-ct sapphire would look very pretty in a bezel setting.

▶ This round Sri Lankan 3.34-ct sapphire has an intense blue body color with a hint of violet.

◀ This 7.62-ct cushion-shaped sapphire has a slightly cloudy appearance and an inclusion in front of the table.

SPINEL

▲ A lively, 1.89-ct pretty pink spinel with a hint of lilac in an oval shape.

▲ A similar color to the cushion shape below, this 2.85-ct spinel contains more brilliance.

▼ The soft red color of this 1.11-ct pear shape is a common shade for spinel.

▲ Cushion-shape, deep blue, natural color spinel of 4.11 ct.

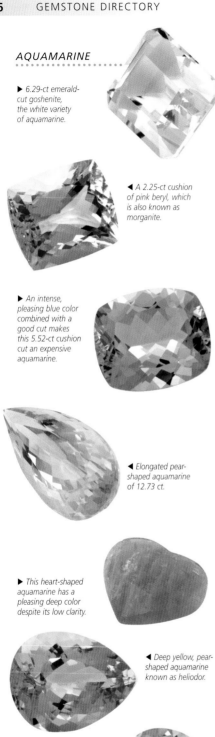

AQUAMARINE

▶ *6.29-ct emerald-cut goshenite, the white variety of aquamarine.*

◀ *A 2.25-ct cushion of pink beryl, which is also known as morganite.*

▶ *An intense, pleasing blue color combined with a good cut makes this 5.52-ct cushion cut an expensive aquamarine.*

◀ *Elongated pear-shaped aquamarine of 12.73 ct.*

▶ *This heart-shaped aquamarine has a pleasing deep color despite its low clarity.*

◀ *Deep yellow, pear-shaped aquamarine known as heliodor.*

▶ *Pale green oval aquamarine. This green is very different to the intense color of emerald, which is also a member of the beryl family.*

Spinel can look very similar to ruby and pink sapphire but at a lower price per carat for a comparable color. Black spinel is a harder alternative to onyx or jet.

CLARITY Inclusions are common but not as abundant as inside a ruby.

QUALITIES
Color and clarity of the stone are important factors as well as a good cut to give a bright, lively appearance.

HARDNESS 8
TOUGHNESS Good
LUSTER Bright vitreous
RI 1.72 to 1.73 (natural)

TREATMENTS To date, spinel is a relatively untreated stone.

SYNTHETICS Synthetic spinels are predominantly created by the Verneuil process and can be identified using basic gemological equipment. A synthetic created by the flux method is possible and more difficult to identify but is currently much less common.

Synthetic spinel often imitates other materials rather than natural spinel.

CARE Be cautious of inclusions when using acid or under a steam cleaner.

STONES WITH A SIMILAR APPEARANCE
Ruby, sapphire, tourmaline, amethyst, iolite, glass, tanzanite, and garnet.

AQUAMARINE

Aquamarines occur in a beautiful range of pale to mid-blues and it is possible to obtain fairly large pieces. They are members of the beryl group that also contains pink, green, yellow, white, and very rarely red stones.

GROUP Beryl
CHEMICAL COMPOSITION Beryllium Aluminum Silicate
COLORS Blue to greenish blue
VARIETIES Other varieties of beryl are:
GREEN BERYL Pale green or pale yellowish green
MORGANITE Peachy pink to rose pink
GOSHENITE White
HELIODOR Pale yellow to rich gold
RED BERYL (Bixbite)
LOCALITIES INCLUDE Brazil, Kenya, Madagascar, Myanmar (Burma), Namibia, Nigeria Russia, Sri Lanka, United States, Zambia, and Zimbabwe.

AVAILABILITY
CUT Available in large sizes, apart from red beryl. Flawed material is mainly used for beads and cabochons.
COLORS Red beryl is very rare. Aquamarines are mainly pale to mid-colors. The more intense the color of beryl, the more expensive the stone. Heated material has a more intense blue color without greenish tones.
CLARITY Large, fairly clean material is available so it is assumed that high-quality aquamarine has few internal flaws.

QUALITIES
The strongest and purest color is most desirable.
HARDNESS 7½
TOUGHNESS Good
LUSTER Vitreous
RI 1.56 to 1.60
BIREFRINGENCE 0.003 to 0.010

TREATMENTS Aquamarine is very commonly heated to remove any yellow tint, so the greenish aquamarines are generally unheated. Some aquamarine can be irradiated but the results may not be stable.

CARE Avoid excess heat; take care if the stone has many inclusions.

STONES WITH A SIMILAR APPEARANCE
Glass, blue topaz, blue synthetic spinel, zircon, sapphire, and tourmaline.

TOPAZ

Topaz is a popular material, particularly in blue. It is available both in bright, treated material and stunning natural colors that are often overlooked.

CHEMICAL COMPOSITION Fluorosilicate of aluminum with hydroxyl
COLORS Blues (mostly treated), yellow to sherry colors, brown, white, pink, orange, and green.
LOCALITIES INCLUDE Australia, Brazil, Myanmar (Burma), Nigeria, Pakistan, Russia, Sri Lanka, and United States.

AVAILABILITY
CUT Faceted and cabochon cuts are readily available. Step cuts particularly suit stronger shades of color.

Topaz is a relatively heavy stone so prices will be high in large material.
COLORS The blue irradiated material is commercially sold under the names "Sky" (light), "Swiss" (bright and electric), and "London" (deeper and smoky).

Natural imperial "sherry"-colored material, along with pink, is the most expensive color. Treated blue and natural white topaz are fairly common and reasonably priced.

CLARITY Large inclusion-free material is available in blue and colorless topaz.

QUALITIES
Large, clean material is pricey to obtain in the natural pink, yellow, and imperial colors. The smoky London blue is more expensive than Swiss, and Swiss is more expensive than Sky.

HARDNESS 8
TOUGHNESS Medium—it contains a direction of easy cleavage
LUSTER Vitreous
RI 1.61 to 1.64
BIREFRINGENCE 0.008 to 0.010

TREATMENTS Blue colors are created from white material using irradiation combined with heat treatment. An unstable brown/yellow material can be produced by irradiation. Pinker tones may be induced from yellows/browns after heating.

It is common for white topaz to be coated to many colors and iridescent effects such as "mystic topaz" and a fuchsia-pink hue.

SYNTHETICS "Synthetic topaz" is often actually synthetic spinel.

CARE Fairly durable, but care should be taken to avoid the easy direction of cleavage when setting and to avoid knocks during wear. Overheating and acids should be avoided.

STONES WITH A SIMILAR APPEARANCE
Quartz, tourmaline, aquamarine, apatite, kunzite, synthetic spinel, zircon, synthetic sapphire, and CZ. Smoky quartz is frequently mistakenly called smoky topaz. Citrine is also mistaken for yellow topaz.

CHRYSOBERYL

The yellowish green and cat's eye varieties have historically been very popular but are less utilized in the current market. Alexandrites, named after the Tsar of Russia in 1831, can be extremely spectacular though are difficult to obtain in a fine quality. Chrysoberyl is a good choice when considering durability.

CHEMICAL COMPOSITION Beryllium aluminum oxide
COLORS Red, yellow, green, and brown.
VARIETIES Alexandrite (shows a color change from green in daylight to red-brown in artificial light). Cat's eye (shows a streak of light across its surface, similar body colors to the transparent variety), also known as cymophane. Cat's eye alexandrite (shows both a color change and streak of light effect). Transparent material (yellowish to greenish to brownish).

LOCALITIES INCLUDE Brazil, Russia, Sri Lanka, Madagascar, and Zimbabwe.

AVAILABILITY
CUT Cat's eyes must be cut as cabochons to reveal their streak of light and oriented properly so the light is central to the stone.

COLORS Fine-quality alexandrite which shows a good color change from red to green is very, very rare and even rarer with a cat's eye. It is therefore very expensive.

Most commercial material shows a patchy color change from green to purple, with the body color often containing a grayish tint. Despite being poorer quality, these still sell for high prices.

CLARITY Less included material is more desirable, apart from the many parallel inclusions inside cat's eye stones.

QUALITIES
A more intense, pleasing color corresponds to a higher value. The quality of the streak of light over a cat's eye stone affects its value.

HARDNESS 8½
TOUGHNESS Excellent to good
LUSTER Bright vitreous
RI 1.74 to 1.76
BIREFRINGENCE 0.008 to 0.010

SYNTHETICS Synthetic alexandrite exists and requires laboratory equipment for identification.

Synthetic color-change corundum is often used as an imitation that changes color from grayish green to grayish purple. Synthetic color-change spinel may also imitate alexandrite and shows a color change of bluish green to purplish red.

CARE Usually very durable. Alexandrite is more sensitive to heat and pressure.

STONES WITH A SIMILAR APPEARANCE
Sapphire, synthetic sapphire, synthetic spinel, color-change garnet, tiger's eye, fiber-optic glass, topaz, beryl, peridot, tourmaline, and CZ.

TOPAZ

▲ *Pear-shape light "Sky" blue topaz. This shade of blue topaz has a very similar appearance to aquamarine.*

▲ *The emerald-cut shape draws attention to the deep, smoky color of this "London" blue topaz.*

▲ *A pear-shape "Swiss" blue topaz; the color of this material is almost an electric blue.*

▶ *The briolette shape of this "London" blue topaz can be simply and effectively mounted into a piece of jewelry.*

▲ *This delicate pink oval topaz's color is of natural origin as opposed to some very bright, coated material on the market.*

▲ *4.53-ct oval-cut yellow topaz, the color of this stone is of natural origin.*

◀ *A simple emerald-cut shape showcases the deep sherry color of this 4.79-ct imperial topaz.*

▶ *"Mystic" topaz; a very thin coating over the surface of this once-white topaz creates an unusual iridescent effect.*

CHRYSOBERYL

▼ *This 3.34-ct olive-toned chrysoberyl is a durable, good-quality stone.*

▲ *Under a single light source this oval chrysoberyl cat's eye shows a bright streak of light across its surface.*

▶ *This 1.49-ct alexandrite appears a deep green color under daylight and reddish-purple under artificial light conditions.*

ZIRCON

▲ Natural-color yellowish brown zircon. It is best to protect zircon from wear so this stone would suit a bezel setting, especially if it is used in a ring.

▲ Colorless zircons like this oval show a lot of fire. Diamonds also show this and the two can look similar.

▶ This ½ in (10 mm) round brilliant-cut zircon has high brilliance and fire with a lovely blue color.

TOURMALINE

◀ When this 10.40-ct cushion-shape tourmaline is viewed from different directions its body color may appear slightly different.

▶ This light green trillion-shape tourmaline shows a darker green color when viewed through the side.

◀ An oval-cut 8.03-ct tourmaline in a beautiful soft pink color.

▶ Carved flower watermelon tourmaline; the petal tips are yellowish green while the centers are pink.

◀ The straight facets of this emerald-cut tourmaline draw attention to its intense greenish blue color.

▶ Emerald-cut tourmalines like this bicolored green and pink stone are prone to wavy fractures widthwise which may be hazardous when setting.

ZIRCON

Natural zircon is a wonderfully brilliant and fiery stone with a sub-adamantine luster, suitable for jewelry as long as it sustains a minimal amount of impact.

CHEMICAL COMPOSITION Zirconium silicate
COLORS Red, brown, green, blue, white, and yellow.
LOCALITIES INCLUDE Australia, Nigeria, Sri Lanka, Thailand, and Vietnam.

AVAILABILITY

CUT Zircon is usually faceted to show off brightness and internal fire.
COLORS Vivid blue, yellow, and white are the most popular. The stones at left have been heat treated. Blue and yellow are the most expensive colors.
CLARITY Usually fairly free from inclusions, zircon may show strong doubling of back facets when viewed through a 10x loupe, depending upon its type.

QUALITIES

Color and cut are very important when judging the quality of zircons. Clarity and size are also factors.
HARDNESS 6½ to 7½. Some types of zircon are softer than others.
TOUGHNESS Poor to medium. Despite being a hard stone, it is brittle.
LUSTER Sub-adamantine
RI 1.78 to 1.99
BIREFRINGENCE None to 0.059

TREATMENTS Blue, bright yellow, and white stones have been heat treated.

CARE Zircons should not be stored together because they can easily damage each other. Avoid knocks, heat, and ultrasonic and steam cleaners.
UV light may affect the color of some stones. It is common for zircon to chip, particularly on facet edges if worn in jewelry that sustains wear.

STONES WITH A SIMILAR APPEARANCE

Diamond, chrysoberyl, glass, synthetic moissanite, sapphire, and CZ.

TOURMALINE

Tourmaline occurs in a large range of colors and is always popular.

CHEMICAL COMPOSITION A complex borosilicate of aluminum, magnesium, and iron.
COLORS A wide range of colors through to black. The color can change dependent on the viewing angle and across the material.

VARIETIES Other varieties of tourmaline are:
WATERMELON Shows color zoning across a rounded triangle-shape cross-section, ideally with a pink center and green rim.
BICOLOR Color zoning along the length of crystals.
PARAIBA Electric blue color
CHROME TOURMALINE Colored by chromium to give a vivid green.
RUBELLITE Red to bright pink color
INDICOLITE Dark blue
SCHORL Black
DRAVITE Brown
Cat's eye tourmaline is possible.
LOCALITIES INCLUDE Africa (Madagascar, Mozambique, Namibia, Tanzania), Brazil, Pakistan, Russia, and United States.

AVAILABILITY

CUT It is common to see long emerald cuts because a tourmaline crystal is naturally long and thin. Large rounds are rare because of the preferred shape of the rough material.
If material contains various colors, the stone is often cut to show more than one of these colors off at a time, e.g. watermelon tourmalines are usually cut as slices, and bicolor as baguette or emerald cut.
COLORS Out of the many colors of tourmaline, pink, green, and blue are most commercially available. These can range from pastel to intense colors. Red, neon blue, and bright green (rubellite, Paraiba, and chrome material) are the most popular colors.
If a contrast of colors across a stone is clear and attractive, the value of the material increases. Bicolored materials usually show two or three colors and could be any combination of many. Tourmaline can show different colors when viewed in different directions. The most desirable color direction will be cut so it is seen through the table, but the effect can be so strong that the two colors may be visible at the same time.
CLARITY It is common for tourmaline to contain wavy inclusions in a vaguely parallel configuration.

QUALITIES

An attractive color is important—strong colors tend to command a higher price especially if combined with relatively inclusion-free material. Brightly colored material is available at medium prices but the clarity is usually sacrificed for the color.
Paraiba, rubellite, and chrome varieties are the most expensive; a Paraiba tourmaline's price can reach thousands of dollars per carat.
HARDNESS 7 to 7½
TOUGHNESS Good
LUSTER Vitreous
RI 1.62 to 1.65
BIREFRINGENCE 0.014 to 0.021

TREATMENTS Some stones may be heated to lighten, darken or intensify color. Irradiation may have produced some red colors.

CARE Be careful using heat, and ultrasonic and steam cleaner, and guard against knocks if the stone contains wavy fractures. Tourmaline attracts dust if rubbed or heated.

STONES WITH A SIMILAR APPEARANCE Quartz, topaz, spodumene, andalusite, beryl, glass, synthetic quartz, synthetic spinel, chrysoberyl, topaz, and CZ.

PERIDOT

Peridot has an extremely distinctive and eye-catching yellow-green color. It is hard to obtain in large sizes but it is worthwhile when this is possible.

GROUP Peridot is a gem-quality variety of the mineral olivine.
CHEMICAL COMPOSITION Magnesium iron silicate
COLORS Green to yellowish or brownish.
LOCALITIES INCLUDE China, Myanmar (Burma), Pakistan, United States, and St. John's Island in the Red Sea.

AVAILABILITY

CUT Large sizes are difficult to find and expensive. It is hard to find rough that is large and gem quality, as well as without inclusions. More included material is often cut as cabochons.
COLORS A stone with a good, pleasing, saturated apple-green color and a lively cut will command the most expensive price, especially if large and clean.
CLARITY A large stone, free from inclusions, will be expensive. Inclusions called "lily pads" are common. Be careful when setting very close to these if they are close to the surface.

QUALITIES

Color is the most important factor, followed closely by clarity.
HARDNESS 6½
TOUGHNESS Medium
LUSTER Dull vitreous/greasy
RI 1.65 to 1.69
BIREFRINGENCE 0.036

GARNET

Garnets occur in a range of colors. They are bright stones and encompass a range of values and rarity. The cheapest garnet is a cloudy purplish-red almandine ranging up to the rare green and fiery demantoid.

CHEMICAL COMPOSITION Magnesium, iron, or manganese aluminum silicate or calcium chromium, aluminum or iron silicate.
COLORS Brownish red, purplish red, orange, green, and black.
VARIETIES Other varieties of garnet are:
PYROPE Reddish to brownish
ALMANDINE Reddish purple to black
SPESSARTINE Orange to red
MANDARIN Orange
HESSONITE Brownish orange
TSAVORITE Green
HYDROGROSSULAR Opaque yellowish green to pinkish, white, and brown
DEMANTOID Bright green
Garnets showing a star effect as well as color change are possible but rare.
LOCALITIES INCLUDE Brazil, Kenya, Madagascar, Namibia, Pakistan, Russia, Sri Lanka, South Africa, and Tanzania.
Pyrope and almandine occur worldwide.

AVAILABILITY

CUT Most garnets are transparent so the majority are faceted. Deep-color almandine garnets were historically cut as carbuncles, with a hollow back to lighten the color. Currently the more included almandine material is cut as shallow cabochons with flat backs.

A large stone in clean material is fairly difficult to obtain. Green garnets are available in smaller sizes than the red. Garnets are heavy so the carat weight may seem high for the size of the stone.
COLORS Shades closest to red colors, green, and orange can be expensive in large sizes. Demantoid garnet is the most expensive variety and can display fiery spectral colors over its body color. Rhodolite is a commercial name for stones in the color range of pyrope and almandine that are light purple.

Pyrope and almandine are the cheapest varieties of garnet, especially those containing inclusions and approaching a black color.
CLARITY Pyrope tends to contain fewer inclusions than almandine. Other types of garnet tend to show some inclusions, and material with few or no inclusions is most desirable.

Hessonite's inclusions sometimes give a hazy appearance and will usually be numerous.

QUALITIES

Color and clarity are the most important factors when judging garnet.
HARDNESS 6½ to 7½
TOUGHNESS Good, except demantoid.
LUSTER Bright vitreous
RI 1.70 to 1.89

TREATMENTS To date, garnet is not usually treated.

PERIDOT

▶ This high-quality cushion-cut 7.91-ct peridot contains few inclusions, meaning it is expensive.

◀ The mixed cut of this oval 5.25-ct peridot reflects a lot of light back through the front of the stone.

▶ Noticeable inclusions and a dark color meant this peridot material was cut as a cabochon.

▶ Dark inclusions are visible in this 9.10-ct baguette-cut peridot, but a clean stone of this size would be very expensive.

GARNET

▶ This long, thin, marquise-shape garnet will require care when setting as the corners are very fine.

◀ A light reddish-purple 5.42-ct oval rhodolite garnet containing few inclusions.

▲ A prong on each corner of this emerald-cut "Mali" garnet would highlight its shape while holding it secure.

▲ This pale green pear-shape tsavorite garnet is a lively stone with a minty hue.

▲ The bright green color of this oval tsavorite is a desirable and beautiful alternative to emerald.

MOONSTONE, LABRADORITE, SUNSTONE, AMAZONITE

◀ A flash of blue is seen across the front of this round, faceted moonstone.

▶ A round cabochon moonstone.

▼ The high, straight sides mean the setting edges for this cabochon moonstone would have to be quite tall.

▼ Inclusions inside this white oval moonstone make it appear milky.

▼ This moonstone is a pretty shade of peach and will show a silvery effect.

▲ A subtle sheen is seen across this gray cabochon-cut moonstone.

◀ This oval labradorite shows predominantly blue iridescent colors across its surface.

▶ White veins create interesting patterns over this vibrant green amazonite.

▼ This lower quality peach moonstone contains larger inclusions and a pinker hue than the stone at left.

▲ The oriented inclusions in this oval cabochon sunstone catch the light, giving a shimmering effect.

CARE Demantoid is the softest of all garnets with a hardness of 6.5.

Avoid heat and sharp changes in temperature but generally the durability of garnets is good.

STONES WITH A SIMILAR APPEARANCE

Ruby, red spinel, glass, tourmaline, composites, fire opal, citrine, emerald, peridot, chrome tourmaline, chrome diopside, and zircon.

MOONSTONE, LABRADORITE, SUNSTONE, AMAZONITE

The reflection effects of these feldspars are wide-ranging and impressive.

GROUP Feldspar
CHEMICAL COMPOSITION Potassium, sodium, or aluminum silicate.
COLORS White, peach, gray, yellow, blue, brown, and green.
VARIETIES
MOONSTONE Usually white and yellowish to transparent with a blue flash just under the surface. It can also be peach, pink, green, gray, or white with a silvery effect.

"Rainbow moonstone" is used to describe feldspar material that shows an iridescent color flash over yellowish and white to colorless material.
LABRADORITE Commonly gray with iridescent effects across the surface. This can also be called spectrolite.
AMAZONITE Blue-green and opaque material with irregular distribution of white areas.
SUNSTONE Usually a pale body color with platy orangey inclusions creating a shimmery effect.

These stones have slightly varying chemical compositions so their properties and appearance all differ.
LOCALITIES INCLUDE Australia, Brazil, India, Canada, Madagascar, Mexico, Myanmar (Burma), Norway, Russia, Sri Lanka, Tanzania, and United States.

AVAILABILITY

CUT Mainly cut as cabochons to show off optical effects, which should be oriented correctly.

Moonstone can be cut to show cat's eyes or star effects.

Poorer-quality moonstone, labradorite, and amazonite are available in large sizes.
COLORS Blue moonstone with a strong, even color flash is very desirable.

Dark-material labradorite with strong iridescence is popular.

Higher quality amazonite has a pretty bluish-green color with as few white streaks as possible.

"Oregon" sunstone has tiny copper inclusions, giving evenly distributed color, and is more

expensive than the ordinary variety of sunstone.
CLARITY Moonstone may contain many inclusions, cracks, and fissures.

Labradorite may also contain inclusions and fractures. Sunstone's inclusions are part of its optical effect and can range in size.

QUALITIES

The strongest or most transparent body color with the best optical effect and least undesirable inclusions gain the highest price. These will be the most attractive stones.

Large, transparent moonstone with a good flash of color and free from inclusions is rare, extremely expensive, and difficult to obtain.
HARDNESS 6
TOUGHNESS Fairly poor
LUSTER Vitreous
RI 1.51 to 1.57
BIREFRINGENCE 0.004 to 0.009

TREATMENTS Some varieties can be oiled or waxed to improve the clarity and appearance.

CARE Avoid wear against other items, as well as heat, ultrasonics, and chemicals. Most feldspars contain two directions of cleavage, so be careful when setting and cutting, and avoid impacts. Poorer-quality moonstone and labradorite is particularly risky.

STONES WITH A SIMILAR APPEARANCE

Synthetic spinel, composites, glass, goldstone, chalcedony, jade, and turquoise.

OPAL

Opal shows a magical iridescent play of color across its surface due to microscopic spheres within its structure. The effect can almost look holographic.

CHEMICAL COMPOSITION Silica with water
COLORS Body colors can be white, black, orange, and yellowish; with and without play of color. Also brown, blue, pink, and green without play of color.
VARIETIES
PRECIOUS OPAL Containing color patches of iridescence, this can be on a pale to dark body color varying from transparent (water opal) to opaque.
COMMON OPAL Material without a play of color including pink and blue Peruvian opal.
FIRE OPAL Yellow to orange, with or without play of color.
BOULDER OPAL Flat area of opal on top of the host rock in which the opal has been deposited.
MATRIX OPAL Host rock fissures filled with opal.

DENDRITIC OPAL Common opal containing dendritic inclusions.
Opal may rarely occur as a cat's eye.
LOCALITIES INCLUDE Australia, Czech Republic, Brazil, Ethiopia, Honduras, Indonesia, Mexico, Peru, and United States.

AVAILABILITY

CUT Cabochons and carvings are most common. Freeform cabochon shapes are cut to make best use of the rough material. Most transparent fire opals are faceted.
COLORS Fine black opals are the most expensive with a good play of color, followed by fire opals, then white. Common opals are the cheapest. The most expensive material with a play of color has large patches of strong colors all over the stone and contains all colors in the spectrum from red to violet. Violet is the commonest shade within the iridescent colors, and red is the rarest. Material containing a cat's eye is scarce.
CLARITY Interfering inclusions are undesirable.

QUALITIES

A stone's quality is judged on body color, iridescent color, size, and transparency. Good-quality material is expensive.
HARDNESS 6
TOUGHNESS Medium to low
LUSTER Below vitreous
RI 1.40 to 1.46 but the RI liquid may stain.

TREATMENTS Porous white opal may be stained to look black or gray.
Resins or oils can be used to fill cracked stones. Thin slices may be used as part of a composite, either on top of an opaque stone as a doublet, or between an opaque material and under a transparent material such as rock crystal to form a triplet.

SYNTHETICS Imitation opals are created using a similar process to nature and are fairly common. To date these can usually be detected with a 10x lens.

CARE Avoid chemicals including perfumes. Clean using a damp cloth only. Opals are best used in jewelry that will not sustain too much wear and in a protective setting.
Care should be taken in storage—avoid heat and dry environments—some material may craze internally over time.

STONES WITH A SIMILAR APPEARANCE

Plastic and glass containing foil or showing a sheen, ammonite, cornelian, spessartine garnet, and synthetic opal.

CHALCEDONY

Chalcedony is a fine-grained multi-crystalline variety of quartz that occurs in a range of colors. The crystals are so tiny that they are barely discernible.

GROUP Quartz
CHEMICAL COMPOSITION Silicon dioxide
COLORS Commercially chalcedony's color is pale bluish-gray. However the material chalcedony is available in many colors.
VARIETIES INCLUDE
CORNELIAN Reddish orange
SARD Brown
PRASE Dark green
CHRYSOPRASE Bright green
AGATE See page 43
ONYX Black
BLOODSTONE Green with red patches
LOCALITIES Worldwide

AVAILABILITY

CUT Used as cabochons, slices, signet stones, beads, and carvings. See agate section for sardonyx information (see page 43).
COLORS Colors with a good saturation and even distribution are desirable. Banding, specks, or patches may add beauty.
Bloodstone is most desirable with a reasonable amount of red specks. Chrysoprase often varies in color depending on its chemical content and may be pale green, emerald green, or even dark green.
CLARITY Blue chalcedony that is pale with a slightly lilac tint is most desirable, containing an even color and no clouds. It is one of the more expensive varieties of the chalcedony family along with chrysoprase. The best chrysoprase should have an intense apple-green color and be translucent with no clouds. Inclusions in the form of black or brown speckled deposits can occur and give a jadelike appearance.

QUALITIES

Evenness and depth of color are important factors. Some banding and inclusions can increase desirability and value but patchy areas can lower the value of the material.
HARDNESS 6 to 7
TOUGHNESS Very good
LUSTER Vitreous
RI 1.53 to 1.55

TREATMENTS Often stained, either to convincing colors such as black onyx or orange cornelian, or to bright colors such as bright pink, bright blue, and bright green. There is a risk that the dye may not have completely penetrated the stone. Most chalcedony on the current market is now dyed. Cornelian may have been heated to a reddish color.

OPAL

▲ Large, intense color patches are desirable in opals such as this 4.88-ct stone.

▲ Fire opal can be tricky to set so be careful around the corners of this intense orange-faceted trillion.

▲ Best use has been made of the uncut rough material to cut this 2.45-ct freeform white precious opal.

▲ Orange cabochon oval fire opal, a less intense color than the above trillion and therefore less expensive.

▲ This transparent opal shows flashes of orange through the stone.

▲ The dark body color of this precious black opal contrasts wonderfully with the bright flashes of blues and greens across its surface.

▲ A freeform opal triplet; if viewed from the side, the top of this stone would appear colorless.

▲ The front of this stone shows the precious iridescent black opal layer.

▲ Opal-filled fissures can be clearly seen in this host rock that has been cut to a cabochon.

CHALCEDONY

▶ Evenly colored lilac-blue pale chalcedony cut as an oval cabochon.

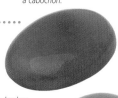

▶ A bright green cabochon-cut chrysoprase, a naturally colored green chalcedony.

◀ The deep green body color of bloodstone accentuates the vivid red areas scattered across this signet stone.

JADE

▶ Mottled grayish-green opaque jadeite jade cabochon.

◀ Finer quality, translucent jadeite jade cabochon with intense green patches.

▶ Stained jadeite jade round cabochon, a budget option when purchasing jadeite.

▲ An intense, natural-color jadeite jade cabochon with a slightly mottled appearance.

▲ Dark green nephrite cut into an oval cabochon shape.

◀ Jadeite jade cabochon that has been stained to produce a deep lavender color.

▶ Oval jadeite jade in an evenly distributed, pale, natural lavender color.

LAPIS LAZULI

▼ This good-quality lapis lazuli has a concentrated, even ultramarine-blue color.

▼ Lapis lazuli's blue color is interspersed with white calcite and pyrite in this freeform stone.

▲ This lapis lazuli looks like the crown of a faceted stone. The flat back allows for a cabochon-style setting.

◀ Intricately patterned lapis lazuli that has been carved by machines in the Far East.

JADE

There are two types of jade: jadeite jade and nephrite jade. Both occur in a range of colors and are very tough materials; however, jadeite's top prices far outreach nephrite's.

CHEMICAL COMPOSITION Jadeite: Sodium aluminum silicate
Nephrite: Calcium magnesium silicate
COLORS Jadeite: green, purple, white, red, orangeish, yellow, and brown.
Nephrite: darker green, brown, orange, bluish, black, and white.
VARIETIES Jadeite and nephrite
LOCALITIES INCLUDE Jadeite: Myanmar (Burma), Guatemala, Japan, and United States.
Nephrite: Canada, China, New Zealand, Taiwan, and United States.

AVAILABILITY

CUT Often cut as cabochons to show their color. Good for carving as the material is very tough and can be found in large boulders.
COLORS Green is classic and the most desirable jadeite color. Paler greens to white are becoming more popular, and lilac colors are also expensive. Nephrite greens tend to be more muted than the brighter jadeites.
   The most expensive jadeite, "Imperial Jade," is a very vivid green.
CLARITY Imperial Jade has a very even color and almost indiscernible individual crystals, so the material appears almost transparent.

QUALITIES

Texture and evenness of color is very important, particularly when judging jadeite material. The purity of the color is also a factor.
   Lack of treatment is desirable and rare in good-quality jadeite material.
HARDNESS Jadeite: 7
Nephrite: 6½
TOUGHNESS Jadeite: Second-toughest gem material
Nephrite: Toughest gem material
LUSTER Greasy vitreous
RI Jadeite: 1.64 to 1.68
Nephrite: 1.62

TREATMENTS Jadeite jade is commonly bleached to remove discolored areas in fractures and between crystals. This would be followed by filling with resin to stabilize and improve clarity and appearance. The filling material can be colored or the material dyed without bleaching and filling. Wax may hide surface cracks.
   Untreated jadeite jade is known as "A jade." Bleached and impregnated material is "B jade." Dyed material is known as "C jade." Both nephrite and jadeite material may also be heated to give the impression of age.

CARE Avoid heat and chemicals. A good choice for delicate carvings. Treatment can lower the stone's durability.

STONES WITH A SIMILAR APPEARANCE

Lower-quality emerald, chrysoprase, aventurine quartz, bowenite, hydrogrossular garnet, glass, and plastic.

LAPIS LAZULI

Lapis has a beautiful ultramarine color and was historically a source of ultramarine paint. It is an opaque rock and may contain white calcite crystals and golden-colored pyrite inclusions.

CHEMICAL COMPOSITION A rock of blue minerals, calcite, and pyrite.
COLORS Blue with areas of white and flecks of gold.
LOCALITIES INCLUDE Afghanistan, Chile, and Russia.

AVAILABILITY

CUT Good for cabochons, beads, inlay, and carvings. May be faceted for interest.
COLORS Intense ultramarine blue is the most desirable.
   Whether material contains or does not contain pyrite inclusions is down to personal preference.
CLARITY If the material is to be engraved, it is preferable that pyrite and calcite inclusions are not present for a smooth engraving surface.

QUALITIES

Color should be even and vivid. If pyrite inclusions are present, these should be lightly scattered.
HARDNESS 5½
TOUGHNESS Good
LUSTER Low vitreous
RI 1.50

TREATMENTS The material may be ground down and reconstructed with resin-producing reconstituted lapis. White and gold inclusions may be added.
   Lapis may also be dyed to improve color and waxed or filled with resin to improve its physical appearance.

CARE The white calcite inclusions will react vigorously with acids and chemicals, resulting in the surface of the stone being damaged, sometimes irretrievably. Avoid heat, ultrasonics, and steam cleaners.

STONES WITH A SIMILAR APPEARANCE
Dyed howlite, dyed jasper, sodalite, and dyed magnesite, fluorite, emerald, onyx marble, and jade.

CARE Avoid acids and bright sunlight if dyed, and also avoid sudden heat changes.

TURQUOISE

Turquoise can be a very stunning blue color and has been used in jewelry since ancient times. A large proportion of material on the market is now stabilized.

CHEMICAL COMPOSITION Copper aluminum phosphate
COLORS Blue to green and light to dark.
LOCALITIES INCLUDE Egypt, Iran, and United States.

AVAILABILITY
CUT Usually beads, cabochons, and carvings. It is a comparatively light material that is suitable for large carvings.
COLORS A strong turquoise blue color is the most popular, but colors can vary down to pale and greenish. Most turquoise turns greener over time.
CLARITY Veins in turquoise can look attractive and individual; however, clean material is more expensive.

QUALITIES
Natural untreated turquoise with a strong color and no veining is most expensive. This is followed by resin-filled material, material with a veining matrix (often filled too), and finally reconstructed.
HARDNESS 5½ to 6
TOUGHNESS Good
LUSTER Dull vitreous
RI 1.62 but the RI liquid may damage the surface.

TREATMENTS It is common for turquoise to be treated with resin or wax to improve stability if it is slightly powdery. Color can be improved if the filling material is additionally combined with a coloring agent.
Extremely small or poor-quality turquoise may be ground to a powder and reconstructed with resin. It is possible for this material to contain black or brown veins.
Turquoise can be dyed without resin filling.

CARE Avoid heat, chemicals, and ultrasonic cleaners. Turquoise can be attacked by acids easily and abraded.
Some material may have only been dyed to reach just below the surface, which should be considered if cutting the material.
Turquoise is porous. It is common for various oils and chemicals to be absorbed over time that will discolor the material.

STONES WITH A SIMILAR APPEARANCE
Glass, dyed howlite, dyed chalcedony, and dyed magnesite.

AGATE

Agates are a group of wonderful, decorative stones. They are tough, extremely popular, and often dyed to very bright colors.

GROUP Quartz, a type of chalcedony
CHEMICAL COMPOSITION Silicon dioxide, a fine-grained multi-crystalline material with curved bands of different transparencies and colors.
COLORS Often dyed blue, green, pink, purple, gray, brown, and black.
VARIETIES Lace agate, banded agate, moss agate, dendritic agate, and fire agate (which contains an iridescent effect).
LOCALITIES INCLUDE Worldwide

AVAILABILITY
CUT Used as cabochons, slices, signet stones, cameos, beads, and carvings.
Some banded material is oriented so one evenly sized color band is cut upon another. When the material is carved or engraved, the different color beneath is revealed, for example, black and white or black and red sardonyx. This precision orientation means it is an expensive cut.
COLORS Many colors are possible, particularly if the material is dyed.
CLARITY Inclusions, some color banding, and patches may be highly regarded features in agate. The beauty of these features affects the value. Moss agate can contain highly decorative examples of inclusions. These make it one of the more expensive varieties of agate.

QUALITIES
Even, well-saturated coloration is most important. Pretty banding patterns, patches, and color combinations may increase their value.
HARDNESS 6 to 7
TOUGHNESS Very good
LUSTER Vitreous
RI 1.53 to 1.56

TREATMENTS Frequently dyed (see chalcedony section, page 41).

CARE Avoid acids and bright sunlight if dyed. Avoid sudden heat changes.

STONES WITH A SIMILAR APPEARANCE
Fluorite, emerald, and onyx marble.

TURQUOISE

▶ *Freeform turquoise that contains veins of the original host rock, adding character to the stone.*

◀ *This stabilized round turquoise cabochon has a strong, even turquoise color.*

▶ *The matrix veins in this oval turquoise have been added rather than originating from nature.*

▲ *An oval turquoise cabochon that has been reconstructed from ground material.*

◀ *This Persian turquoise shows a pretty green color.*

▶ *Turquoise can easily be carved into attractive shapes such as this flower.*

AGATE

▼ *This white agate with dendritic inclusions is unusual because it has been faceted.*

▲ *Delicate patterns are seen in this freeform dendritic agate cabochon.*

◀ *This cabochon agate contains interesting treelike inclusions.*

▶ *Dyed red-and-white striped agate cabochon. Stained agates like these are usually cheap.*

▼ *This fire agate appears to have iridescent bubbles just below the surface.*

▲ *Agate's tough nature means it is a good stone for practicing setting. This black-and-white striped agate cabochon would look striking in a simple mount.*

HEMATITE

HEMATITE

◀ *These faceted hematite beads will feel very heavy compared to other materials of the same size and cut.*

▲ *The metallic luster of hematite can be seen on this oval cabochon stone.*

◀ *A racehorse has been carved on the front of this flat hematite intaglio.*

IOLITE

◀ *Marquise-cut faceted iolite.*

◀ *This princess-cut iolite has been cut so the strongest blue color can be seen through the front of the stone.*

▶ *If you were to view this round iolite from the side it would appear almost colorless.*

KUNZITE

◀ *Kunzite has two directions of cleavage; by fashioning it as an emerald cut, the danger of breaking a stone's corner when setting is lessened.*

▶ *Kunzite can range from a strong pink to the pale peach color of this oval stone.*

◀ *This cushion-cut kunzite is a desirable color of pink with a hint of violet.*

HEMATITE

A dark gray gemstone with a metallic luster, hematite actually appears red when in powder form or very thin slices and is used as a type of jeweler's polishing compound.

CHEMICAL COMPOSITION Iron oxide
COLORS Dark gray
LOCALITIES Brazil, UK, and United States.

AVAILABILITY

CUT Usually cabochon, signet stones, or intaglios, but may be faceted. Large beads will feel noticeably heavier than other beads of the same size.

QUALITIES

An inexpensive material. Higher-quality material will take a higher polish.
HARDNESS 5½ to 6
TOUGHNESS Fair
LUSTER Metallic
RI 2.94 to 3.22

TREATMENTS A lot of material on the market is now reconstituted hematite that can be press molded rather than carved.

CARE Hematite is soft, so is good for carving but can be a difficult material to work because it is prone to chipping. It is also soft, so avoid abrasion if possible. Hematite can be damaged by acids.

STONES WITH A SIMILAR APPEARANCE
Glass, plastic, and steel.

IOLITE

Sometimes sold as water sapphire, iolite's most striking feature is visible when the stone is viewed in different directions. It can show a deep blue color in one direction, but pale yellow in another.

GROUP Cordierite
CHEMICAL COMPOSITION Magnesium aluminum silicate
COLOR Blue to colorless. From one direction the body color is blue, from another it is pale yellow to colorless.
LOCALITIES India, Madagascar, Myanmar (Burma), and Sri Lanka.

AVAILABILITY

CUT If possible, iolite is cut so the strongest blue is visible through the table, not the pale yellow. Low-grade material is cut as cabochons.
COLORS A saturated blue color is most desirable when viewed through the table or top of the stone.

CLARITY Inclusions can be red. If these are numerous, the material may be called bloodshot iolite.

More transparent material is preferable but inclusions are common.

QUALITIES

Color is most important when judging quality, closely followed by clarity.
HARDNESS 7 to 7½
TOUGHNESS Medium to poor
LUSTER Vitreous
RI 1.54 to 1.56
BIREFRINGENCE 0.008 to 0.012

CARE Iolite does have one direction of cleavage so take care with storage and avoid knocks during wear. Avoid heat.

STONES WITH A SIMILAR APPEARANCE
Sapphire, tanzanite, and spinel.

KUNZITE

Kunzite is a violet-pink-colored variety of the spodumene family. Its color makes it a popular choice. However, customers should be warned that kunzite is best suited for occasional wear because of its brittle nature and instability under UV rays, even in sunlight.

GROUP Spodumene
CHEMICAL COMPOSITION Lithium aluminum silicate
COLORS Various shades of pink.
VARIETIES Other colors of spodumene can be: green, yellow, white, and violet.
LOCALITIES INCLUDE Afghanistan, Madagascar, Myanmar (Burma), Pakistan, and United States.

AVAILABILITY

CUT Stones are cut so the most desirable color is visible through the table. Emerald cuts are popular because this material can be prone to breakage.
COLORS Strong pink with a purplish tint is rarest and most expensive. Colors range down to very pale pink.
CLARITY Cleaner material is most desirable.

QUALITIES

Color and clarity are the main valuation factors.
HARDNESS 7
TOUGHNESS Fair
LUSTER Vitreous
RI 1.66 to 1.68
BIREFRINGENCE 0.015 to 0.016

TREATMENTS Brownish material may be heated to improve color. Some unstable colors can be produced using irradiation.

CARE Avoid knocks—kunzite contains two directions of cleavage. UV light (even in sunlight) can fade the material.

STONES WITH A SIMILAR APPEARANCE

Topaz, spinel, sapphire, morganite, tourmaline, rose quartz, and synthetic sapphire.

QUARTZ

Quartz is one of the world's most abundant gemstone materials. Some quartz material is found as transparent single crystals, and others are made up of many tiny crystals. These are semitransparent to opaque. The quartz family is popular; gemstones are often fairly cheap and can be available in large sizes.

CHEMICAL COMPOSITION Silicon dioxide
COLORS Purple, green, yellow, brown, pink, orange, reddish, and colorless.
VARIETIES
SINGLE-CRYSTAL QUARTZ
Amethyst: Purple
Citrine: Yellow to gold to goldish-brown
Prasiolite or green quartz: Green (sometimes misleadingly called green amethyst).
Rose quartz: Pink
Rock crystal: Colorless
Rutilated quartz: Colorless with golden needles
Smoky quartz: Brown
Tourmilated quartz: Colorless with black needles
Cat's eye: Usually muted greens, grays, yellows, and browns
POLYCRYSTALLINE QUARTZ
Jasper: There are many sub-varieties of jasper.
Aventurine: Green flecks in a whitish body color.
Tiger's eye: Yellow to brown silky-looking stone (can show a cat's eye); blue material is called "hawk's eye."
Chalcedony: (see Chalcedony, page 41).
Agate: (see Agate, page 43).
Silicified wood: Quartz-replaced wood.
LOCALITIES INCLUDE Africa, Australia, Brazil, India, Japan, Myanmar (Burma), Russia, and Sri Lanka.

AVAILABILITY

CUT Quartz can be faceted, carved, or cut as a cabochon depending on the quality of the material. It can be available in large stones with many or few inclusions.

Tiger's eye is usually domed to reveal lines of light across a silky, sometimes wavy texture.
COLORS Amethyst and citrine of a deep, vibrant color command the highest value. However, both materials can occur from very light to dark. Ametrine is a material that contains both the violet of amethyst and the yellow of citrine. Rose and green quartz are mid- to pale colored. Smoky quartz is cheap and can range from very light to dark.

CLARITY Rose quartz is usually quite cloudy and very rarely can contain enough fine inclusions to produce a star effect.

Cat's-eye quartz contains enough parallel inclusions to produce a streak of light across the surface.

Most single-crystal material is fairly clean but some inclusions are inevitable in large natural pieces. Overall, a clearer material is desirable but there are many beautiful inclusions possible that may add interest to the material and be marketed under specialist titles.

QUALITIES

Saturated colors are most desirable unless inclusions are of sufficient interest to increase the value of the stone.
HARDNESS 6 to 7
TOUGHNESS Good to very good
STABILITY Good
LUSTER Vitreous
RI 1.53 to 1.56
BIREFRINGENCE 0.009

TREATMENTS Most treatment of quartz is carried out with the aim of producing different colors.

Multi-crystalline quartz is commonly dyed to many colors (see also chalcedony and agate sections). Fractured material from a single crystal may also be dyed.

Irradiation can change rock crystal to smoky quartz and citrine to amethyst. Heating can lighten smoky quartz and turn some amethyst to green quartz but most to citrine. Tiger's eye can be heated to red.

SYNTHETICS Synthetics are available.

CARE Avoid sudden changes in heat that can dramatically fracture the material.

Avoid leaving dyed materials, amethyst, and rose quartz in strong sunlight.

Be careful of ultrasonics and strong acids.

STONES WITH A SIMILAR APPEARANCE

Glass, topaz, tourmaline, chrysoberyl, sapphire, synthetic sapphire, synthetic spinel, and CZ.

QUARTZ

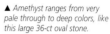

▲ Amethyst ranges from very pale through to deep colors, like this large 36-ct oval stone.

▲ Smooth rock crystal cut as a briolette drop shape.

▲ This slender oval citrine has an interesting "checkerboard" top with a flat back.

▲ An elongated pear-shaped faceted pale-green quartz.

▲ Rose quartz often has a misty appearance because of many very fine inclusions.

▲ This nebula jasper has the appearance of paint being splashed across it.

▼ Many beautiful pictures can be seen in landscape jasper, as seen in this oval cabochon.

▲ Very fine green inclusions seem to float inside the transparent body of this pear-shape "phantom" quartz.

▲ Tiger's eye has a silky appearance and often shows wavy patterns, as in this round cabochon.

▲ Rutile needles criss-cross over each other inside this oval-shaped rutilated quartz.

▼ A white matrix is pierced by long, thin tourmaline crystals in this striking cabochon trillion stone.

▲ Mica flakes are speckled over this rectangular rock-crystal piece, showing the vast array of inclusions possible inside quartz.

TANZANITE

◄ *Oval 3.11-ct pale purplish tanzanite.*

▲ *High-quality bluish pear-shape tanzanite; the apex should be treated with care when setting because tanzanite is a brittle material.*

◄ *The greenish hue of this oval tanzanite lowers the value of a high-clarity, deep-colored stone.*

DIOPSIDE

▲ *Bright green emerald-cut chrome diopside, a soft material best suited to earrings, brooches, and pendants.*

▲ *Oval-faceted chrome diopside with a hint of yellow in its body color.*

▲ *Round cabochon black-star diopside that will show an asymmetric four-rayed star under a single light source.*

TANZANITE

A beautifully colored stone that is only mined in the Merelani area of Tanzania. Most are heat treated to a blue color that can range from quite violet to a much purer blue. The material is quite brittle but this is compensated for by its stunning color.

GROUP Tanzanite is a blue gem-quality variety of zoisite.
CHEMICAL COMPOSITION Calcium aluminum silicate with hydroxyl
COLOR Purplish blue
VARIETIES Green gem-quality zoisite is possible.
LOCALITY Tanzania

AVAILABILITY

CUT Gem-quality tanzanite is usually faceted, often step cut to show off its color.

Emerald cuts are an advantage because tanzanite is quite a brittle stone.
COLORS A strong blue color with a violet tint is usually most expensive. Less expensive are stones with grayish tones.

Colors can be very strong down to pale lilac, and differ with directions between bluish and purplish. The material is mostly oriented to allow the most attractive color to be seen through the table.
CLARITY Included material is increasingly being cut as cabochons. Unincluded material is the most expensive.

QUALITIES

A vivid blue color is most desirable, particularly in clean, large materials that are cut well.
HARDNESS 6½
TOUGHNESS Medium to poor; quite brittle.
LUSTER Vitreous
RI 1.69 to 1.70
BIREFRINGENCE 0.006 to 0.013

TREATMENTS Many tanzanites are heated.

CARE Avoid wearing when knocks or rough handling may occur. Also avoid rapid changes of temperature and ultrasonic or steam cleaners. The material is soft, so it is not advisable for everyday wear, particularly without a protective-style setting.

STONES WITH A SIMILAR APPEARANCE

CZ, sapphire, spinel, iolite, glass, YAG, synthetic forstorite amethyst, iolite, and synthetic sapphire.

DIOPSIDE

Chrome diopside has a strong, attractive color and can be mistaken for chrome tourmaline. It is best used for areas that do not sustain abrasion because the material is very soft. Star diopside is very striking and is sometimes used as a simulant of black star sapphire.

CHEMICAL COMPOSITION Calcium magnesium silicate
COLORS Green to brown, white, and black.
VARIETIES
STAR DIOPSIDE Four-rayed asymmetric star effect.
CHROME DIOPSIDE Colored by chromium and a very bright green.
VIOLANE Opaque purple to violet–blue.
LOCALITIES INCLUDE Brazil, Italy, Myanmar (Burma), Pakistan, Russia, and Sri Lanka.

AVAILABILITY

CUT Chrome diopside is often faceted. Large chrome diopside can be expensive, but smaller material is of a medium price. Chrome diopside beads are available but can be costly.

Star material is cut as cabochons to reveal the optical effect. The material is relatively inexpensive.
COLORS Chrome is the more expensive variety. A bright green color is desirable without being too dark.
CLARITY A large, clean stone can be hard to find in chrome diopside, so may be expensive.

QUALITIES

Transparent chrome diopside is judged for its color and freedom from inclusions.

Star stones should be dark with a sharp star, cut to lie in the middle of the stone with as few additional inclusions as possible, other than those creating the star.
HARDNESS 5½
TOUGHNESS Fair
LUSTER Vitreous
RI 1.67 to 1.70
BIREFRINGENCE 0.024 to 0.030

CARE Diopside is soft so it is best suited to jewelry that sustains a low amount of wear.

It has two directions of internal cleavage, so beware of breakage.

Avoid using heat near the stone, acids, steam cleaners, and ultrasonics.

STONES WITH A SIMILAR APPEARANCE

Tourmaline, peridot, green garnet, sapphire, and black star sapphire.

CAT'S EYES

See Aquamarine (page 36), Chrysoberyl (page 37), Tourmaline (page 38), Opal (page 40), and Quartz (page 45).

FLUORITE

Fluorite is transparent, occurring in soft colors, often with beautiful internal banding. Take great care with this material; it is soft and extremely prone to breakage.

CHEMICAL COMPOSITION Calcium fluorine
COLORS Almost any except red or black.
VARIETIES Blue john from Castleton in Derbyshire, UK. This is translucent and banded purple, white, and pale yellow.
LOCALITIES INCLUDE Argentina, Austria, France, Germany, Myanmar (Burma), Namibia, UK, and United States.

AVAILABILITY

CUT Mostly cabochons due to the material being soft and delicate; however, beads, carvings, and crystals are also available. Fluorite is very soft and challenging to cut.
COLORS White, purple, green, and yellow are common colors. Attractive banding combinations and good depths of color command a higher value.
CLARITY Good clarity is desirable because there is less chance of breakage. Cleaner material is comparatively more expensive.

QUALITIES

Poor-color, very included material is cheaper. Blue john is often more expensive due to its specific mining location and ever-decreasing output. Other material is abundant and fairly inexpensive.
HARDNESS 4
TOUGHNESS Poor
LUSTER Dull vitreous
RI 1.43 to 1.44

TREATMENTS Stones may be irradiated, heated, and filled to improve resilience.
    Some types of fluorite may be made into a doublet or a triplet to improve the stone's durability.

CARE Fluorite is extremely easy to break because it has four directions of easy cleavage. Take care to avoid knocks; even heat may cause the material to break. Some may fade in the sun.

STONES WITH A SIMILAR APPEARANCE

Tourmaline, glass, synthetic spinel, and quartz varieties.

MALACHITE

An opaque, banded green gemstone.

CHEMICAL COMPOSITION Hydrated copper carbonate
COLOR Green, including shades of green in bands that can grow concentrically with radiating fibers intersecting the bands.
VARIETIES If malachite is intergrown with azurite, this is known as "azurmalachite."
LOCALITIES INCLUDE Australia, Russia, United States, and Zambia.

AVAILABILITY

CUT Malachite is a soft material so it is common to see cabochons, beads, carvings, and inlays.
COLOR The quality and shades of color varies.
CLARITY Banding is often desirable and patterns can be very attractive.

QUALITIES

Concentric banding in a pleasing arrangement is most expensive.
HARDNESS 4
TOUGHNESS Fair
LUSTER Silky or low vitreous
RI 1.85

TREATMENTS Malachite may be reconstituted from powder with resin, enhanced with oil or wax, or larger pieces may be held together with resin or plastic.

CARE Malachite is very susceptible to damage by acids and can be damaged by heat. Do not use in steam cleaners or ultrasonics and avoid use in jewelry that will be heavily abraded.
    Ensure any work on the stone is undertaken while wet to avoid breathing in its dust.

STONES WITH A SIMILAR APPEARANCE

Green agate and aventurine quartz.

OBSIDIAN

Obsidian is a type of natural glass and typically contains inclusions that are either decorative or create iridescent effects. Remember that this material is glass and is therefore quite fragile.

GROUP Natural glass
CHEMICAL COMPOSITION Silica
COLORS Generally muted colors: black, brown, gray, blue, green, and red.
VARIETIES
SNOWFLAKE Black material with white inclusions resembling snowflakes.

FLUORITE

▲ A low-quality example of blue john; the variety of fluorite from the Derbyshire mine.

▲ This cabochon shows characteristic colors and zoning of blue john.

▲ A green fluorite cabochon that is very prone to breakage.

▲ Fluorite should be treated with care; this unusual faceted stone will be fragile as well as possessing a delicate appearance.

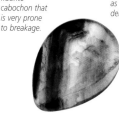

◄ This pear-shape cabochon shows dramatic color zoning that is typical of fluorite.

MALACHITE

▲ Malachite cabochon containing varying banded shades of green.

▲ Concentric bands of green have been cut to emphasize their dramatic appearance in this oval malachite.

OBSIDIAN

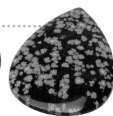

▲ Subtle colors are seen across the surface of this pear-shape rainbow obsidian.

▲ Inclusions have the appearance of little snowflakes across this appropriately named "snowflake" obsidian.

▲ Many inclusions can be seen inside this dark green moldavite oval.

▼ Emerald-cut natural glass known as moldavite.

CORAL

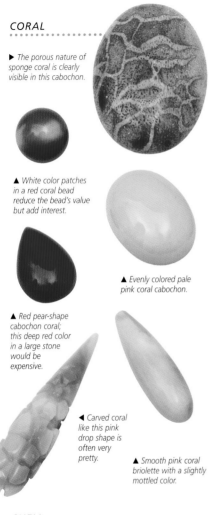

▶ The porous nature of sponge coral is clearly visible in this cabochon.

▲ White color patches in a red coral bead reduce the bead's value but add interest.

▲ Red pear-shape cabochon coral; this deep red color in a large stone would be expensive.

◀ Carved coral like this pink drop shape is often very pretty.

▲ Evenly colored pale pink coral cabochon.

▲ Smooth pink coral briolette with a slightly mottled color.

SHELL

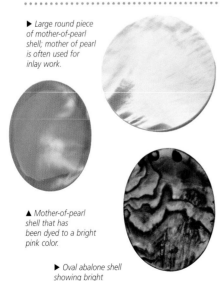

▶ Large round piece of mother-of-pearl shell; mother of pearl is often used for inlay work.

▲ Mother-of-pearl shell that has been dyed to a bright pink color.

▶ Oval abalone shell showing bright iridescent colors.

RAINBOW Material which shows iridescent colors.
BANDED Material containing color banding.
GOLDEN A dark body color with a golden effect.
MOLDAVITE A green and transparent type of natural glass.
LOCALITIES INCLUDE Mexico, Russia, and United States.

AVAILABILITY
CUT Usually cabochons and carvings if not transparent. Moldavite is often faceted.
COLORS Colors may be uniform or banded. Moldavite's green color is muted and so is often more valued by collectors than jewelers.
CLARITY Moldavite often has a sleepy appearance because of the presence of many bubbles and swirl effects. It is comparatively more expensive than other varieties of natural glass.
   Obsidian may contain many tiny inclusions, necessary to produce optical effects and patterns.

QUALITIES
Good-quality material requires an even color and few other inclusions except those necessary for patterns or interesting effects.
HARDNESS 5 to 5½
TOUGHNESS Medium
LUSTER Vitreous
RI 1.50

SYNTHETICS For man-made glass see the Man-made section on page 51.

CARE Avoid knocks, heat, and sudden changes in temperature. Glass is fairly soft and particularly vulnerable to damage if the material is very included for wear and for cutting.

STONES WITH A SIMILAR APPEARANCE
Man-made glass, plastic, onyx, dyed chalcedony, agate, and CZ.

CORAL

Coral originates from an organic polyp that grows in the sea. It occurs in beautiful colors such as red, orange, black, and gold.

CHEMICAL COMPOSITION Precious coral is mainly calcium carbonate.
COLORS Red, pink, orange, white, blue, black, and gold. Currently trade is restricted to protect the species of black and gold coral.
VARIETIES Red, pink, orange, white, black, and gold. Sponge coral has the appearance of a sponge and is red to orange with brown to yellow veins. Blue coral also has a porous appearance.
LOCALITIES INCLUDE Japan, Hawaii, West Indies, Australia, and southern waters toward Antarctica.

AVAILABILITY
CUT Coral is often cut as cabochons, drops, or carvings.
   Large cut pieces of coral are rare and costly. Coral is soft, easily carved, and easily polished.
COLORS Red is the most expensive and sought-after. Darker red (called moro) is rarest and commands the highest price.
   Red coral can contain white color patches that reduce its value.
   Other colors of precious coral range from mid-red to pale pink.
CLARITY Better quality material contains no fissures or cavities; however, sponge coral is porous by nature.

QUALITIES
Coral is judged by color, surface smoothness, and size.
   Sponge coral is cheap.
HARDNESS 2½ to 3½
TOUGHNESS Poor
LUSTER Below vitreous

TREATMENTS Coral can be ground up and "reconstituted" into blocks. The color of this is quite bright and uniform.
   Sponge coral is often filled with resin to improve color and stability.
   Paler coral may be dyed to achieve dark red color.

CARE Coral is easily attacked by even mild acids; avoid heat and avoid abrasion as the material is soft.
   Clean with water and a soft cloth.
   If cutting coral, it is important to do this under water to avoid breathing in the dust, which can be harmful if inhaled.

STONES WITH A SIMILAR APPEARANCE
Ceramic, stained bone, glass, plastic, and red jasper.

SHELL

Shells can contain iridescent linings that may be used for jewelry, inlay, and beads.

CHEMICAL COMPOSITION Calcium carbonate
COLORS Black, white, multicolored, pink, and brown.
VARIETIES
MOTHER-OF-PEARL Pale or grayish material, often showing iridescence.
ABALONE Dark material with blue-green iridescent colors.
CONCH SHELLS Contain pink, white, and brown layers; often ideal for carving.
LOCALITIES INCLUDE Australia, Indo-Pacific, New Zealand, and United States.

AVAILABILITY

CUT Cameos are commonly cut from banded material. As the material is cut away, a new color is visible underneath. The size of the finished product is dependent on the size and depth of the original shell, but this material is soft and easily carved to many shapes.

COLORS Most shells are fairly cheap whatever their color.

INCLUSION-FREE MATERIAL A smooth surface, with good iridescence or strong differentiation between banding, is most desirable.

QUALITIES

Color, surface smoothness, and quality of bands or iridescence are quality factors.

HARDNESS 2.5
TOUGHNESS Fair
LUSTER Often pearly
RI 1.53 to 1.69

TREATMENTS Shell can be coated, and mother-of-pearl in particular is commonly dyed.

CARE Extremely sensitive to acids and heat. When working with marine materials, make sure they are immersed in water or that the dust produced is washed away—it can be harmful if inhaled.

The surface may be damaged by acids, chemicals from the skin, or detergents.

Shell is easy to file, polish, and drill. However, beware if the material is dyed—the dye may only be surface deep.

STONES WITH A SIMILAR APPEARANCE

Ceramic, glass, and plastic.

PEARL

Pearl is an organic gem material and has a very subtle, luminescent beauty. A pearl does not need to be cut and its luster is unique. Natural pearls are extremely rare, so cultured pearls are usually sold. These may be either freshwater or seawater in origin.

GROUP Organic mollusk origin
CHEMICAL COMPOSITION Calcium carbonate, conchiolin, and water.
COLORS White, gold, gray, brown, black, pink, and peach.
VARIETIES
NATURAL Extremely rare and expensive.
CULTURED FRESHWATER Grown by man in mussels without a bead core.
CULTURED SEAWATER (AKOYA) Grown by man in oysters and contain a bead center.
SOUTHSEA Large pale pearls cultured in larger shells.

TAHITIAN Large dark pearls cultured in larger shells. Abalone shells rarely produce pearls, but blister pearls are possible.
LOCALITIES INCLUDE Persian Gulf, Red Sea, China, Japan, Polynesia, and the Cook Islands.

AVAILABILITY

CUT Shapes available are:
CYST Fully round.
BOUTON Squashed round.
BLISTER Grown attached to the inside of the shell.
BAROQUE, BIWA, KESHI Misshapes.
MABE A composite.
DROP Elongated fully round. Small pearls are available cut in half. Pearls may be sold on strings or half drilled.
COLORS A combination of body color, additional tint, and iridescence creates a pearl's overall color. Coloring should be even.

Freshwater pearls are naturally a peachy pink color, and other varieties depend on the host's shell or may be treated to a different color.
SIZE Currently, Akoya pearls are available up to about $^{6}/_{16}$ in (9 mm), freshwater up to about $^{8}/_{16}$ in (12 mm), Southsea/Tahitian approximately $^{5}/_{16}$ in (8 mm) to $^{5}/_{8}$ in (14 mm), Mabe from about $^{1}/_{2}$ to $^{6}/_{8}$ in (10 to 17 mm). These sizes are ruled by the size of the shell or the bead nucleus.

QUALITIES

A combination of color, luster, shape, surface evenness, size, and origin dictates the price and quality of a pearl.

Natural pearls are by far the most expensive, then Southsea and Tahitian, followed by akoya, and finally freshwater.

Pearls produced by the conch shell are rare and very desirable.
HARDNESS 3½ to 4
TOUGHNESS Surprisingly good considering their lack of hardness.
LUSTER Uniquely iridescent and pearly.

TREATMENTS

BLEACHING Lightens a pearl's color.
DYEING Changes a pearl's color.
POLISHING This is a specialist procedure aimed at improving the luster.
IRRADIATION Used to turn a pearl gray or black.
COATING Carried out to improve the surface appearance.

It is common for white pearls to have been bleached, colored pearls to have been dyed, and some gray and black pearls to have been irradiated. Mabe pearls are composites. Blister pearls are grown on the inside of a shell, sawn off, attached to a piece of mother of pearl, and then filled with resin between the pieces. This process enables pearls to look very large if the join is not visible when set in jewelry.

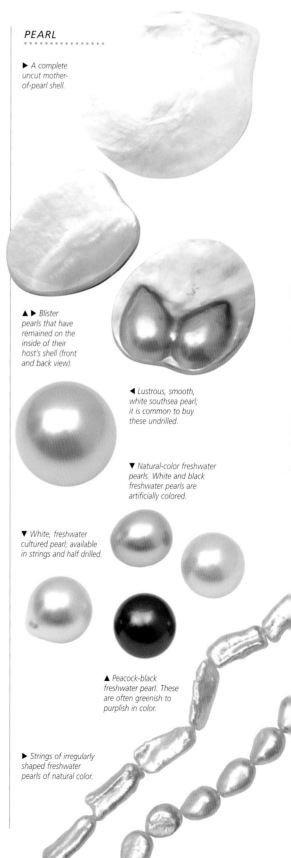

PEARL

▶ A complete uncut mother-of-pearl shell.

▲ ▶ Blister pearls that have remained on the inside of their host's shell (front and back view).

◀ Lustrous, smooth, white southsea pearl; it is common to buy these undrilled.

▼ Natural-color freshwater pearls. White and black freshwater pearls are artificially colored.

▼ White, freshwater cultured pearl; available in strings and half drilled.

▲ Peacock-black freshwater pearl. These are often greenish to purplish in color.

▶ Strings of irregularly shaped freshwater pearls of natural color.

AMBER

▶ *Oval cabochon amber containing sun spangles produced by heating the amber in oil.*

◀ *Freeform amber specimen containing minute insects that are millions of years old.*

▶ *Freeform pear-shape amber containing insects and plant debris from millions of years ago.*

▶ *"Green" amber oval; take care not to scratch the coating off the back or you will lose the green color of the stone.*

▲ *This dark amber cabochon has probably been treated to obtain its dark color and it will only be surface deep.*

▲ *Amber drop clearly showing a drill hole used to attach the material to jewelry.*

CARE Pearls are very sensitive to acids and chemicals, even hairspray and perfume. Contact with these is best avoided. It is common for pearls to turn yellowish over time due to absorption of chemicals during wear, which can even be from the skin.

Clean with water and a soft cloth but be aware of the possibility of damaging the thread if it is strung. If you are drilling a pearl, make sure you do it while the pearl is immersed in water to avoid inhaling dust.

STONES WITH A SIMILAR APPEARANCE
Coated glass beads, "shell pearls" (shell that has been ground up and reconstituted), coated plastic beads.

AMBER

Amber is a fossilized plant resin from over 15 million years ago. It can contain organic inclusions such as plant matter or insects that were trapped while the material was still sticky. It is very light and can be imitated by modern plastics and resins.

COMPOSITION Fossilized plant resin
FORM Amorphous
COLORS White, yellow, brown, and reddish brown, rarely with a green or blue tint.

VARIETIES

COGNAC Cognac amber can cover a range of shades from mid-golden brown to deep brandy colors.

YELLOW Bright, transparent yellow is considered the most desirable and expensive color of amber. However, many jewelry buyers prefer the spangled effect caused by inclusions.

GREEN Green amber is always popular, but it is not easy to source.

WHITE Only 10 percent of Baltic amber production is white. It is sometimes called bone amber and is full of small bubbles. It ranges in color from pure opaque white to pale cloudy cream. It often occurs alongside yellow amber material, and fabulous swirling patterns can result where the two colors meet.

RED Red amber occurs naturally but is quite rare. Most red amber in jewelry is imitation, often cognac amber backed with red foil.

VIOLET Violet amber is extremely rare and not commercially available.

LOCALITIES INCLUDE The Baltic, Dominican Republic, and Mexico.

AVAILABILITY

CUT Amber is a soft material, so is commonly fashioned as cabochons, beads, and carvings. If a stone contains desirable internal features, it may be cut to show these to best effect.

Large, natural material can be fairly expensive. Amber can be polished using jeweler's Tripoli and rouge compounds.

COLORS Yellows to oranges tend to be the more popular colors.

CLARITY Insects and other organic matter are desirable according to personal preference; both transparent and sun-spangled materials are popular. Opaque material is less valuable than transparent.

QUALITIES
Transparency, color, and inclusions all affect the price of amber.
HARDNESS 2.5
TOUGHNESS Fairly brittle
LUSTER Resinous
RI 1.54

TREATMENTS
Amber is frequently treated to enhance clarity. "Sun spangles" can be induced during this process and are now viewed as desirable features.

Surface color can be darkened by heat. Color can be changed by coating and dyeing.

Ambroid is a composite amber that is created by heating small pieces of real amber at a high temperature and compressing them together. It is often dyed and is much stronger than natural amber. Ambroid usually has a misty look and will frequently contain trapped elongated air bubbles that can be seen through a loupe.

Copal resin is often sold as amber (for amber prices). It is actually a resin produced by a type of tropical tree.

Use a hot needle held on an unobtrusive place on the stone with tweezers to distinguish amber from synthetics. Real amber will produce smoke that smells a bit like incense, while plastic will melt and show a black mark.

CARE Avoid heat, strong light in shop windows, chemicals, acids, and cleaning products. Color treatments may only be surface deep, recutting and even heavy polishing may remove this. Amber is easily carved and drilled but this material burns readily if it becomes too hot. The whole stone can crack if an inclusion is penetrated during drilling.

STONES WITH A SIMILAR APPEARANCE
Plastic, copal resin (very similar to amber but simply tree resin), and glass.

MAN-MADE STONES

Synthetic stones such as sapphire, ruby, and emerald all have the same chemical composition as their natural counterparts but have been created artificially. Synthetic stones may be challenging to identify using only handheld gemological equipment and may need to be sent to a laboratory for further testing. Popular man-made materials include:

MATERIALS

CUBIC ZIRCONIA (CZ)
This occurs in a vast range of colors. It is a very good diamond imitation with a hardness of 8.5. Nearly all material is clean; the main quality factor is its cut.

YAG, GGG
These are historical diamond simulants that are now rare since the invention of the CZ.

SYNTHETIC MOISSANITE T
This is a good diamond simulant, however it often shows a tint of color. It shows doubling of the stone's back facets, which is a valuable indication that this material is not diamond. It currently has limited production and is much more expensive than CZ.

PLASTIC
A very cheap material that is usually betrayed by its extremely light weight.

GLASS
This has been a popular gemstone simulant for thousands of years. It is commonly molded into shape and stones often betray their origin by showing mold marks, internal swirls, and bubbles. A high-quality glass may have been recut to hide mold marks but the internal features may remain. There are many different chemical variations possible for man-made glass that will affect their properties. It has a much larger RI range compared to natural glass; from 1.50 to 1.70. Man-made glass can be a component of composite stones. Hard-mass, paste, and alpinite are commercial names for types of man-made glass.

STONES

SYNTHETIC RUBY AND SAPPHIRE
Synthetic corundum (which includes both ruby and sapphire) can currently be created using a few methods. The Verneuil method of production is the easiest to identify. Internally, color zones in synthetics produced by this method are curved as opposed to the straight zones of natural stones or other types of synthetic material. This curvature is due to molten corundum dropping onto a rotating "boule." Bubbles may also be present individually or in clouds, which does not occur in natural stones. Stones produced by other processes such as flux melt and hydrothermal methods of production are more difficult to identify. Features such as platinum inclusions, characteristic feathers, and hazy zoning may indicate man-made production. The various colors of sapphires and ruby are created by additions of chemical coloring elements to pure corundum, which is naturally colorless. For example, chromium would be added to create synthetic ruby.

SYNTHETIC SPINEL
The most common method of synthetic spinel production is the Verneuil process, as mentioned above. These may also show the curved zoning and bubbles; because of a slightly differing proportion of chemical elements from a natural stone, stones can usually easily be proved to be synthetics using standard gemological equipment. Synthetic spinels have a slightly higher RI of 1.727 rather than the 1.717 of natural stones and also show recognizable effects under a gemologist's polariscope. Other methods of production are more difficult to identify, but are currently less common on the gemstone market.

SYNTHETIC EMERALD
Synthetic emerald may be created by the flux melt and hydrothermal methods. Each of these methods may leave identifying features within the gemstone to indicate man-made origin. These may include platinum inclusions, characteristic partially healed fractures, hazy zoning, and sometimes low RI and birefringence values. If a clear combination of factors cannot be seen, the stone may have to be tested in a laboratory. Emeralds naturally contain many inclusions; if a stone appears very clean, large, and cheap, it is wise to be suspicious of its original source.

GENERAL GEMSTONE CARE

- Store separately to avoid gemstones damaging each other.
- Wash in mild, soapy water.
- Avoid chemicals, heat, knocks, and abrasion wherever possible.
- If cutting or drilling gemstones, make sure the dust created is constantly washed away by a water flow or by immersion in water.

FURTHER NOTES
Material availability and relative prices are subject to change from time of publication and based upon the author's experiences and research.

MAN-MADE

▲ Lavender pear-shape cubic zirconia.

▲ The facets on this emerald-cut pink cubic zirconia are triangular, which is known as a radiant cut.

▲ Oval, white cubic zirconia; currently a very popular choice as a cheap diamond simulant.

▲ The chemicals used to color the deep blue of this tanzanite-colored cubic zirconia make it slightly more expensive than other hues.

◀ Orange synthetic sapphire in a radiant emerald-cut shape.

▲ Marquise-cut yellow cubic zirconia.

▲ Synthetic ruby contains the same chemical composition as a natural stone but has been created artificially.

▲ Bright blue synthetic spinel; this particular shade of blue is different from natural blue spinels.

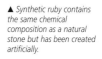
▲ Radiant emerald-cut hard mass green glass, which can be used as a cheap, man-made alternative to emerald.

▲ Elongated radiant-cut white cubic zirconia.

Metalworking skills allow you to use a vast range of methods for setting stones. For many of the techniques described in this section, metal is compressed over or around a stone to hold it securely in position, but the methods by which this is done vary greatly. Diagrams are used to explain each style of mount and suggest possible variations. Stone setting is not easy, but with practice and perseverance, your success rate will improve, and it will be a very rewarding experience.

CHAPTER 3

Techniques Directory

Getting Started

From making sure the correct tools are readily available to wearing safety goggles, you should incorporate safe and sensible working practices into your everyday routine of working in a studio —this includes how the studio itself is set up.

▲ *Safety glasses*

▼ *Cup mask*

▲ *Protective finger tape*

▲ *Leather finger protectors*

A Safe Workspace

Most health and safety is common sense, whether you have a workshop or studio space in your home or not. It is sensible to arrange the workspace in a practical way, having enough storage and space for tools to lie on surfaces while you work, and isolated areas for heating metal, pickling, and other chemical processes. Work surfaces need to be securely fixed to a wall, or screwed to the floor to prevent them from moving when force is applied. This is essential for accurate working, as is good lighting, especially for stone setting; a daylight bulb in an adjustable lamp that is fixed to the bench is a worthwhile investment.

It is important to have clear floor space around working areas, and heavy equipment such as vises and rolling mills bolted down to a sturdy surface at the correct working height. Flexshaft motors can be fixed with either a stand screwed onto the bench, or suspended from a bracket attached to the wall at the correct height. Rotary machines such as drills and polishing motors can be dangerous if not used correctly—always wear safety glasses and tie hair and loose clothing back. Polish chains in a barrel polisher and never on a polishing motor.

Take general precautions to reduce the noise created by certain tasks as good working practice. Place a sandbag under tools such as dapping blocks when hammering punches, so that some of the noise will be absorbed, and use a mallet rather than a hammer wherever possible, since the tone is much less sharp.

Storing, Using, and Disposing of Chemicals

Store chemicals in a labeled, lockable metal cupboard, and always wear gloves, goggles, and a mask when handling toxic, corrosive, or harmful chemicals. Choose the safest possible option when using chemicals to limit the risks involved; many safer alternatives to chemicals commonly used in jewelry making are now readily available, with citric acid solution preferable to traditional pickle, for example. Spent pickle must be disposed of responsibly—allow the liquid to evaporate so that just crystals remain, thus reducing the volume of the waste. It is not safe to dispose of the resulting sediment in household waste because it contains heavy metals—you will need to find out where to dispose of chemical waste locally.

The area of the studio in which you use heated pickle should be well ventilated, either by extraction or an open window, since it is dangerous to breathe in the fumes. Soldering also creates fumes, and ventilation is equally important but don't let drafts interfere with the flame or its effectiveness will be reduced.

Turn off bottled propane gas at the bottle after use, and check the gas pipe on a regular basis. The area of the studio you use to heat metal should be lined with house bricks and covered with a heatproof mat to prevent damage to the underlying surface.

Health and Safety Equipment

It is vital to take adequate preventative measures when using chemicals, machinery, or processes that could damage your health.

Wear eye protection whenever you use rotary machinery such as drills, flexshaft motors, or polishing motors. Safety glasses are used to protect the eyes, and should even be worn over glasses. They are made from a shatterproof plastic that will withstand impacts from flying debris or pieces of work, and also provide a barrier to chemical splashes.

Cup masks are a barrier prevention against dust, and you should wear one whenever you carry out work that produces dust, including using abrasives with a flexshaft motor and filing soft

▲ *Eyewash solution*

▲ *Rubber gloves*

IDEAL STUDIO SETUP
The studio shown below is well organized, the tools are arranged and stored in a safe and practical way, and there is enough space in which to work.

1. Racks and containers for frequently used items.
2. Heat-resistant soldering mats or blocks to avoid burning the bench.
3. "Skin" to collect dust and scraps of precious metals for recycling.
4. Gooseneck lamp with a bright daylight bulb.
5. Bench peg: The jeweler's primary support tool for holding metal steady during many making processes.
6. Storage containers with multiple drawers.
7. Files and different grades of emery paper.
8. Pliers stowed point-end upward on a rack.

materials such as wood or plastics. The mask should fit closely over your nose and chin and you can push the metal strip around your nose to stop dust from being drawn in at the sides of the mask.

NEVER wear gloves when operating rotary machinery such as drills and polishing motors—if your fingers need to be protected from abrasive mediums, or the work quickly gets hot when polishing, wear leather finger protectors. If the polishing wheel does catch on the leather protector, it will simply slip off. These are also useful for holding small, awkward-shaped pieces while filing.

Other essential items for any workshop are a first-aid kit for minor cuts and burns, which are an occupational hazard, and a small fire extinguisher, just in case.

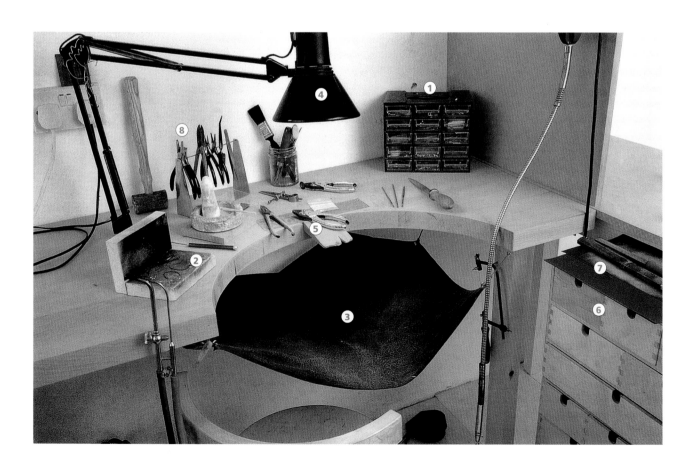

Useful Tips and Troubleshooting

Choosing the correct tools for a job is only part of achieving a successful outcome when setting stones. Judging whether a tool is working effectively and knowing what to do when things don't quite work out as planned all come with experience.

As with each particular branch of jewelry making, a specific set of tools is required for stone setting. As your skill level increases, so will your number of tools. A few basics such as a pusher, triblet, and a couple of gravers will be enough when you start out with basic stone-setting techniques, and these can be sourced relatively inexpensively. Keep tools organized and protected and in a good state of repair so that they are always ready to use when required. Magnetic organizers and sectioned drawers or stands made from blocks of wood with drilled holes are all good solutions.

A few other sundry items are also invaluable and these include protective finger tape, also called "alligator" tape, which can be wound around fingertips to protect them from abrasion when cleaning up pieces, and as a preventative measure against cuts and blisters. The tape is loosely woven with a texture, making it easier to grip small pieces of work while working on them.

Hold pieces in clamps or with a support wherever possible; this can spare your fingers from hours of holding parts that are too small to comfortably hold. Insert wooden doweling into bezels and tapered bezels to prevent them from becoming misshapen during the cleaning up process.

Chamois leather covers for the bench pin will prevent finished or polished work from becoming scratched or bruised while you are setting stones.

Making Best Use of Holding Media

Supporting the work so that you can use adequate force makes all the difference when setting stones. Setters' wax has the optimum consistency for holding pieces of work during stone setting, being very firm but slightly flexible and tacky; warm the wax with a soft yellow flame, such as that of a spirit lamp, so that it does not char. The shape of the wax on the end of the stick will depend on the type of setting and the shape of the form being held. Roll the warmed wax on a flat steel block to even out its overall shape and warm it again to soften the surface so that you can set the piece into it with tweezers; take care not to touch the wax while it is hot—it can be cooled quickly in cold water.

Jett Sett can be used in a similar way but is a bit less versatile. It is, however, much cleaner to use as it only requires hot water to soften it—but being less sticky, it does not grip work as well. This means it is only really good for holding larger pieces that can be covered by the plastic while still allowing enough access to set the stone.

ORGANIZE YOUR TOOLS
Keeping your tools and workbench organized will help you to approach your work in a methodical manner.

PREVENTING AND RECTIFYING MISTAKES

- When cleaning up a fine silver or gold bezel, it may accidentally get squashed, compressed, or deformed if you put too much pressure on the wall, so that the stone will not fit in. Open up the bezel carefully with a burnisher or a steel rod of a similar diameter to the stone.

- Always make sure solder seams are a strong join—the forces used in stone setting mean that any weak points can be stressed to the point of breaking. Even a small nick in the solder seam that joins a bezel to itself or to a base can open up during setting, so file it out if possible.

- If the stone is wrongly set, you need to make a decision as to whether the stone or the bezel is more important. If the stone is, the bezel can be cut and torn to release the stone, before being remade. If the stone is cheaply and easily replaced but the bezel will take too long to reconstruct, heat and quench the stone several times to encourage the stone to crack—it can then be prized out and the bezel carefully opened up to put a new stone in.

- When burring a seat for the stone, if the mid-point of the burr passes the level of the top of the tapered bezel or bezel and the stone still doesn't fit in—stop. This usually means the stone is fractionally bigger than the burr; if the burr is used at an angle, it will widen the seat more than if used straight on as ball burrs are not perfectly round. Work with the burr angled at north, south, east, and west before trying the stone again. Increase the angle and repeat the process until the stone is seated.
    If that still doesn't work and the next size of burr is far too large, use a spitstick to engrave metal away from around the seat—this is the method of cutting seats for oval stones.

- If a stone does not sit straight in a mount, try to work out why. Is a part of the seat preventing it from sitting level? Hold it up to the light to see where the stone is actually touching—that is where you should remove the metal. Do not attempt to set the stone until you have resolved the problem.

- If, once you have started setting, the stone moves and is no longer level, it may be possible to tap it down on the higher side using a piece of hardwood, or if in a bezel, by setting the higher side more than the lower side.

- If prongs break, get them laser-welded back on, or have new tip applied—this is inexpensive considering it might otherwise mean you have to make the mount again—and laser welding can be done with the stone in situ.

- Silver, yellow, and white gold all move differently and their malleability will affect how easily a stone can be set.

- There are ways to disguise mistakes—such as further engraving to cover slips and little tricks to fool the eye; but there are also plenty of scenarios that mean starting again—removing a tapered bezel from a shank by reheating the solder, or using a jewelry saw to cut it out. In these cases, it's best to take a break or do something else for a while—everyone has bad days. It is important to learn from mistakes because if you can understand why something didn't work—if it was a fault in making or a design flaw—you will deepen your knowledge in a way that informs a very individual way of working.

SETTING ERRORS
Sometimes the only way to fit a stone into a mount is to engrave metal out from the inner edge of the seat with a spitstick.

▶ Saw blades (1)

◀ Jewelry saw (1)

Hand Tools

A few basic metalworking tools will be sufficient when you start out in jewelry making, and you can expand the range as your skill level increases.

Tools that are used to shape, join, and refine the surface of metal are vital for accurately constructing mounts for stones. The range of tools required will depend on the techniques that you use. A small range will suffice for general working, but you are likely to acquire a small number of more specialist tools as you need them for specific tasks, particularly burrs—to begin with only certain sizes will be required, but as you set more stones of differing sizes, more burrs will be required of incrementally closer sizes. It is also a good idea to have a range of "consumables" such as solder, saw blades, and abrasive media in the workshop so that it is not necessary to stop work because something is missing, or to have to use a less appropriate item as a compromise, which only usually has the effect of making the whole process take much longer.

The range of tools may also depend on the metals you are working with—harder metals such as platinum and palladium require special saw blades, files and polish, and an oxyacetylene torch rather than a propane gas torch in order to reach the temperatures required for soldering and annealing these metals.

JEWELRY SAW AND SAW BLADES (1)

Jewelry saws are sprung steel frames set into a wooden or plastic handle. The frame is slightly flexible and holds a saw blade under tension, secured by two nuts. Fixed and adjustable saw frames are available. The frame is lightweight and can be used to cut very accurate detail in a range of materials with the aid of a suitable saw blade—size 2/0 is good for general-purpose uses, and 4/0 or 5/0 should be used for fine detail; the grade determines both the thickness of the blade and the size of the teeth that run down one side. Specially hardened saw blades are available for platinum; these can also be used for piercing stainless steel.

Spiral saw blades should be used for cutting soft materials, such as wax, acrylic, and wood, because the spiral arrangement of the teeth prevents the blade from becoming stuck.

FILES (2)

Hand files are used to remove metal and refine surfaces in preparation for other techniques. Files are usually supplied without handles—these are sold separately and need to be fitted before use. Files cut as they are pushed forward across a surface, but do not cut on the return stroke.

A wide range of cuts, sizes, and profiles of hand files are available. It is useful to have one half-round cut 0 file for quickly removing material, and a small range of cut 2 hand files. See page 67 for file shapes.

Needlefiles are used for more intricate work than hand files because they are smaller and available in a greater range of profiles.

Needlefiles made from a harder alloy are available for platinum and stainless steel.

Wax, or rasping, files have widely spaced rough teeth that allow wax to be removed without clogging the file, and are available as both hand and needlefiles, with a range of profiles.

CHENIER VISE AND CUTTERS (3)

Chenier vises are useful for holding tube while a length is cut with a jewelry saw, and can also be used to file the cut end of the tube, or rod, absolutely true at 90-degree or 45-degree angles. A chenier vise is something of an investment, but invaluable for accuracy.

Chenier cutters can be used to cut identical lengths of tube, using the adjustable stop to set the length. The tube is placed in the base of the "V," and the lever secures the tube with pressure from the left thumb. A jewelry saw is then used to cut the tube, using the gap in the cutter as a guide.

▼ Needlefiles (2)

▼ Hand files (2)

▼ Chenier cutter (3)

▼ Chenier vise (3)

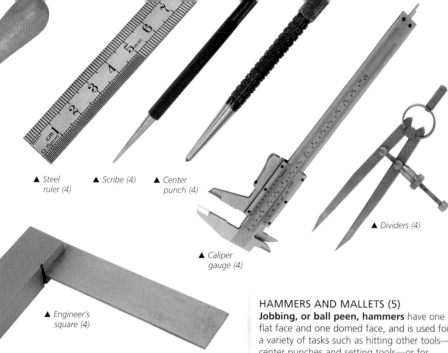

▲ Steel ruler (4) ▲ Scribe (4) ▲ Center punch (4)

▲ Dividers (4)

▲ Caliper gauge (4)

▲ Engineer's square (4)

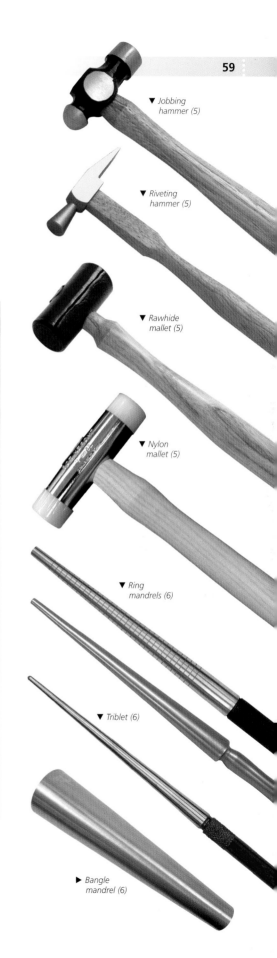

▼ Jobbing hammer (5)

▼ Riveting hammer (5)

▼ Rawhide mallet (5)

▼ Nylon mallet (5)

▼ Ring mandrels (6)

▼ Triblet (6)

▶ Bangle mandrel (6)

MEASURING AND MARKING TOOLS (4)

Steel rulers are often used in conjunction with a scribe or dividers that mark the metal once the correct measurement has been decided. Rulers usually have both metric and imperial scales, and are either 6 in (15 cm) or 12 in (30 cm) in length.

Engineer's squares can be used to mark perpendicular lines on metal with the use of a scribe, and is also useful for checking the accuracy of right-angles.

Scribes are used in combination with a steel ruler or an engineer's square for very precise marking of measurements—the fine point means that it is accurate. Designs can also be drawn freehand.

Center punches are used to create a registration mark in sheet metal before drilling so that the drill bit has a reference point. The punch is tapped with a general-purpose hammer.

Dividers are useful for marking circles on metal, and to make parallel marks by using the side of a metal sheet as a reference.

Gauges are used for measuring the thickness of metal sheet and the diameter of rod or gemstones, and a variety of gauges is available—sliding gauge, digital display, and dial.

HAMMERS AND MALLETS (5)

Jobbing, or ball peen, hammers have one flat face and one domed face, and is used for a variety of tasks such as hitting other tools—center punches and setting tools—or for making textures on metal.

Riveting hammers have one flat circular face and a narrow rectangular flat face. The lightweight head can be used for many small tasks in jewelry, including hardening and straightening wire, as well as for making flat-headed rivets and tapping pins into hinges.

Mallets will form metal without marking the surface, but can also be used for hitting other tools, such as dapping punches, with less force and noise than a hammer. Both rawhide and nylon mallets are suitable for use in jewelry making.

MANDRELS AND TRIBLETS (6)

Mandrels are most often used for forming a ring with a mallet, truing the form once it has been soldered, and forcing the piece up the mandrel to enlarge it. The ring mandrel is usually held horizontally in a vise, but can be supported in the "V" of a bench pin while sizing or truing a ring. The most common profile (cross-section) is round, but oval and square mandrels are also useful. Other styles available include pear-shaped, mandrels with a groove (for sizing or truing stone-set rings), and mandrels marked with ring sizes.

Bangle mandrels are either round or oval, and are of a suitable size for forming and truing bangles and cuffs.

Triblets are basically small ring mandrels, for forming and truing bezels.

The shape of triblet used will depend on the shape of the stone that is being set—round, oval, square, cushion, or pear-shaped. Larger bezels may be formed on the tip of a ring mandrel if it is of a suitable diameter.

▲ *Dapping block (7)*

▲ *Steel dapping punches (7)*

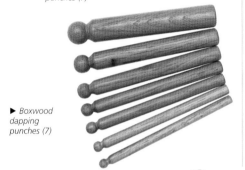

▶ *Boxwood dapping punches (7)*

DAPPING BLOCK AND PUNCHES (7)

Dapping blocks are used in conjunction with dapping punches to curve sheet-metal forms. The block should be placed on a sandbag—a leather cushion filled with sand—to reduce the noise produced when the dapping punch is struck. Dapping blocks and cubes are made of either steel or brass, and have a graduating range of depressions. The most common range is ⅟₁₆–1¼ in (2–30 mm) diameter. Outsized blocks have single or double depressions and are often sold with the corresponding punch.

Dapping punches have a polished ball on one end, and are designed to be hit with a mallet or jobbing hammer on the other. When used with a dapping block in the corresponding depression, they will force metal to form a hemisphere; they can also be used as punches for spreading rivet heads. Dapping punches are made from either steel or boxwood, and are sold individually or in sets.

BENCH VISE (8)

Every workshop needs a vise, predominantly to hold tools while working, such as mandrels, ring clamps, or pieces of jewelry secured in setter's wax on a piece of wood; they can also be used to make press forms. Protective pads are often used to protect work from the rough surface of the jaws, and can be made from leather. Vises must be fixed to a sturdy bench with bolts.

Small vises that are fixed to the bench top with a C-clamp are suitable for small-scale work such as riveting. You can find reasonable-quality second-hand vises cheaply.

PLIERS (9)

Pliers generally open with a scissor action and are used for a variety of techniques in jewelry making. Many styles of pliers are available plain, or sprung, meaning that they will automatically reopen after being closed.

Round-nose pliers are good for making small loops, but can mark wire if it is gripped tightly.

Half-round pliers will not mark wire, but cannot make such small loops.

Chain-nose pliers have tapered tips and so can get into smaller spaces than other, wider pliers, and are particularly useful for tightening wire that has been wrapped around itself.

Flat-nose pliers with two flat-faced jaws are used to bend and fold sheet and wire, and are also useful for pulling rivets or pins through a hole.

Parallel pliers open with a parallel action, unlike other pliers, and can therefore be used to hold work without damaging it. This makes them useful for bending right angles and straightening kinks without marking the metal. Wires can also be hardened through twisting with these pliers.

CUTTERS (10)

Top (also called end or flush) cutters can be used to cut wire of less than 17 gauge (1.3 mm) if it is soft, and up to 24 gauge (0.5 mm) hard wire. For larger-diameter wires, use heavy-duty cutters or a jewelry saw. These cutters allow wires to be accurately cut flush or close to another surface, but do leave a pointed end on the wire and should not be used to cut steel wire because it will damage the cutters.

Memory wire cutters are suitable for cutting steel and other hard metals, leaving a reasonably flat end.

Tin snips or shears are most often used for cutting solder pallions, but also for cutting thin sheet metal and binding wire; they cut with a scissor action.

Heavy-duty scissors can also be used for cutting soft, thin sheet metal such as fine silver bezel strip.

◀ *Bench vise (8)*

▲ *Flat-nose pliers (9)*

▲ *Round-nose pliers (9)*

▲ *Half-round pliers (9)*

◀ *Parallel pliers (9)*

◀ *Top cutters (10)*

◀ *Memory wire cutters (10)*

◀ *Tin snips (10)*

◀ *Chain-nose pliers (9)*

▶ *Double-ended pin vise (11)*

◀ ▶ *Pin vises (11)*

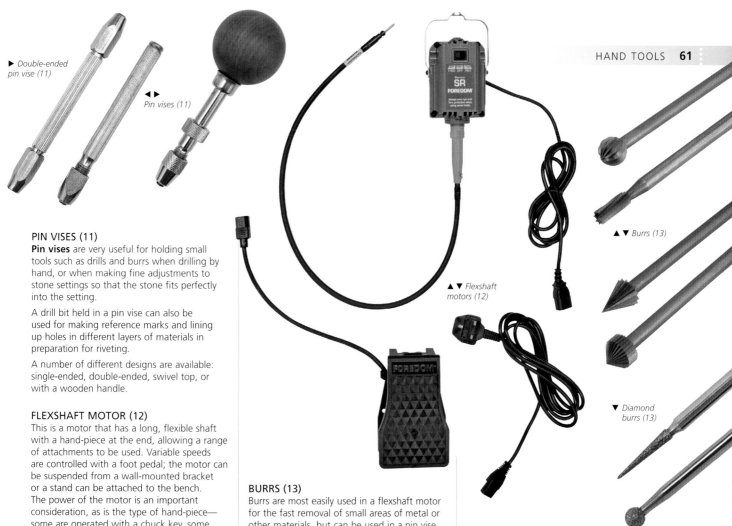

▲ ▼ *Burrs (13)*

▲ ▼ *Flexshaft motors (12)*

▼ *Diamond burrs (13)*

PIN VISES (11)

Pin vises are very useful for holding small tools such as drills and burrs when drilling by hand, or when making fine adjustments to stone settings so that the stone fits perfectly into the setting.

A drill bit held in a pin vise can also be used for making reference marks and lining up holes in different layers of materials in preparation for riveting.

A number of different designs are available: single-ended, double-ended, swivel top, or with a wooden handle.

FLEXSHAFT MOTOR (12)

This is a motor that has a long, flexible shaft with a hand-piece at the end, allowing a range of attachments to be used. Variable speeds are controlled with a foot pedal; the motor can be suspended from a wall-mounted bracket or a stand can be attached to the bench. The power of the motor is an important consideration, as is the type of hand-piece—some are operated with a chuck key, some work with tapered bezels, and others are quick-release at the flick of a lever. It is a worthwhile investment because it is such a versatile piece of machinery and is invaluable for cleaning up, carving, polishing, applying surface textures, drilling, and stone setting. Many types of attachments and tools can be used in a flexshaft motor, from abrasive media to shaped felt polishing bobs.

Many different makes of motor, and several styles of hand-piece, are available, so stick to one brand to ensure compatibility. Small, hand-held motors are a more affordable alternative, but they will not withstand heavy use.

BURRS (13)

Burrs are most easily used in a flexshaft motor for the fast removal of small areas of metal or other materials, but can be used in a pin vise to tidy drilled holes or for adjustments to stone settings. For burring out seats for stones, the burr should be the same diameter as the stone. See page 67 for the different shapes of burr.

Burrs should be stored upright in a block or rack with individual holes to prevent the burrs from touching, and should always be used with a lubricant to help keep them sharper for longer.

A diamond burr has a coating of industrial-grade diamond powder. For grinding or carving hard materials such as stones, they are used with water as a lubricant, which also keeps the dust in solution; the burr is dipped into a small pot of water at regular intervals to keep the surface of the material wet. Special care must be taken when using water with electrical tools.

DRILL BITS (14)

Drill bits are used to make holes, which may be decorative or act as a starting point for other techniques such as piercing or riveting. They are often made from high-speed steel, but may be tungsten carbide, which will not blunt as quickly; lubricants can be used to prolong the life of drill bits. More expensive drills have a thicker shank, which reduces vibration when drilling. Drill bits are available in a range of very small increments from 30 gauge (0.2 mm) to 1 in (25 mm).

Diamond drill bits are coated with diamond grit, and are used to drill very hard materials such as semiprecious stones, and they should be lubricated with water while cutting. A range of diameters between 20 gauge (0.8 mm) and 12 gauge (2.0 mm) is available.

Pearl drills are specially designed to prevent chipping of the nacre when drilling pearls, and can be used to enlarge predrilled holes as well as half- or full-drill pearls. A limited range of sizes is available.

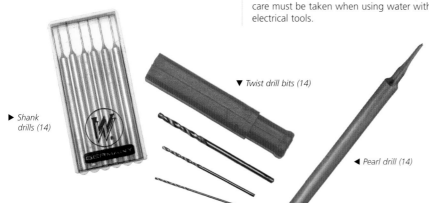

▶ *Shank drills (14)*

▼ *Twist drill bits (14)*

◀ *Pearl drill (14)*

◀ *Abrasive papers (15)*

▶ *Gas torch (17)*

▼ *Emery sticks (15)*

▼ *Wire wool (15)*

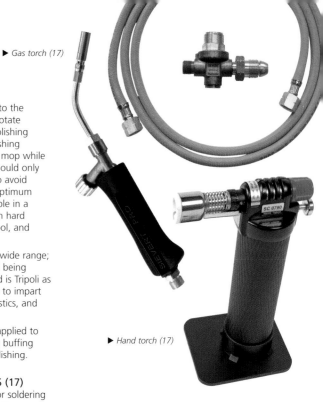

▶ *Hand torch (17)*

POLISHING (16)

Polishing wheels are screwed onto the spindle of a polishing motor, and rotate at high speed, enabling the fast polishing of surfaces, particularly metal. Polishing compound must be applied to the mop while the motor is running, and mops should only be used with one type of polish, to avoid cross-contamination and achieve optimum results. Polishing wheels are available in a number of different materials, from hard to felt, through muslin, cotton, wool, and swansdown, which is very soft.

Polishing compounds come in a wide range; many are particular to the material being polished. The most commonly used is Tripoli as an initial polish, followed by rouge to impart a high shine. Vonax is used for plastics, and Hyfin for steel.

Polishing compounds can also be applied to polishing threads and felt or suede buffing sticks, which are used for hand polishing.

SOLDERING TOOLS—TORCHES (17)

Hand torches are most suitable for soldering chain and other fine work. Filled with lighter gas (butane), the small flame means that the hand torch is only suitable for small-scale soldering and annealing jobs, because larger pieces of metal would take too long to reach temperature.

Gas torches are an essential tool for soldering and heating. If these two processes are going to be frequently used in jewelry making, a good quality gas torch is a necessity. The gas torch needs to be connected to bottled propane with a reinforced rubber hose and a gas pressure regulator. A range of different-sized heads that can be interchanged on the hand-piece is available, and these allow different sizes of flame to be used, as appropriate for the work being done. Ask your supplier for advice on setting up the torch to the gas supply, and follow the manufacturer's guidelines.

ABRASIVES (15)

Abrasive papers are used to remove file marks, scratches, and firestain from metal and other materials. A rough grade of paper is used initially, before finer grades are used to refine the surface, often in preparation for polishing. A number of different types of paper are available. The most commonly used are emery paper, which must be used dry, and waterproof silicon carbide paper, otherwise known as wet-and-dry paper, which is available in grades from 180 to 2500; the most commonly used grades are 600 to 1200.

Abrasive papers can be stuck onto wooden sticks to aid the cleaning up process.

Other abrasives such as steel wool, pumice powder, and Scotchbrite are often used to degrease and prepare metal surfaces for processes such as patination, or may be used as a final finish on a metal surface. Steel wool is also useful for refining the surface of carved wax models.

PICKLE (18)

Pickle solution removes oxides and flux residues from precious metals. Pickle powder needs to mixed with warm water in the correct proportions. Because the solution is heated it will give off fumes, so use it in a well-ventilated area and wear gloves and goggles when mixing.

Safety pickle powder contains sulfuric acid, so some jewelers prefer to use less toxic solutions such as alum or citric acid. Spent pickle should be allowed to evaporate before it can be properly disposed of, because it contains heavy metal residues.

Pickle tanks are used to hold the pickle solution, usually with the facility to heat it. It is a good idea to have a timer switch on the socket as an extra safety device.

Heated pickle will work much faster than cold, but an electric unit may be a luxury for a small workshop where a bain-marie will suffice.

▼ *Polishing wheels (16)*

◀ ▼ *Polishing compounds (16)*

◀ *Pickle powder (18)*

▶ *Pickle tank (18)*

▶ *Polishing thread (16)*

PICKELEX
HEATED ACID BATH

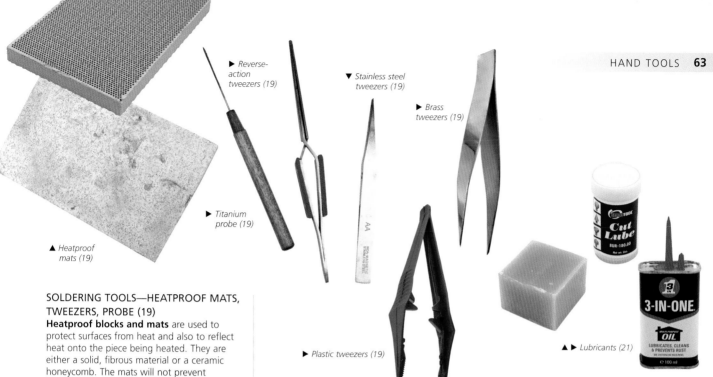

▲ *Heatproof mats (19)*

▶ *Reverse-action tweezers (19)*

▶ *Titanium probe (19)*

▼ *Stainless steel tweezers (19)*

▶ *Brass tweezers (19)*

▶ *Plastic tweezers (19)*

▲ ▶ *Lubricants (21)*

SOLDERING TOOLS—HEATPROOF MATS, TWEEZERS, PROBE (19)

Heatproof blocks and mats are used to protect surfaces from heat and also to reflect heat onto the piece being heated. They are either a solid, fibrous material or a ceramic honeycomb. The mats will not prevent prolonged heating from damaging the surface underneath, so build a platform from house bricks to go underneath.

Steel reverse-action tweezers can be used to hold elements of a piece in position while soldering and also to absorb heat out of thinner parts. Tungsten-tip tweezers should be used when soldering platinum. Plastic tweezers are ideal for working with acids and other chemicals because they will not scratch metal, but cannot be used for hot work. Brass tweezers should be used for placing work into pickling solution.

Titanium probes are used to position or apply solder to a piece while it is being heated, and can also be used to spread molten solder across a surface.

FLUXES (20)

Fluxes are used to prevent oxides from forming on metal when it is heated, and will therefore help metal or solder flow better when they are molten. All fluxes have specific working temperatures—Easyflo works best with low-temperature solders such as easy and extra-easy, while the high temperatures required for soldering gold mean that the most suitable flux is Auroflux. This will not degrade before the solder melts.

Borax is suitable for most soldering jobs—most commonly for silver. It has a good working range and is easily prepared by adding water to the dish and grinding the cone to make a thin paste which is applied with a fine paint brush.

When using flux, work in a well-ventilated area.

LUBRICANTS (21)

Machine oil is used to lubricate machinery or tools when in use; drill bits and burrs will work more efficiently with less resistance, friction, and heat and will therefore stay sharp for longer if a lubricant is applied. Use generous amounts of oil when sharpening tools on an oilstone to aid the process.

Beeswax can be rubbed onto saw blades so that they cut more smoothly.

Other lubricants are available as creams, liquids, and in solid form for specific purposes, such as prolonging the life of burrs.

A regular application of oil to tools helps prevent rust, by forming a physical barrier against moisture, and keeps them in good working order.

ADHESIVES (22)

The choice of adhesive will depend on the flexibility and porosity of the materials being joined, and the degree of permanence required. Epoxy resin is suitable for many jobs and provides a strong and durable bond; some types cure faster or more clearly than others. Cyanoacrylate (crazy glue) is powerful but rather brittle for jewelry applications; however, it is useful for tacking elements together temporarily. Adhesives are available that will dry completely clear and are cured by the action of UV light.

Work in a well-ventilated area when using adhesives, and follow the manufacturer's instructions for use.

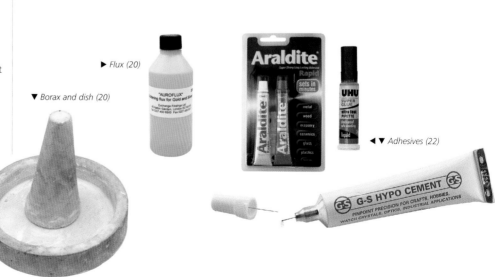

▶ *Flux (20)*

▼ *Borax and dish (20)*

◀ ▼ *Adhesives (22)*

Stone-setting Tools

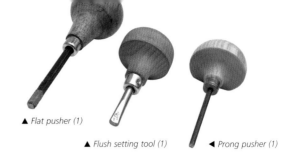

▲ Flat pusher (1)

▲ Flush setting tool (1)   ◀ Prong pusher (1)

Tools for stone setting fall into three basic types: those for forming the metal settings for stones, devices for holding and securing the settings while the stones are being set, and tools for refining the setting and manipulating the metal around the stone. Tools and materials for stringing beads are also described in this section, and range from silks to needles and knotting tools.

The specialist tools for setting stones have perhaps the greatest range because each one needs to be appropriate for the job in hand. It is often necessary to make a tool, or adapt an existing one in order to successfully set a stone. Shaped steel rods can be fitted into short wooden handles; basic toolmaking skills are very useful—although "tool" steel is a hard metal, it can be cut, filed, cleaned up, and polished much in much the same manner as nonferrous metals. Certain tools may need to be tempered, a process that makes the steel harder or softer depending on the function of the tool.

Engraving tools, or gravers, are also commonly used in stone setting, and must be kept sharp and clean, as must grain tools to ensure accurate working and less room for error.

The storage of so many small tools can be problematic—drilled wooden blocks or magnetic stands can provide a solution, but shallow drawers with plastic dividing trays are invaluable. It is important that the tools do not knock against each other and are kept dry to ensure their proper working condition.

PUSHERS (1)

Bezel pushers are used for rub-over settings on cabochon stones to apply pressure to the bezel surrounding the stone. A slightly matte surface on the end of the pusher will help to prevent it from slipping. Bezel pushers usually have square or rectangular faces with slightly rounded edges, or are curved in one plane so that they can rock backward and forward to move the metal.

Prong pushers are similar to bezel pushers, but with a groove in the flat face of the tool so that it will push the prongs of a prong setting down without slipping. These tools can be easily made by filing a groove in the end of a steel rod and mounting it in a wooden handle.

Flush setting tools have an angled end and a curved face, allowing the tool to be used at a more acute angle than other pushers. It is also useful where there is restricted access to a bezel because the tip is narrower than a flat-ended pusher.

BURNISHERS (2)

Polished steel burnishers are versatile tools, used for a number of different techniques.

Because steel is harder than precious metals, the burnisher imparts a shine to areas it is rubbed across—this technique is often used for the final rubbing of the metal around a stone and will also work-harden the metal. Burnishers must be kept highly polished so that the surface does not scratch the metal. Polished steel burnishers are either curved or straight and come in a range of lengths and widths.

Hematite burnishers have rounded ends, which makes them more suitable when stone-setting. Other nonmetallic burnishers are made from agate or bone. Plastic burnishers can be made for setting very soft materials such as shell or amber with fine silver bezels.

BEZEL SETTING PUNCHES (3)

Bezel setting punches, or stakes, are steel tools with a concave recess in one end that is placed over the stone once it is in its mount. The tool is rotated firmly around the bezel to force it around the stone. These setting tools are sold in sets with an interchangeable handle; they can be used for rub-over setting around stones that have diameters of between ⅛ and ⅝ in (3 and 9 mm).

BEZEL BLOCKS AND PUNCHES (4)

Bezels are metal frames that hold stones, and may be formed from tubing, or a soldered strip of metal. A bezel block is used to true the angles of the tapered bezel, and will also shrink or stretch the setting if required. It is used in much the same way as a dapping block, the punch being struck with a hammer or mallet to force the setting into shape.

Bezel blocks have angles of either 17 or 28 degrees; after round, the most common shapes are square, emerald-cut, oval, and pear-shaped. Punches are sold with the blocks and have a corresponding angle and profile to their block.

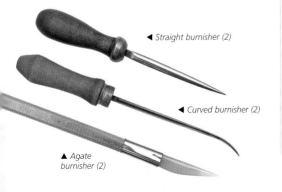

◀ Straight burnisher (2)

◀ Curved burnisher (2)

▲ Agate burnisher (2)

▲ Bezel setting punches (3)

▶ Bezel block and punch (4)

GRAVERS (5)

Gravers are used to engrave designs, textures, and lettering on metal, as well as for accurately carving seats for stones within a mount. They are sold without handles, and need to be correctly mounted at the right length for an individual's hand.

Specific gravers are suitable for specific tasks: Square gravers are used for cutting lines and some lettering, spitsticks are used raise grains, and flat scorpers to carve out stone seats. See page 67 for different graver profiles.

Oilstones are used with machine oil to grind down steel tools such as gravers and give them a sharp cutting edge. An Arkansas stone is then used to refine the faces of the tool so that it cuts more brightly and cleanly.

GRAIN TOOLS (6)

When a spur is raised with a graver, the grain tool with a round depression in the end is used to push and roll the spur down into a neat ball, or grain. These grains are used to hold stones in position, or for purely decorative effect. Graduated sizes of grain tool are available, in sets or individually. Grain tools are interchangeable in a wooden handle that is usually supplied as a part of the set.

Grain tools quickly wear down, or the edges become deformed through use, and they will need reshaping and sharpening periodically with a fion.

Milgrain wheels are rotating wheels set in a handle that is run along a metal edge to produce the effect of many grains. It is traditionally used along the borders of pavé pieces to mimic the visual effect of the grains that hold the stones. Milgrain wheels are available in sizes of 1 (smallest) to 15, which is the largest and makes grains of 1/32 in (1 mm).

MAGNIFIERS (7)

Eyeglasses and loupes are used to view small work magnified. This becomes a necessity as one's eyes age, and is important in techniques such as stone setting where accuracy is paramount. Eyeglasses fit neatly around the eye and can be used hands-free while fine work is being carried out. The degree of magnification of eyeglasses is measured by their focal length, with a short focal length giving a higher magnification. Focal lengths range from 2 to 4 in (5 to 10 cm). Loupes are hand-held, and are used to inspect progress at a higher magnification, x10 or x20.

Binocular head-pieces or attachments that can clip onto glasses are also available, as are freestanding magnifying lamps.

HOLDING MEDIA (8)

Setter's wax is melted onto the top of thick wooden doweling or a flat block of wood so that the piece can be easily held at the bench or fixed in a vise, and is used for holding small items of work when performing techniques such as stone setting or engraving. The wax is warmed with a soft flame until it is pliable enough to sink the piece into the surface and secure it. The piece can be carefully chipped out afterward, or the wax very gently warmed, depending on the item. Wax residue can be removed by soaking the piece in acetone.

Jett Sett (Polymorph) is a thermoplastic that can be softened in boiling water and sets hard at room temperature—it can be used in a similar way to setter's wax.

CLAMPS (9)

Ring clamps are used to secure rings while stones are being set. They are best suited to rings with narrow or parallel shanks or for holding other pieces of small work. Clamps are made from either plastic or wood and are closed with a screw or wedge mechanism, and the jaws are often lined with leather to protect the ring. It is possible to make custom clamps for unusual-shaped pieces of work.

Clamps can be secured in a vise for added stability.

STRINGING TOOLS (10)

Silks and threads are used for stringing semiprecious beads and pearls, and are usually knotted between beads or pearls to stop them from knocking against each other and getting damaged. The thread is used doubled up, and fed through the beads with a wire needle.

French wire (gimp) is fine, coiled wire that is used at the ends of strings of beads and pearls to protect the thread from rubbing thin on the catch fittings.

Wire needles are used to easily insert thread through the holes in beads or pearls. They are thin and flexible, with eyes that will flatten and fit through very small holes in beads. Some silks are supplied with needles attached.

Chinese clippers are used to cut silk or thread ends close to the knot, giving a neat finish with no trace of stray threads.

Diamond reamers are tapered, diamond-coated steel points that will enlarge drilled holes, especially in glass or semiprecious stones.

Knotting tools allow knots to be pulled tightly against the previous bead or pearl on a string and will help form neat, uniform knots, making a tidy string of beads.

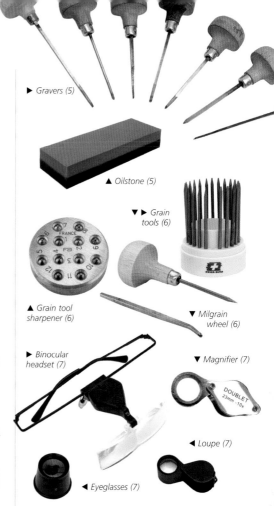

▶ *Gravers (5)*

▲ *Oilstone (5)*

▼ ▶ *Grain tools (6)*

▲ *Grain tool sharpener (6)*

▼ *Milgrain wheel (6)*

▶ *Binocular headset (7)*

▼ *Magnifier (7)*

◀ *Loupe (7)*

◀ *Eyeglasses (7)*

▼ *Custom clamp (9)*

▲ *Setter's wax stick (8)*

▼ *Silk and thread (10)*

▼ *Diamond reamer (10)*

▼ *Ring clamps (9)*

▼ *French wire (gimp) (10)*

▼ *Wire needles (10)*

▶ *Chinese clippers (10)*

▼ *Knotting tool (10)*

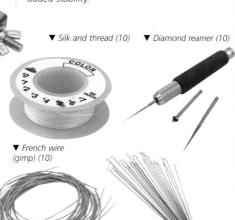

Tool Shapes

Selecting the correct tool for a particular technique is essential for good results. The shape of a tool directly influences the effect it will have when used.

Most setting tools are made of steel stock, and are shaped according to function. Flat and curved pushers are used for setting bezels and tapered bezels, flush setting tools have an angled face so that the tip can push metal closer around a stone, and prong pushers have a gap for wire prongs so that the tool does not slip.

Pliers are used for bending and shaping metal, and the profile of the jaws influences their effect.

A jobbing hammer and a mallet will be sufficient for many processes, but other shaped hammers are required for riveting, forging, or chasing. The shape of the hammer head directly affects the way it moves the metal.

Files come in many shapes, and the profile of the file determines the groove it cuts—always try to match the shape of the file to the shape of the area being filed, especially when cleaning up intricately pierced fretwork with needlefiles.

The shape of a graver determines the mark it will make when it cuts; oval or onglette gravers are used in stone setting to carve a seat for the stone and square gravers are used for engraved line work.

Seating, ball, and hart burrs are all used predominantly in stone setting, and should be the same diameter as the stone. Other shaped burrs are generally used for carving or making surface textures, and all burrs come in a wide range of sizes.

Setting tools

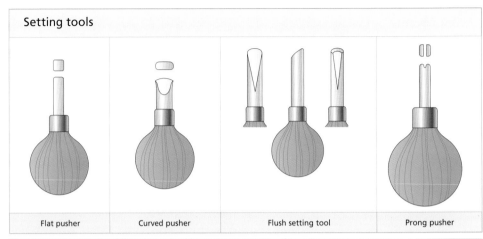

Flat pusher   Curved pusher   Flush setting tool   Prong pusher

Pliers

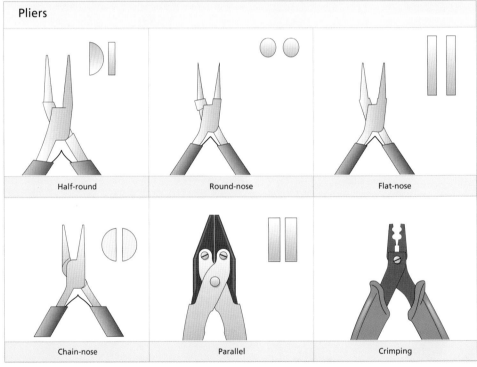

Half-round   Round-nose   Flat-nose

Chain-nose   Parallel   Crimping

Hammer heads

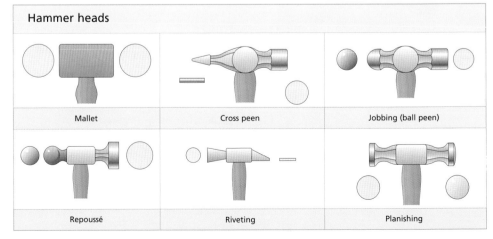

Mallet   Cross peen   Jobbing (ball peen)

Repoussé   Riveting   Planishing

File shapes

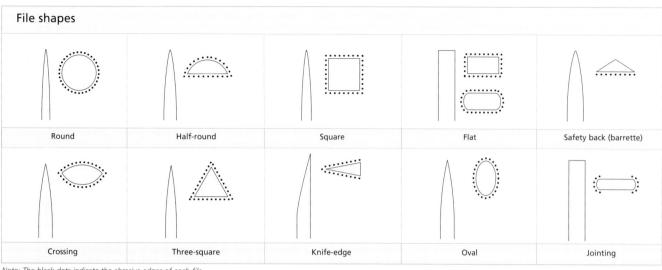

Round	Half-round	Square	Flat	Safety back (barrette)
Crossing	Three-square	Knife-edge	Oval	Jointing

Note: The black dots indicate the abrasive edges of each file.

Graver shapes

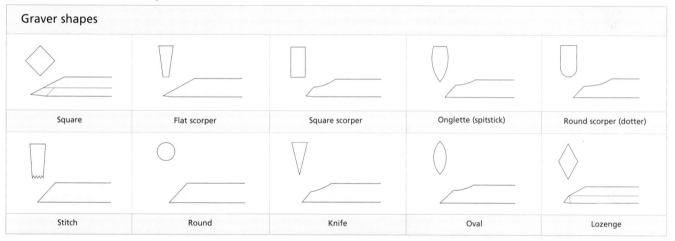

Square	Flat scorper	Square scorper	Onglette (spitstick)	Round scorper (dotter)
Stitch	Round	Knife	Oval	Lozenge

Burr shapes

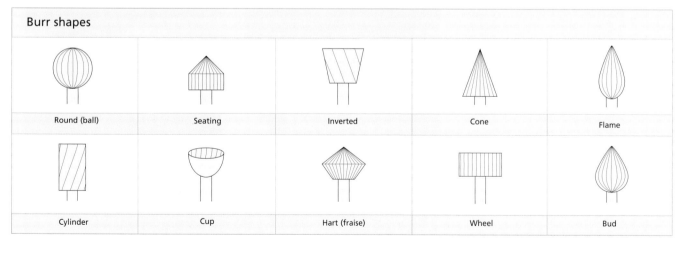

Round (ball)	Seating	Inverted	Cone	Flame
Cylinder	Cup	Hart (fraise)	Wheel	Bud

Basic Fabrication Techniques

Jewelry making techniques such as cutting, filing, soldering, and polishing metal are essential for constructing jewelry pieces, as well as for creating the mounts for gemstones.

skill level

Cutting and Piercing

Many different tools can be used to cut metal, and while snips, bench shears, and end cutters all offer speed and convenience, their shearing action tends to distort the metal when cutting. Piercing with a jeweler's saw is more time consuming, but it offers a much greater degree of accuracy and versatility of movement. A jeweler's saw can hold incredibly fine blades (size 2/0 is suitable for general-purpose cutting), which must be held in the saw frame under tension. The saw can be used to cut outlines by working to a template, or if the saw blade is inserted through a drilled hole, it can be used to cut intricate fretwork. Designs can be marked out directly on metal using a scribe or dividers, or a design drawn on paper may be stuck down onto the metal.

When piercing flat metal sheet, the saw is used with the blade perfectly vertical and is moved lightly up and down to cut; the teeth on the saw blade should point down so that the blade cuts on the downstroke. The saw blade can be lubricated with beeswax or machine oil to aid smooth cutting.

BASIC FABRICATION TECHNIQUES
Piercing, filing, cleaning up, and polishing are all vital jewelry-making skills. It will take many hours of practice to achieve proficiency.

TOOLKIT
- Jeweler's saw and blades
- Hand and needlefiles
- Abrasive papers
- Polishing compounds
- Flexshaft motor

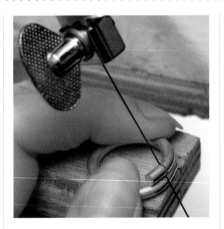

PIERCING
The most accurate method for cutting metal is with a jeweler's saw because it does not distort the edge of the metal. For piercing through rings to size them, intricate fretwork, and for the general shaping of metal, this type of saw is invaluable.

FILING
Hand files are used to remove metal or excess solder from a surface, shaping and refining the form. Files cut on the forward stroke; flat files should be used for flat and convex surfaces, and round or half-round files for concave curves. Needlefiles are used for more intricate filing.

Filing

Filing is used to remove marks caused by cutting techniques, such as piercing, as well as for truing forms. For removing large areas of metal from a piece, it is faster to use a rough file, such as cut 0; for most other jobs cut 2 files, which are finer, should be sufficient. Hand files should be used for larger areas, and needlefiles for more intricate work.

Files only cut with the forward motion and pulling the file backward against the metal will eventually blunt it. The profile of the file should match the job in hand—flat files for flat surfaces and convex curves, and the most similar curved profile for concave curves. The half-round file is one of the most useful profiles, because it can be used for flat and curved surfaces.

Specific files are available for platinum, which are tougher than other files, and will not become blunt from use with harder metals.

Annealing

Annealing is a process used to soften metal once it has been work-hardened. By heating the metal to a specific temperature, which is gauged by its color changes, stresses within the metal are relaxed and it becomes much more malleable. Each metal alloy has its own optimum temperature for annealing and for quenching (the process of cooling the piece rapidly in water). After annealing, the metal will usually have a thin layer of oxides on the surface, making it appear dirty—the oxides can be removed in a weak acid solution called pickle. If a piece a of metal is being heavily manipulated—for example, in forging or in a rolling mill—it is common for it to require annealing several times during fabrication, because working with hardened metal can cause cracking or the tendency to use excessive force. However, in some circumstances, it is preferable to leave metal work-hardened so that it does not bend out of shape, for example with earring hooks.

SINGLE SPHERE BAROQUE RING
Even complex pieces start with basic techniques. The layers of the metal in this ring, made by Elizaveta Gnatchenko, were made using techniques such as piercing, casting, and soldering. Tube-set champagne diamonds stud the outer surface and a large garnet is held on a stem between pavé-set white-gold rings.

CLEANING UP
Emery, or wet-and-dry, paper is used to remove the marks left by filing and can be used loose or adhered to wooden sticks. Rough grades of paper are used to start, followed by successively finer grades of paper to refine the surface. Working across the grain of the direction of the last paper used helps scratches to be seen more easily, and subsequently removed.

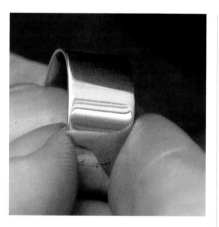

POLISHING
Polishing motors are used to apply a bright, shiny finish to metal pieces. Apply polishing compound to the wheel while it is running—Tripoli is used for initial polishing, and rouge for the final finish. Wash the piece thoroughly between the two steps, and afterward to remove any traces of polishing compound.

FLEXSHAFT MOTORS
Flexshaft motors are used to increase the speed of cleaning up. A large number of attachments can be used, from a split pin, in which emery paper is used, to polishing bobs, which are ideal for putting the final finish on the insides of rings. Hold the piece steady, and keep the tool moving constantly with firm, even pressure.

Annealing temperatures for different metals

Metal	Annealing temperature		Annealing color	Method of cooling
Sterling silver	1200°F	650°C	Dull red	Quench in cold water when metal has cooled to black heat
Yellow gold	1200–1300°F	650–700°C	Dull red	Quench in cold water when metal has cooled to black heat
White gold	1400°F	750°C	Dull red	Quench in cold water when metal has cooled to black heat
Red gold	1200°F	650°C	Dull red	Quench above 930°F/500°C
Platinum	1850°F	1000°C	Orange–yellow	Allow to air cool
Palladium	1500–1650°F	800–900°C	Yellow–orange; hold for 30–60 seconds	Quench in cold water when metal has cooled to black heat

BASIC FABRICATION TECHNIQUES

Annealing, drilling, and basic dimensional shaping of metal are processes necessary for creating jewelry designs. Not every process will be used in every piece, but these basic techniques form part of a useful metalworking repertoire.

TOOLKIT
- Sheet metal and wire for forming
- Heat brick
- Gas torch
- Mandrel
- Mallet
- Pliers
- Dapping block and punch
- Pillar drill and drill bits

ANNEALING
Prop sheet metal up against a heat brick during annealing. Bring the piece up to temperature as quickly and evenly as possible with the gas torch until it begins to glow a dull red. Check the table above for the treatment of specific alloys.

BENDING METAL WITH A MALLET
Annealed metal sheet or wire can be formed using tools such as a mandrel or other steel former. When the metal is hit with a mallet, it is forced over the mandrel into a curve; start at one end and gradually move the metal strip forward as it is hit.

Pickling

Pickle is a solution used to dissolve both oxides and fluxes, which adhere to the surface of metal after annealing and soldering. The solution is usually heated to make the chemical reaction work more quickly. Many jewelers use safety pickle, or dilute sulfuric acid, but less toxic solutions can be equally effective—citric acid solution is one alternative; see page 62.

Metal should be placed into the pickle using brass, stainless steel, or plastic tweezers, and should take around five minutes to be cleaned, depending on the strength and temperature of the pickle solution. Once removed, wash the piece well with clean water and detergent to remove any traces of pickle.

Bending Metal

It is often necessary to bend metal within the fabrication process, whether you are forming ring shanks, making earring hooks, or creating chain links. There are innumerable methods for bending metal, but you can achieve the best results using annealed metal. Wire and sheet metal can be shaped around a former and hammered into the desired form using a mallet—mallets will not mark the metal. Forming tools such as triblets, mandrels, dapping and swaging blocks, bearers, and jigs are all useful for this purpose.

Pliers can also be used to shape metal, but take care not to mark the metal. Ring or half-round pliers do not mark metal if they are used carefully, and parallel pliers are also very useful.

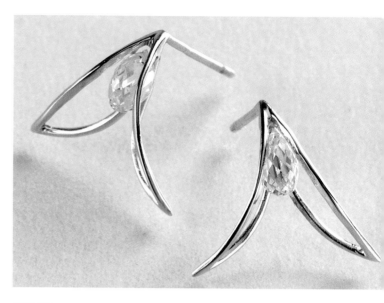

WINGED DIAMOND BRIOLETTE STUDS
The diamond briollettes in this delicate pair of ear studs by Zoe Marie are held by thin wires to the carefully formed structures of the white-gold frames.

BENDING METAL WITH PLIERS
Pliers are very useful for forming or adjusting the shape of a piece of metal. The profile of the jaws of the pliers determines how the metal will bend; half-round pliers form a curve, with the curved side of the jaws being on the inside of the curve.

DAPPING
Metal disks are the most common forms used when dapping, but other shapes can be dapped to give them three-dimensionality. Start in a much larger hole than necessary, hammering the correct size of punch into the hole; work down through the sizes until you have achieved the desired curve.

DRILLING
A motorized drill is the quickest way to drill holes in metal, whether a flexshaft motor or a pillar drill, which makes perfectly vertical holes for better accuracy. Always center punch metal before drilling, and use lubricant to reduce friction.

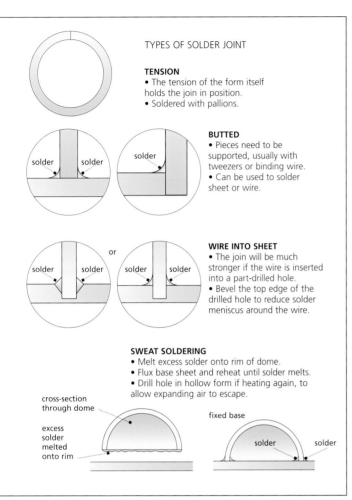

TYPES OF SOLDER JOINT

TENSION
• The tension of the form itself holds the join in position.
• Soldered with pallions.

BUTTED
• Pieces need to be supported, usually with tweezers or binding wire.
• Can be used to solder sheet or wire.

WIRE INTO SHEET
• The join will be much stronger if the wire is inserted into a part-drilled hole.
• Bevel the top edge of the drilled hole to reduce solder meniscus around the wire.

SWEAT SOLDERING
• Melt excess solder onto rim of dome.
• Flux base sheet and reheat until solder melts.
• Drill hole in hollow form if heating again, to allow expanding air to escape.

cross-section through dome

excess solder melted onto rim

fixed base

Soldering

Solder is an alloy that has a melting point lower than the metal it is joining; it is used to form strong, permanent bonds. Solder alloys are specific to their parent metals, having a corresponding range of melting points, so 18-karat yellow gold requires 18-karat yellow gold solder. Solders for each metal come in hard, medium, and easy, with hard solder having the highest melting point. This range allows subsequent solder joins within one piece without the risk of melting previous joins.

There are several methods for soldering and the one you choose will depend on the type of join. The most common method is to flux the join and apply "pallions," or chips, of solder, then heat the piece until the solder melts along or around the join, before pickling to remove oxide and flux.

Cleaning Up

Cleaning up is the process of removing excess solder, scratches, and file marks, and the preparation of work for polishing. First, remove all unwanted marks with a rough grade of abrasive paper—600 or 800—before methodically working up through the grades to 1200 or 1500. The cross-grain method gives the best results, revealing scratches so that they can be efficiently removed. The first grade of paper is used in one direction only and the next grade is used across the grain made by the first, and so on. Emery sticks or a split pin used in a flexshaft motor can greatly reduce cleaning-up times. Once you have worked through all the grades of abrasive paper, there should be a fine satin finish on the surface of the metal. At this stage it is ready to be polished, unless satin is the desired finish.

Polishing

Polishing involves using finely abrasive compounds applied to fabric polishing wheels, or mops, and the use of a polishing

PALLION SOLDERING A BAND RING
Soldering is a key process for jewelers, allowing metal to be joined to metal. A good solder seam, once cleaned up, should be virtually indistinguishable from the surrounding metal.

TOOLKIT
■ Ring shank
■ Solder
■ Tin snips
■ Flux (borax)
■ Heatproof mat and heat brick
■ Gas torch
■ Cold water for quenching
■ Pickle
■ Soft brush and detergent

1 The join that is to be soldered must be close fitting and clean. Cut the solder into "pallions" (chips); use tin snips to cut a fringe on one end of a piece of silver solder and then cut across the fringe. Cutting a range of sizes of pallion is useful if you are doing a lot of soldering.

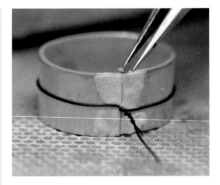

2 Apply flux around the join to prevent it from oxidizing when heated, and put the solder pallions into position while the flux is still damp. Position the piece on a heatproof mat with an upright heat brick behind to reflect heat back onto the piece.

DRILLED RINGS
This set of rings by Liz Hancock consists of perforated silver bands decorated with 18-kt gold dots and bezel-set cabochon stones. Holes were drilled in the silver before it was formed, giving the wide bands a visual lightness.

motor. The high-speed rotation of the mop buffs the metal to a high shine. The compounds used are a matter of personal taste but often, a compound called Tripoli is used first because it is abrasive and will remove fine scratches from the surface of the metal. The piece should then be washed to remove any traces of Tripoli polish, and a separate mop used with rouge, a fine iron compound, which imparts a high shine to the metal. Special polishing compounds are available to give optimum results when polishing platinum, steel, plastics, or certain alloys of gold.

Hand polishing with felt or suede-covered sticks is an alternative to using a motor, and the same polishing compounds can be used. Another alternative is a motorized barrel polisher, which rotates a container of steel shot and barrel soap with the work inside. The steel shot burnishes, polishes, and work-hardens the softer metals jewelry is made from, but this process is not suitable for fragile pieces and stones softer than 7 Mohs.

Drilling

Drilled holes have many uses within jewelry making, from allowing wires to be inserted for riveting to creating circular recesses in which stones can be set. Metal must be center-punched before it is drilled to make a registration mark. Whether using a bench drill, flexshaft motor, or hand drill, the metal must be held securely, either by hand or clamped, and steady, even pressure should be applied until the desired depth of hole is drilled. Safety glasses should be worn when drilling. Drill bits can be lubricated with machine or cutting oil to aid drilling and keep them sharp.

SOLDERED RING
Multiple solder joins are necessary to join elements of different-colored metals together. The small tube settings have been soldered onto the larger yellow-gold bezels for the opal and peridot, which were soldered to the white-gold shank in this ring by Guntis Lauders.

3 Warm around the piece to dry out the flux before heating it directly. It is important that all parts of the piece are heated evenly; thicker parts will require more heating than thin ones, and both sides of the join need to be heated. It is the heat from the metal, rather than the flame, that should melt the solder.

4 Once the piece reaches the correct temperature, the solder will melt and run along the join. As soon as this happens, remove the flame from the piece and allow it to cool for a few seconds before quenching it in cold water. Remove any binding wire.

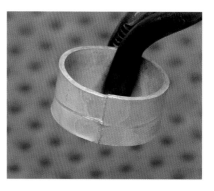

5 Clean the piece up in a heated pickle solution to remove oxides and flux. Ensure that all traces of flux are completely gone before washing the piece thoroughly with a soft brush and detergent to remove any residue of pickle. Dry the piece.

Advanced Fabrication Techniques

Incorporating different construction techniques into a piece allows for a greater range of designs. The techniques here are used in conjunction with basic skills to create more complex forms and surfaces.

skill level 👁 👁

Press Forming

Three-dimensional forms can be created from sheet metal with the use of an acrylic die, rubber sheet, and a hydraulic press or vise. Thick acrylic sheet has a shaped hole cut in it to form the die, and a sheet of metal is placed centrally over the hole and secured in position with tape. A layer of rubber is then placed over the metal and the whole sandwich is placed either in a hydraulic press or a vise. When the pressure is increased, the rubber compresses and forces the metal into the recess in the die, forming a cushion shape whose profile is dictated by the parameters of the hole. Curved forms tend to work best, because angular profiles can cause the metal to split. This technique can also be used to form metal over solid objects.

Forging

The technique of shaping metal with steel hammers working over a steel stake is usually referred to as forging. The metal is shaped between the two steel surfaces each time the hammer strikes. Forging can be used to rapidly change the dimensions of a

FORGED RING
This ring, by Kara Daniel, has been formed from a length of stainless steel rod that was forged to taper it. The prong setting for the princess-cut topaz was made by cutting the top of the rod into four sections and opening out the ends.

ADVANCED FABRICATION TECHNIQUES
Techniques such as press forming, forging, and granulation are useful for forming and embellishing metal forms. The use of several techniques within one piece of jewelry allows designs to be explored more creatively.

TOOLKIT
- Metal for forming
- Pierced acrylic die, rubber sheet
- Vise
- Hammer
- Gas torch
- Tweezers
- Liver of sulfur
- Goggles and gloves

PRESS FORMING
Sheet metal can be forced into a cushion-shaped three-dimensional form with the aid of a pierced acrylic die and rubber sheet. A hydraulic press or vise is used to compress the rubber, which forces the sheet metal down through the hole in the die. Regular annealing is necessary to achieve deep press forms.

FORGING
Metal hammers can be used to plastically distort metal. The shape of the hammer affects the way in which the metal will move. Forging is used to taper, spread, or distort metal in a variety of ways. See page 66 for hammer shapes.

piece of metal, whether rod or sheet. The shape of the face of the hammer affects the way in which the metal will move, as will the shape of the stake that is being worked on—domed surfaces cause metal to move radially, while hammers with cylindrical heads will make the metal stretch in one plane only.

Processes such as tapering, thinning, and upsetting can be used to alter the section and form of a piece of metal. Hammers and stakes are also used in combination for more specialist silversmithing techniques, such as raising, anticlastic raising, and sinking and raising.

Riveting

Riveting involves pinning two sections of a piece together using wires or tubing inserted through drilled holes. It is very useful for

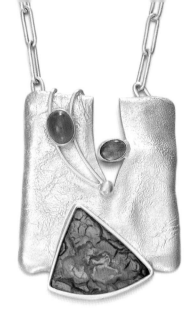

RETICULATED PENDANT
Reticulated silver forms a textured background for this pendant by Irena Maria Varey. The silver has been cut after reticulation, and the gold decoration and bezels soldered into place. The large stone is a boulder opal, and is set from behind.

Cross-section diagrams of some commonly used forms of rivet (see page 76)

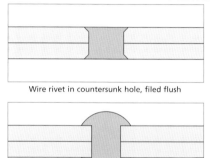

Wire rivet in countersunk hole, filed flush

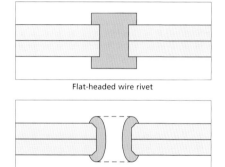

Flat-headed wire rivet

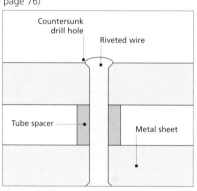

Wire rivet joining two metal sheets, with a tube spacer

Domed wire rivet

Tube rivet in countersunk hole

RETICULATION
A rippled surface can be created on silver (or gold) by heating the piece until the surface turns liquid. For the best results, the silver should be annealed several times to bring the fine silver to the surface, but the addition of fine silver scraps will accentuate the effect of the technique.

GRANULATION
Tiny balls of metal are applied to a form to create a granulated surface. The balls may be soldered into position or, if all elements are copper-plated, the pieces can be fused together without the use of solder. Granules sit best between wires or in depressions in sheet metal so that they do not roll away.

PATINATION
A warm solution of liver of sulfur can be used to oxidize silver, copper, or brass. The process must be carried out in a well-ventilated area and goggles and gloves should be worn. Rinse the work thoroughly to remove all traces of the chemicals.

combining elements which would otherwise be damaged by the heat of soldering, such as plastics, stones, and natural materials, as well as metals with heat-sensitive finishes, such as gold leaf, anodization, or patination.

The ends of wires or tubes are hammered to spread them, increasing their diameter so that they will not slip through the drilled hole. If a burr has been used to countersink both sides of the rivet hole, and the piece is made from the same metal as the rivet, then it is possible to file the rivet head flush with the surface of the piece, making it almost invisible, or a perfect circle if used on a contrasting material. Multiple rivets through more than one layer require careful planning so that all the drilled holes line up perfectly—the holes on the front or top surface should all be drilled first.

Texturing

There are many different ways of applying textures to metal, whether graphic, experimental, or traditional. Several texturing techniques involve compressing the metal to create an uneven surface—this can be done with hammers, punches, and stamps, with the shape of the tool head determining the corresponding impression in the metal. This method can be used to create a field of texture, or more specific patterns. A rolling mill can also be used to create impression textures, by layering materials, such as dried leaves or paper templates between metal sheets and rolling them through the mill. Texturing processes often distort the metal, so it is advisable to cut and shape the metal after it has been textured, taking care not to damage the surface. There are, however, some types of textures that can be applied once a piece has been fabricated, such as those made with engraving tools and burrs. Engraving can also be used to create images or inscriptions, and is also very useful for carving out seats for stones.

Etching removes metal from the surface of a piece by dissolving it in acid. Areas of the metal are masked off, leaving the exposed areas to be etched. Very precise drawings, text, or graphic images can be applied using this method.

ENGRAVED RING
Advanced techniques such as engraving and enameling can be used to enrich the surface of a piece, allowing greater freedom of design and the incorporation of complementary or contrasting colors. This design is by Henn of London Ltd.

USING WIRE RIVETS TO COLD-JOIN SHEET METAL

When metal parts cannot be soldered because surface effects would be damaged or difficult to clean up, riveting is often a good solution. It can also be used as a pivot point, creating moveable parts.

TOOLKIT
- Sheet metal
- Center punch
- Drill
- Ball burr
- Wire for rivet
- Vise
- Needlefile
- Ball peen hammer
- Top cutters
- Masking tape

1 Mark, center punch, and drill holes the same diameter as the wire that will be used for the rivet. Always mark the position of the hole on the uppermost surface first, because this will dictate the position of the rivet.

2 Use a small ball burr to bevel the edges of the drilled holes. This removes any sharp burrs from the metal and is important if the rivet head will be filed flush once hammered, because the portion of the rivet head filling the bevel holds the rivet in place.

Reticulation

This a process that uses heat to distort the surface of silver or gold sheet, by exploiting the differences in melting points within an alloy. If a piece of sterling silver is repeatedly annealed and pickled, a thin layer of fine silver is brought to the surface, which has a higher melting point than the rest of the sheet. When the surface is heated to melting point, the tension caused by the different temperatures within the piece and their differing rates of contraction upon cooling causes an attractive rippling effect. Adding scraps of fine silver can help to intensify the dramatic effects, because they will disrupt the tension of the molten surface.

Granulation

Tiny balls, or granules, of silver or gold can be applied to a surface, either individually, in groups, or as a field of texture. The granules can be held in position for soldering between two wires, in depressions in sheet metal, or with organic gum, which burns away when heated. The solder may be applied as paste, ground up with a file and mixed with flux, or as pallions. It is also possible to fuse the granules to the base piece. Fusing works better if the piece is copper-plated first, causing a eutectic reaction when the metal is heated, which effectively lowers the melting point of the surfaces involved, so that they fuse more quickly.

Patination

Patination is the process of coloring metal with chemicals, which artificially accelerate the natural process of tarnishing. This can be carried out on metals such as silver, copper, and brass. Very few patinas will work on less reactive metals unless they are copper- or silver-plated first.

Patination is very useful for adding contrast to textured surfaces, but it is just a surface finish and will eventually wear away with use, so is better applied in protected recesses.

OXIDIZED EARRINGS
Oxidization has been applied to the silver surfaces of this pair of earrings by Daphne Krinos, echoing the color and internal forms of the tourmilated quartz cabochons on an exaggerated scale.

3 Secure the wire for the rivet in protective jaws in a vise, with a small amount protruding. File the top of the wire flat with a needlefile, and then hammer the end of the wire to make it spread outward. Start in the center of the end and hammer out in a spiral to create a domed nail head.

4 Insert the rivet through the drilled holes in the sheets—you can achieve neater results if the pre-formed rivet head is placed on the front side of the piece. Cut the wire with top cutters, leaving a small amount protruding, and file the end flat, protecting the metal with masking tape if necessary.

5 Working on a steel block, hammer the flat end of the rivet until it forms a neat head and makes good contact with the sheet. Tap down any sharp edges of the rivet head. Check the piece from the front—this rivet head will be flattened a bit, but may not need to be hammered further.

Wax Carving and Casting

The lost wax casting process involves carving a form in jewelers' wax, which is then cast into an exact metal replica. Carving wax is much faster than working in metal, and the same high degree of detail is possible.

skill level

SCULPTURAL OPAL RING
Wax carving can be used to create large sculptural forms in metal, which would otherwise be difficult to fabricate. Ornella Ianuzzi made this ring specifically for this particular stone, displaying two polished sides of the opal to their best advantage.

Lost Wax Casting
When compared to sand, clay, or cuttlefish casting, lost wax casting produces the most accurate replicas of a wax form. A sprue (wax rod) is attached to the finished wax model, and this, along with other waxes, is connected to a thicker wax rod—this forms a "tree." The tree is placed in a flask and a special type of plaster called "investment" is poured into the flask. Once the investment has set, the flask is placed upside-down in a kiln and the wax is melted out. With the flask still hot, molten metal is poured in, often with the aid of a vacuum, and it fills up the void left by the wax, thereby creating an exact metal replica of the wax form.

The main benefit of casting is that it allows forms—which would otherwise be very time consuming to make—to be quickly realized. Complex forms and incised details can be executed in wax far more easily than in metal, and when working with very hard metals such as platinum, white gold, and palladium it is often preferable to have an item cast in one piece, rather than several elements soldered together. Another advantage is the smaller amount of scrap metal produced in comparison to fabrication which, for expensive metals like higher-karat golds and platinum, can make a great deal of difference.

CARVING A RING FROM WAX
Jewelers' wax has been formulated to give the best results for both carving and burn-out during lost-wax casting. Incredibly intricate forms can be created using this technique.

TOOLKIT
- Jewelers' wax ring tube
- Wax ring stick
- Permanent marker pen
- Wax files
- Ball burr
- Wax needlefiles
- Wax carving tools
- Steel wool
- Flexshaft motor

1 It is a good idea to have a design ready before starting to carve. You can make the design from modeling clay for reference. Start with a slice from a wax ring tube of a suitable thickness for the design. Use a wax ring stick to open up the hole in the ring tube to the correct ring size before marking the outline of the design on the wax with a permanent marker pen. Carve down to this line with a wax file.

2 Mark the design around the outer circumference of the ring and carve to the line. Very thin areas will be weak, so leave them slightly thicker than required to prevent breakage. Use a ball burr to create a seat for a stone, carving to the depth of the widest part of the burr.

GOLD STATEMENT RING
Paul W. Leathers carved the form for
the shank of this statement ring in
wax before casting it into 18-kt
yellow gold. He then soldered the
mount for the stone into place.

Carving Wax

A three-dimensional model of the design to be carved can be made from modeling
clay for reference. Wax is commonly carved using the subtractive method: wax files
and carving tools are used to remove areas of wax until the desired form is achieved.
Pieces of wax can be fused together using a heated blade or heat-pen—both surfaces
must be made to melt otherwise the join will be weak. This technique can also be used
to sculpt the wax, or to add small areas to increase the volume of the form, as well as
to repair breaks. Once the basic form has been produced, wire wool can be used to
refine the surface and remove scratches. Fine tools can then be used to add detail.

It is always a good idea to check the weight of the wax before having it cast—you
do not want the piece to be too heavy—or too expensive! Try to reduce the weight
by thinning or hollowing out the piece wherever possible. You can check the thickness
of the wax by holding it in front of a light source; if the wax appears white and
translucent it is probably thin enough. Wax has a specific gravity which is close to 1;
multiplying the weight of the wax by the specific gravity of the metal in which it will
be cast gives a reasonable estimate of the weight of the final metal article. Once the
form has been cleaned up and the weight checked, it can be taken to a professional
caster (see page 28).

The casting will be returned to you with a remnant of the sprue still attached, and
you will need to file this away, taking care to retain the original form. You can then
clean the piece up with further filing if needed, then use emery or wet-and-dry paper
to refine the surfaces, before polishing (see page 72).

SPECIFIC GRAVITY VALUES OF METAL ALLOYS USED IN CASTING

Metal	Specific gravity*
Bronze	8.8
Sterling silver	10.4
Palladium	11.7
18-k yellow gold	15.5
18-k white gold	16.2
Platinum	20.6

* Figures may vary depending on the
exact composition of the alloy.

Wax weight x specific gravity of metal
= weight of final object

For example:

0.45 g (wax) x 15.5 (18-kt yellow
gold) = 7 g

3 Carve the final shape of the ring using wax
needlefiles and carving tools. Round off
the form, and carve the details—incised
patterns, drilled holes, or recesses.

4 Clean up the form with steel wool—use a
rough grade to remove file marks quickly,
followed by a finer grade to polish the surfaces
and refine the details of the design.

5 If possible, to reduce its weight, hollow
out the ring using a small ball burr in a
flexshaft motor. Regularly check the thickness
of the wax by holding it up to a light; areas
that appear pale are thinner. Check the weight
and hollow out further if necessary, before
having the ring cast.

Computer-aided Design and Manufacture

CAD/CAM is used to construct virtual two- or three-dimensional designs that can be rendered as photo-quality images, or exported for use in a number of processes, including rapid prototyping and laser cutting. Jack Meyer explains how.

DIGITAL REALISM
With the help of rendering software like V-Ray we can take CAD models and make them look like real objects.

What is CAD/CAM?

CAD/CAM stands for computer-aided design and computer-assisted manufacturing. CAD itself is a catch-all term used to refer to any software that allows you to visualize two- or three-dimensional design using a computer, while the term CAM refers to any machine that can create a physical object from a CAD design.

Different Types of CAD

CAD itself is a very broad subject. Dozens of software packages are available, each designed for a particular task or for use in a specific area of product design. While there may be some generic CAD design tools, each specialty of product design has specific tools that help their designers work more productively (see list at right).

All CAD software tools are based on a real-world analog. There are two-dimensional design tools that can emulate a painter's brush, two-dimensional vector drawing tools that work like a technical draftsperson's drawing table, three-dimensional design tools that can build objects with architectural precision, and there are other three-dimensional design tools that enable users to sculpt surfaces as if they were clay.

Designing Jewelry Using CAD

The design process for CAD is similar to wax carving. As with wax carving, you will start with a drawing done by hand; however, instead of tracing it or pasting a copy onto the surface of a wax block, you scan the image and import it into your chosen CAD software application. From there, you build up the shape of your piece based on the chosen measurements.

While there are many similarities between the working process of building objects in CAD and building the object with hand tools, there are some important differences—in CAD, measurements and tolerances are more important. Since a computer will give you exactly what you ask for, you must be more specific than you would be when working by hand. In addition, knowing how big the intended dimensions of an object will be in the real world will help you keep your sense of proportion and scale when working with a CAD model.

Unlike carving by hand, anything you make on a computer screen can be remade or changed relatively quickly. Since the object hasn't yet been physically made, the only thing lost if you make a mistake is time.

RAPID PROTOTYPING

Rapid prototyping (RP) is a form of CAM that produces parts that closely match the models you see on the CAD program. Examples of RP include the Solidscape T-66 3D printer (above) and the REVO CNC mill (above right).

CAD SOFTWARE PACKAGES

As of this printing, there are several CAD design software packages being used for computer-based jewelry design. Many other programs can be used for product design, but the following are the ones most likely to be seen in jewelry manufacturing. Screenshots from a variety of software programs are also shown.

Two-dimensional design tools (based on pixel graphics):
Adobe Photoshop
Corel Paint
Gemvision Design Studio

Two-dimensional vector drawing tools (based on vector graphics):
Adobe Illustrator
Corel Draw
Inkscape
TypeEdit

Three-dimensional precision design tools:
3Design
DelCAM PowerShape
Gemvision Matrix
Firestorm CAD
JewelCAD
Monarch CAD
Rhino (with either the RhinoGold or RhinoJewel plug-ins)

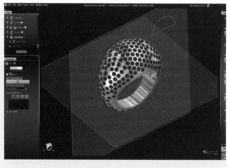

▲ 3Design

▲ Gemvision Matrix

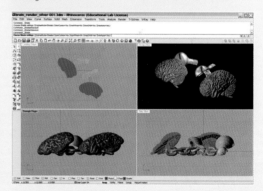

▲ Rhino (with RhinoJewel and RhinoArt)

Three-dimensional sculptural design tools:
ArtCAM Jewelsmith
Claytools
Mudbox
Zbrush
(3Design and Matrix also have built-in tools for handling some aspects of sculpture)

◄ Zbrush

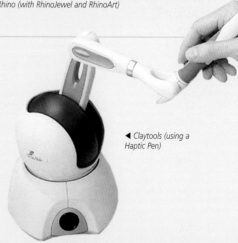

◄ Claytools (using a Haptic Pen)

MAKING A RING USING DIFFERENT TYPES OF CAD

skill level ⚭⚭

METHOD 1: USING THREE-DIMENSIONAL SURFACE-MODELING CAD SOFTWARE

The following is an example of one way to build a basic ring design using three-dimensional surface-modeling CAD software, such as Rhino, Matrix, or JewelCAD.

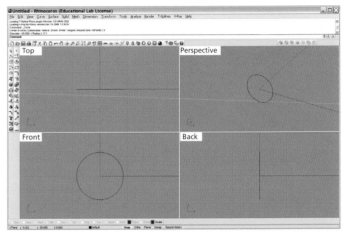

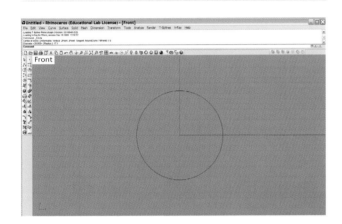

1 Start with a ring circle, measured in terms of inner diameter. This will be made in the front viewport. Some software will have a tool to automatically generate this. This circle will be referred to as the "ring rail" for the rest of this exercise.

2 Lay out a profile curve to build the stone shape. "Revolve" the profile curve along an axis parallel to the profile curve itself to create a basic round stone. (Given its central placement, this axis will likely be the Z-axis.)

Note Some software will have a tool to automatically generate stones. The stone will be placed at the top of the ring, above the finger hole. The stone should be at least 1/64 in (0.5 mm) above the finger hole to allow for clean-up when the ring is made.

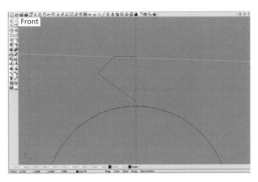

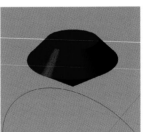

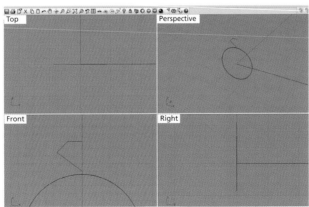

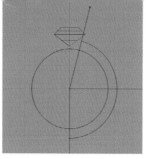

3 You will build this ring style using a basic form of the "Sweep" command. This will require cross-sections that will define the shape, and a "rail" along which the cross-sections will pass, generating the shape as it morphs between each cross-section.

Place the first cross-section along the ring rail, sitting at the bottom of the rail, and sitting perpendicular to the rail itself. This cross-section will be built up as a series of simple curves and joined together into a closed shape when finished.

Once the shape is made, adjust its size with a "Scale" command, and adjust its position with a "Rotate" command used in the same viewport as the ring rail.

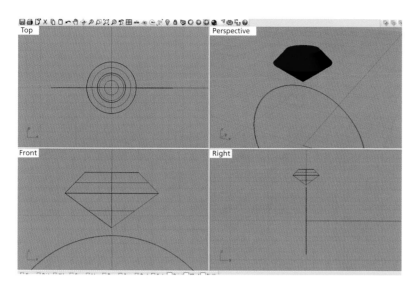

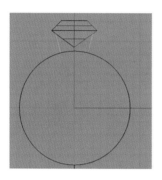

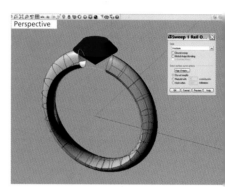

4 Place additional cross-sections along the ring rail, and "Scale" and "Rotate" each one into place. The goal is to have one cross-section at about 6 o'clock along the ring rail, and the other two cross-sections just in line with the outer edge of the girdle of the gemstone at the top of the ring.

5 Once the cross-sections are in place, "Sweep" the ring. Use the ring rail as your rail, and select the cross-sections in order, working around the ring. This will be made as an open sweep to allow for the stone.

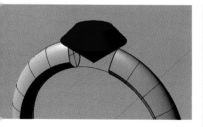

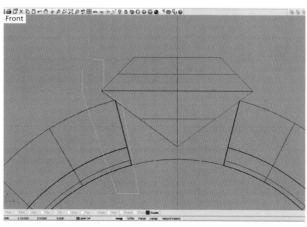

6 Depending on the software, once the shape has been swept, make sure the ends are closed. To close the ends, use the "Cap" command (or similar).

7 For the rub-over setting, use another "Revolve" command, but this time, make a curved profile shape for the setting itself. Once it has been made, revolve it around the same axis as you used for the stone. Note that some software will have a tool for automatically generating one of these based on your specifications.

Continued over

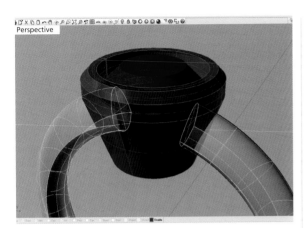

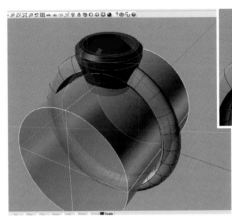

8 Now that the setting (or bezel) and the ring (or shank) have been made, you must make a cut into the shank to accommodate the bezel. This can be done with a "Boolean Difference" command. Use "Boolean Difference" to subtract the bezel from the shank. (Using a semitransparent "Ghosted View" mode on the viewport can help you see what you're doing.)

9 Once the ring has been cut to accommodate the setting, you can now cut the bottom of the bezel to better fit the finger hole. Do this by "Extruding" the finger hole into a straight cylinder, and using "Boolean Difference" to subtract this cylinder from the bezel.

10 Your ring design is now ready to show the client, render into a photorealistic image, or export to a rapid prototyping machine for production.

USING PARAMETRIC SOLID CAD SOFTWARE

Parametric solid CAD modeling works in much the same way as surface modeling, with a few small differences. The tools produce solid shapes that are then refined and reshaped to fit the finished design. Also, rather than building up an object in a three-dimensional grid space, you're building one object based on another.

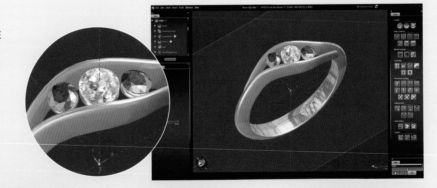

MAKING CHANGES
With parametric solid CAD, every shape you make can be changed later, just as the center stone is being changed in the images at right.

METHOD 2: USING SCULPTURAL MESH CAD SOFTWARE

The following is an example of one way to build a basic ring design using three-dimensional surface modeling CAD software (such as Claytools, ArtCAM Jewelsmith, Mudbox, or Zbrush).

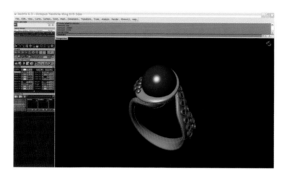

1 Start with a basic shape. This can either be a shape imported from another CAD program, or a primitive shape such as a sphere or cube. With this type of design software, the mesh quality (or resolution) of the surface makes a big difference to your ability to make a clean shape. Start off at a rougher resolution and work your way up as you add more details.

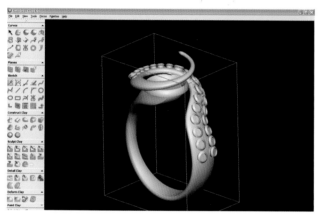

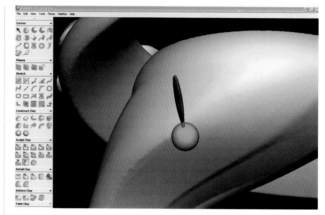

2 As reference to work from, you can do one of two things. Either you can "Import" a jpeg image of the item you wish to model into the program, sizing it as closely to its real-life proportions as you can. Or alternatively, you can work directly from an image or drawing in front of you.

3 Using the various carving and pulling tools, manipulate the surface in sections. Start by using larger tools to roughly shape the surface.

4 As you work, switch over to a blending tool (see above) to soften the edges every so often to give you a smoother shape.

5 Work your way down to smaller and smaller tools to refine the piece.

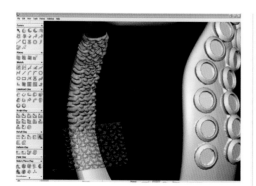

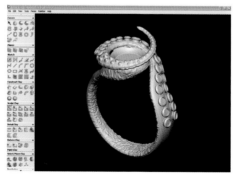

6 Use a texturing tool, such as "Emboss," to apply textures and patterns to the surface, adjusting the angle and size as needed to make the texture "Tile" properly.

7 Once you've reached a sufficient quality of detail, export the piece back to a product-design CAD program to verify dimensions and tolerances.

THE FINISHED MODEL
A render of the finished model (design courtesy Roux Fine Jewellery Ltd).

Rub-over Settings

Metal is "rubbed over" or around the edge of a stone in this style of setting. Although this technique is commonly used to secure cabochon stones, it can be just as suitable for faceted or other cuts of stone.

There are many variations on the basic requirements for a rub-over setting, from closed-back bezels made from constructed walls that enable a great variation of designs to be made, to tube settings that are simple and quick. Flush setting utilizes drilled holes in a form to hold the stones and provides a sleeker, cleaner solution for setting small faceted stones than other methods. Bezels with corners and channel settings are more technically challenging but offer many more design options for including stones within a piece.

BASIC BEZEL SETTING

(see page 88)   skill level

This 14-kt reticulated gold ring by Irena Maria Varey features a large bezel-set tourmaline cabochon, and a small tube-set diamond. The polished inside of the closed-back bezel creates subtle internal reflections within the tourmaline. Variations on the basic bezel cup include piercing out the back to leave a ledge for the stone to rest on, making an internal ledge so that the stone sits higher, and creating a decorative or scalloped edge around the top of the bezel.

TUBE SETTING

(see page 92)   skill level

The focal point of "Kissing Stones Pendant" by Alex Clamp is the two brilliant-cut stones set culet to culet centrally within the piece. The rub-over settings that hold these stones are in turn held in position by three double-ended tube settings containing smaller stones of contrasting colors. Tube settings are incredibly useful for adding stones to structural elements of a piece, forming visual punctuation.

DOME SETTING

(see page 94) skill level 👁👁

Dome setting involves a different approach to the fabrication of the bezel, because it is often formed from a single piece of metal that is shaped into a dome and does not have a solder seam. The dome setting on this silver ring set with an onyx bullet-shaped cabochon, by Sian Hughes, is made from a cast form. The metal is compressed around the stone in the same way as in a bezel setting.

BEZELS WITH CORNERS

(see page 100) skill level 👁👁

This aquamarine pendant by David Fowkes uses a bezel setting to fit the contours of the stone—the irregular angles of the stone have been matched perfectly. The mount is constructed from 18-kt yellow gold, which is quite a hard metal, so the bezel was made thin enough for the stone to be set without damaging it. The bezel is open-backed to allow light to pass through the stone.

FLUSH SETTING

(see page 102) skill level 👁

The central band of this silver ring by Jeanette Buer is flush set with cubic zirconia, and flanked on each side by a row of grain-set brilliants. Flush setting is ideal for rings because the result is very comfortable to wear, with no raised areas to catch on clothing.

CHANNEL SETTING

(see page 104) skill level 👁👁

Vintage emeralds have been channel set in this stainless steel ring by Kara Daniel. Recycled gold has been applied to the steel and set over the edges of the emeralds. Channel-set stones are often used to form a continuous line or area of square or baguette-cut stones. The stones sit girdle to girdle in the channel and no metal is visible between them.

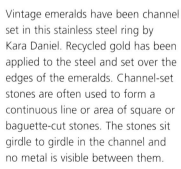

Basic Bezel Setting

Rub-over settings provide a simple solution for securing gemstones with a band of compressed metal. While a basic procedure must be followed for each type of rub-over setting, the scope for variation is immense, making this a very versatile technique.

skill level

SATELLITE RING
22-kt gold bezels have been used to set the Andean and fire opals in this ring by Tanja Ufer. The bezels have been soldered to the sides of a thick sterling silver ring shank which has been covered on one side with fused fine gold foil.

Choosing Stones

This method is traditionally used for setting cabochon stones, utilizing the curve of the stone itself to make the setting work. Cheap cabochon stones are readily available—lower-grade gem material is often used for cabochons, so stones like rubies and sapphires may seem relatively inexpensive. It is also possible to source higher-quality stones.

Metals

Softer metals are often used to make setting the stone easier. Fine silver and gold can be burnished around a stone far more easily than their alloys, with little reduction in the strength of the finished setting. Using less force or pressure to set a stone significantly reduces the risk of damaging softer stones, such as turquoise or amber.

Construction Details

The first step is to work out how long the strip of metal for the bezel needs to be. For a round stone, add the metal thickness to the diameter of the stone and multiply by 3.14 (π)—this will give the length of the strip required for that particular stone.

MAKING A BEZEL FOR A CABOCHON
Bezels for cabochons need to be made exactly the right size for the stone to be placed in from above.

TOOLKIT
- Strip of fine silver for bezel
- Jeweler's saw
- Files
- Soldering equipment
- Pickle
- Oval triblet
- Mallet
- Abrasives

1 Having calculated the length of the strip of fine silver required for the bezel, mark the measurement on the metal and pierce to the right of the mark to remove the excess metal. File both ends of the strip flat before bending the ends to meet. Pierce through the join so that the ends match up perfectly.

2 Prepare the piece for soldering—flux the join and place a pallion of hard solder on top, so that it touches both sides of the join. Heat the bezel until the solder melts and runs along the seam, then pickle and dry the piece.

Cut and file the ends of the strip of metal which, if fine silver, should be between 20- and 26-gauge (0.4 and 0.8 mm thick), depending on the size of the stone. The height of the strip will depend on the degree of curvature of the cabochon; some stones are very shallow and curve away from the base acutely, while others are taller and do not curve as quickly, see diagram on page 91. Ultimately, the height depends on the curvature of the cabochon stone; if the wall is too high then it will cover too much of the stone once set and if it is too low then it is likely the stone will eventually become loose. A millimeter or two above the start of the curve of the stone is sufficient to be able to secure it.

Bend the metal strip so that the ends meet neatly, with no light visible through the join, and solder closed with hard silver solder. Once pickled, the piece can be trued on a triblet, taking care not to hit too hard with the mallet because this can stretch it. Test the size of the bezel by dropping the stone in from above—it should be a snug fit, but not too tight or too loose. Bezels that are too tight can be stretched on the triblet until they are the right size, but oversized bezels will need to be cut shorter and re-soldered. When the bezel size is correct, test the stone from both sides just to make sure it fits, then rub one side of the bezel flat with emery paper and solder it onto a base sheet. Do not be tempted to try to put the stone in at this stage because it may be very difficult to get out again!

QUARTZ RING
This sterling silver ring by Catherine Thomas holds a bezel-set quartz cabochon with inclusions. The stone is transparent enough to show a fused gold textured surface protected beneath the stone.

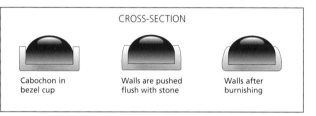

CROSS-SECTION

Cabochon in bezel cup

Walls are pushed flush with stone

Walls after burnishing

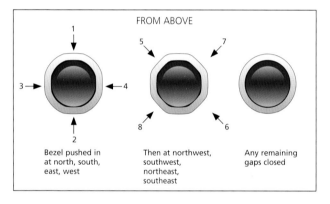

FROM ABOVE

Bezel pushed in at north, south, east, west

Then at northwest, southwest, northeast, southeast

Any remaining gaps closed

3 True the bezel on an oval triblet, making sure the solder join is on a long side. The stone should slip snugly into the bezel from above, and from both sides. If the bezel is too tight it can be stretched gradually on the triblet, but if it is too big then it must be cut and re-soldered.

4 Use a sheet of emery paper on a flat surface to true the top and bottom edges of the bezel until they are perfectly flat; work in a figure-eight motion. Solder the bezel to a base sheet with medium solder placed around the outside.

5 Once pickled and dried, pierce the excess base sheet away from the bezel. Use a file to remove the ledge of remaining metal—the bezel and base should look as if they are one piece of metal. Clean up the mount with emery sticks before soldering it to a bail or other fitting.

Continued over

DIAMOND RING
The lost wax casting process was used to create this 22-kt gold ring by Leo Pieroni, which holds an uncut 7-ct diamond crystal. The soft gold is easily rubbed over the stone to secure it.

CALCULATING THE LENGTH OF A BEZEL

To find the bezel length for a round stone:
diameter of stone + metal thickness x 3.14

To find the bezel length for an oval stone:

$$\frac{(stone\ length + width)}{2} + metal\ thickness \times 3.14$$

For example:

$$\frac{(16.2\ mm + 12.2\ mm)}{2} + 0.7\ mm \times 3.14 = 46.8\ mm$$

The excess sheet from around the bezel can be pierced off, filed true, and rubbed with emery paper before the mount is combined with a ring shank or fittings to make it into a piece of jewelry. The base of the mount can be pierced out, leaving a ledge if it suits the design and the back of the cabochon is polished—which is not always the case. At this stage, check the height of the bezel by holding the stone up to it, and filing it down if it is too high—take care to keep the top edge parallel with the base. Before setting the stone, all soldering needs to be completed and the piece polished, including the inside of the setting if the stone is not fully opaque.

Secure the piece in setter's wax, a ring clamp, or against piece of wood—choose the method most appropriate for the type of piece being made. Position the stone in place using a wax-stick, which will help to keep it level as it goes in and ensure that it is sitting on the base of the mount. Using a flat-ended pusher side-on to the bezel wall, push in at "north," "south," "east," and "west." Use a firm forward thrust, a gentle rocking action may be applied, but do not rub the bezel with the pusher. The bezel will flatten against the stone where it has been pushed. Continue working at opposite points—this is so that the metal compresses evenly around the stone—pushing in at "northeast," "southwest," "northwest," and "southeast." Then use the pusher to close any remaining gaps. Repeat the process, but this time with the pusher at a higher angle, so that the bezel begins to follow the curve of the stone. Continue until the top edge of the bezel is fully flush around the diminished circumference of stone.

Use a burnisher to further compress the edge of the bezel around the stone—the piece may need to be removed from the clamp or wax to make this possible. The inside edge of the bezel can be burnished, just where it meets the stone but take care not to slip. Any irregularities in the bezel surface caused during setting can be carefully removed with a fine emery stick, before the piece is given a final polish with rouge, taking care not to touch the stone, or cause the piece to become too hot through prolonged polishing.

SETTING AN OVAL CABOCHON PENDANT
Methodically compressing the fine silver bezel is key to a secure and even setting, ensuring that the metal is evenly compressed around the stone and then burnished level.

TOOLKIT
- Stone for setting
- Flat file
- Emery paper and scraper
- Polishing materials
- Flat-ended pusher
- Emery stick and leather
- Burnisher

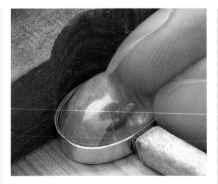

6 Check the height of the bezel against the curve of the stone—if the bezel is too tall it will cover too much of the stone once it is rubbed over. Remove any excess height with a flat file, taking care to keep the top edge parallel to the base. Use emery paper to smooth the edge, and remove any burrs from the inside of the bezel with a scraper.

7 Polish the inside of the setting before inserting the stone. Secure the piece in setter's wax or use a custom-made jig to support the piece during setting. Use a flat-ended pusher at a low angle to firmly push the bezel against the stone at "north," "south," "east," and "west."

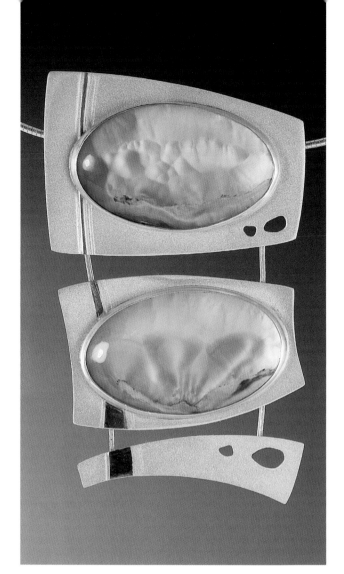

SKETCH OF THE DESERT
Two large agate cabochons have been used as the main feature of this pendant by Aleksandra Vali, chosen for their evocative patterns and set in silver bezels.

STYLES OF SETTING

Height of stone increased by step inside bezel cup

Open-back bezel setting

Filed edges scalloped

BEZEL HEIGHT IN RELATION TO STONE SHAPE/CURVATURE

Bezel is too short and will not hold stone

Bezel is too tall and will cover too much of stone

Correct bezel height

Tips

Transparent stones in closed settings will show water-staining from everyday wear. The insides of settings can be oxidized to alter the appearance of a stone.

8 Continue setting the stone, working across opposite sides until all gaps are closed. Then repeat the process with the pusher at a higher angle so that the top of the bezel is compressed around the stone. Check carefully that there are no gaps between the edge of the bezel and the stone.

9 Carefully clean up any marks left by the pusher using an emery stick. Place a piece of leather over the bench pin to prevent scuffing and use a burnisher to rub over the very the top edge of the bezel so that it feels smooth against the stone.

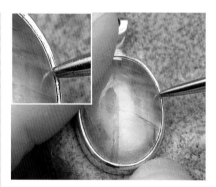

10 The tip of the burnisher can be run around the inside edge of the bezel to highlight it, but do take care not to scratch the stone. You can now give the piece its final polish, but do not allow it to get hot, particularly in the case of sensitive stones.

Tube Setting

Tube settings provide the quickest method for constructing bezel settings. For round stones this may be preferable to constructing a bezel because there will be no solder seam.

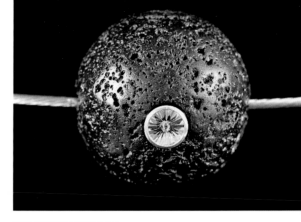

CREATIONS PENDANT
A Canadian diamond is tube-set in silver and set into a carved sphere of lava in this pendant by Ko Park.

STYLES OF TUBE SETTING

Double-ended

Smaller tube soldered inside larger tube

Wire ring soldered inside tube to support cabochon

skill level ☽

Choosing Stones

If faceted, round gemstones are the most suitable for this technique. Cabochons can be round or oval if the tube will be used in place of a simple constructed bezel. Due to the choice of metals, this method of setting is not suitable for very soft stones.

Metals

Store-bought tube is usually only available in the most commonly used metal alloys—sterling silver and the standard karats of gold. Some sizes of tube are available with thicker walls than standard tube. The advantage of using prefabricated tube is that it does not have a solder seam, which eliminates the potential for harder or weaker areas if there was too much or too little solder on the join. Although prefabricated tube has a higher fashion charge (price per gram) than sheet metal, the time saved in making the setting often justifies the extra cost.

Construction Details

Tubing used to make bezels for cabochons needs to be of a large enough diameter for the stone to fit inside the tube. If the tube is too small, sections of cut tube can be

---

MOUNTING FACETED STONES IN TUBE SETTINGS

Tube settings are reasonably simple, but the ball burr used to make the seat for the stone must be the correct size, as must the tube itself, otherwise the wall will end up too thin, or too thick to easily rub over.

TOOLKIT
- Tubing
- Chenier vise
- Ring shank
- Soldering equipment
- Ring clamp
- Ball burr and flexshaft motor
- Stones for setting
- Wax stick
- Flat-ended pusher and burnisher
- Polishing materials

1 First, cut sections of tubing to make the settings from. The inside diameter of the tube needs to be slightly smaller than that of the stone, and the height of the tube must allow for the stone's culet once the stone has been seated. Use a chenier vise to file the ends of the tubes perfectly flat. Solder the tubes into position on the ring.

2 Secure the ring in a ring clamp, and use a ball burr the same diameter as the stone to burr down to the mid-point of the burr. A flexshaft motor can be used to speed up the burring, but once the mid-point of the burr is reached further burring should be done with the burr in a pin vise to avoid going too deep.

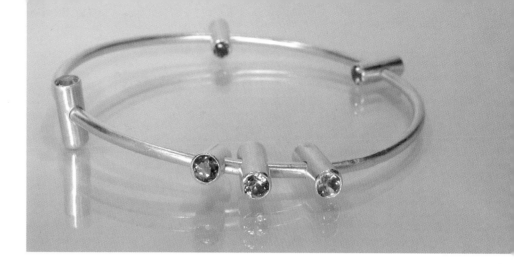

SPINNING BANGLE

This satin-finish silver bangle by Lilian Ginebra has free moving double-ended tube settings, which swivel when worn. The tubes are set with faceted synthetic ruby, yellow topaz, aquamarine and natural peridot.

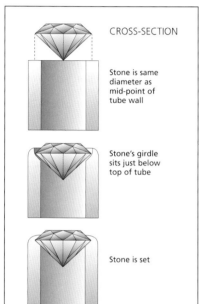

CROSS-SECTION

Stone is same diameter as mid-point of tube wall

Stone's girdle sits just below top of tube

Stone is set

annealed and stretched on a round or oval triblet, or a ball burr can be used to increase the internal diameter. The outside edge of the top of the bezel may need thinning with a file to make setting easier. Small sections of tube can be cut using a chenier vise or tubing block. The chenier vise allows the ends of the tube to be filed absolutely true.

For faceted stones, choosing the correct size of tube for a particular stone requires some planning. The inside and outside diameter of the tube in relation to the diameter of the stone needs to be known. Ideally, after seating the stone, a 26-gauge (0.4 mm thick) wall should remain; otherwise the setting will be weak. If the inside diameter of the tube is too large and only a small amount of metal is burred out during seating then there is the potential for the stone to slip down out of position during setting. The tube needs to be tall enough to allow the culet not to poke out underneath the tube—burring out the seat will cause the stone to sit deeper in the setting than is immediately obvious.

The seat for the stone can be burred out before or after the mount is soldered onto a piece. If before, in theory, a small lathe can be used to aid perfectly central burring, but often the burring will be done afterwards, because it can be more easily held. A ball burr is used to remove enough metal for the stone's girdle to sit below the top edge of the tube, and if the stone sits level then it can be set with a flat-ended pusher and burnisher.

3 Apply the stone to the seat with a wax stick—once in position, the stone's girdle should sit just below the top of the tube. If the stone sits too deeply, file away the top of the tube to the correct level. If the stone sits too high, continue burring until the position is satisfactory.

4 Set the stones with a flat-ended pusher. Secure the ring clamp in a vise so that both hands are free—use a small hammer to tap the pusher, "chasing" the metal over the stone. Work "north," "south," "east," and "west" as previously described, until the stones are set.

5 Burnish around the outside and inside edges of the tube settings before giving the piece a final polish.

Dome Setting

A dome setting is a closed type of setting with a pillow-shaped base, deep enough to enclose the lower part of a faceted or cabochon stone. The closed design of the mount intensifies the color of pale stones.

skill level

Choosing Stones

This type of setting can be used for both cabochons and faceted stones. Because the setting covers the girdle of the stone it is suitable for brittle or softer stones. The color of pale stones can be intensified with a highly polished or foiled mount interior.

Metals

Fine metals and standard alloys can be used. If the rub-over portion of the setting is integral rather than applied, fine metal can be used because it is softer. The curved nature of the form means that it will be more robust than if it were flat sheet, so it is suitable for use with softer or thinner metals with no loss of structural strength. For harder stones, use harder metal alloys.

Construction Details

True domed settings are restricted to round or oval stones. A perfect brilliant-cut stone should fit into a perfect hemisphere with no problems, but not all stones will be of perfect proportions, so you may need to make adjustments to the height of the dome.

DOME-SET CABOCHON EARRINGS
On these earrings by Sian Hughes, cast silver caps hold bullet-shaped garnet cabochons. Oxidized silver and gold components contrast well with the color of the stones, and the earrings are articulated to give the pieces movement when worn.

DOME SETTING
Before beginning the doming process, anneal the metal to make it more malleable. This prevents the metal splitting or breaking when it is being worked.

TOOLKIT
- Sheet metal
- Jeweler's saw
- Dapping block and punches
- 8 mm cabochon
- Soldering equipment
- Jump ring
- Ring shank
- Ring clamp
- Flat-ended pusher
- Burnisher

1 Using the formula on page 198, calculate the size of disk needed for the diameter of the stone being used. A slightly smaller disk can be used if a shallower dome is required. Pierce out the disk and anneal it before dapping in a dapping block.

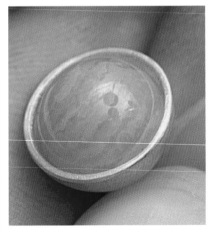

2 The stone should sit inside the dome with a clear ledge around it—this is the portion of the dome that will be rubbed over. If the stone sits too high, make the dome one size bigger in the dapping block; if the stone sits too low then continue dapping it smaller until it is the correct size.

DOME SETTING
A blue lace agate cabochon was set into a fine silver dome to make this ring, which was given a matte finish.

The depth of the dome must be enough to accommodate the pavilion of the stone, and account for the burring in as well—the stone will drop a little lower in the setting once it has been seated. There also needs to be enough metal above the girdle to rub over. Because the seat for the stone is being burred out, slightly thicker gauge sheet should be used—at least 20-gauge (0.8 mm) for gold, and 19-gauge (0.9 mm) for silver.

Calculate the size of disk needed for the stone, and pierce it out from sheet metal. Dome the disk in a dapping block, starting in a large size and gradually working down to smaller sizes, until the diameter of the inner edge of the dome is the same diameter as the stone—it should not quite fit inside. The top edge of the dome can be opened up with a larger dapping punch if necessary. Emery the edges of the dome so that there is a perfectly flat surface and, as for tapered bezel setting (see page 96), the girdle should sit midway across the edge. Solder the mount to the rest of the piece. Secure the piece and use a ball burr of the same diameter as the stone to make the seat—the girdle should sit just below the edge of the dome with enough metal left above to set it.

Variations

For cabochons and faceted shapes other than round, where burring a seat would be problematic, you can solder an inner metal rim in place to keep the stone level.

You can increase the height of the dome by soldering a bezel onto it; this could be of a different color metal, or slightly bigger than the rim of the dome, which would leave a seat for the stone to rest on (see diagram at right).

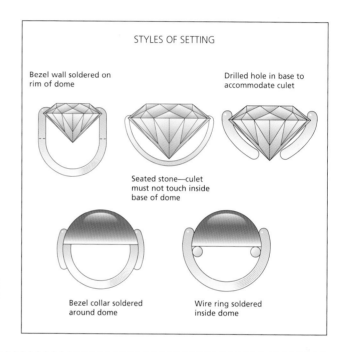

STYLES OF SETTING

Bezel wall soldered on rim of dome

Drilled hole in base to accommodate culet

Seated stone—culet must not touch inside base of dome

Bezel collar soldered around dome

Wire ring soldered inside dome

3 Solder a flattened jump ring inside the dome to support the stone—the jump ring should allow the stone to sit at the correct depth and prevent it from moving when being set. Solder the dome onto a ring shank and clean up the piece.

4 Support the piece in a ring clamp and set the stone, working "north," "south," "east," and "west" first, with the flat-ended pusher perpendicular to the ring shank. Continue setting until the bezel is neatly pushed around the stone.

5 Use a burnisher to rub the edge of the bezel flush against the stone; this will also polish the rim of the dome.

Tapered Bezel Setting

A popular choice for contemporary settings, tapered bezels provide very secure and protective mounts, with a conical shape that echoes the profile of the stone.

skill level 👁 👁

SWEETIE RINGS
Tapered bezels have been used to hold stones of contrasting colors in this set of stacking rings by Francis Levis. The satin finish on the silver contrasts with the sparkle of the citrine, peridot, and iolite faceted brilliants.

Choosing Stones

Because it protects the girdle of the stone, this type of setting is suitable for brittle stones that may be prone to chipping. However, very soft stones are less suitable because fine metals should not be used to make this type of mount.

Faceted round and oval stones are the most simple to make tapered bezels for. Other shapes of stone can be used, but the construction of the bezel is more difficult.

Metals

Due to the degree of construction required, standard alloys of silver, gold, platinum, and palladium are the most suitable for this setting. The sheet metal used to make the bezel needs to be at least 20-gauge (0.8 mm) to allow for burring.

Cast precious metal tapered bezels can be bought in standard shapes and sizes. These are a good alternative to handmade ones because they will save time and reduce the amount of metal wasted as scrap. This is particularly important when working with gold and platinum, because they are so expensive.

Construction Details

It is important to start with an accurate template when fabricating a tapered bezel, otherwise it will not have the correct proportions for the stone being used. Formulas for

---

FORMING A TAPERED BEZEL FOR A FACETED STONE
Calculating the correct size of a tapered bezel for a stone is not easy; mark out the template accurately and do a test run in base metal first so that if the bezel is too tall or short, the template can be adjusted before starting on the final piece.

TOOLKIT
- Tracing paper and pencil
- Double-sided tape or glue
- 22-gauge (0.6 mm) silver sheet
- Jeweler's saw
- File
- Round or half-round pliers
- Soldering equipment and pickle
- Bezel block and punch, mallet

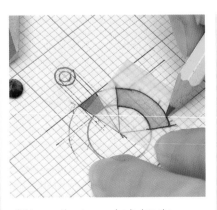

1 Measure the stone and calculate the template for the tapered bezel using the formula described on page 198. Carefully copy the outline created with tracing paper. Keep a copy of the template in case adjustments need to be made to the size.

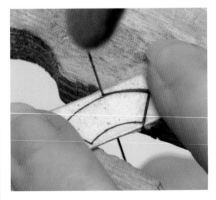

2 Use double-sided tape or glue to stick the template to a piece of 22-gauge (0.6-mm) silver sheet, and pierce around the outline with a jeweler's saw. File the flat ends true.

GOLD GARNET RING
A checkerboard-cut oval garnet has been set in a handmade tapered bezel in this ring by Marianne Anderson. The detailed surface texture of the gold shank contrasts with the geometric cut of the stone.

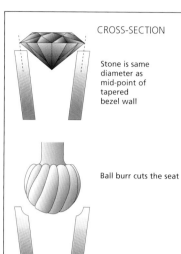

CROSS-SECTION

Stone is same diameter as mid-point of tapered bezel wall

Ball burr cuts the seat

Stone's girdle sits just below top of tapered bezel

Set stone

calculating the dimensions of tapered bezels can be found on page 198. Pierce out the template from sheet metal, file the flat ends, and use a pair of half-round pliers to curve the sheet—the shorter curve should be topmost in the pliers, to follow the taper of the jaws—and make the ends meet. Cut through the seam with a jeweler's saw, close with the pliers again, and hard solder the seam. File and emery the bezel both inside and out.

Tapered bezels made from tube have the advantage of no solder seam. Choose a diameter of tube a little smaller than the diameter of the stone; the annealed tube will shrink at its base and stretch at its top edge when hammered with a mallet into the bezel block. If the tube protrudes above the surface of the bezel block, it can be compressed into the block by tightening in a vise.

Bezel blocks are used for truing tapered bezels and they determine the angle of the walls of the bezel. They are available with 28 or 17 degrees angles—17 degrees will produce a narrower profile than 28. Place the bezel into the smallest hole in the block that it will fit into completely, and use a mallet to tap the punch inside.

Rub the top end of the bezel with emery paper until it is level, and check its size against the stone. The outer edge of the girdle should sit halfway across the width of the bezel wall—if the stone sits inside the bezel, further sanding down is needed. At this stage the bottom of the bezel can be leveled as well. Remember that the stone

3 Anneal the silver and bend it into a cone shape with round or half-round pliers—the narrow end of the cone should be at the top of the pliers. Make the flat ends meet, ensuring there is a good join before using hard solder to solder the join.

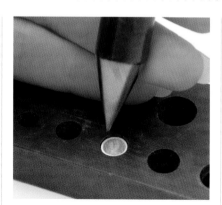

4 Pickle the bezel, and remove any excess solder on the outside of the bezel with a file. True the bezel by placing it in a bezel block and tapping the bezel punch with a mallet. This corrects the angle of the walls of the cone, but may distort the top and bottom out of alignment.

5 File the top and bottom of the bezel so that they are in alignment with the walls of the cone. If the stone sits very deeply inside the bezel then enough metal needs to be removed so that the stone sits on the top edge of the bezel. If the bezel is too small, stretch it with the bezel punch.

Continued over

will sit a little lower in the bezel once it has been seated, so do not remove so much metal that the culet will protrude from the bottom. Lightly clean up the outer surface of the bezel with emery sticks before soldering it into position on the piece of jewelry.

Use a ball burr of exactly the same diameter as the stone to carve out the seat. Enough metal needs to be removed so that the girdle of the stone sits just below the top of the bezel and is level—any slight angle of the stone will cause problems when setting. Check this using a loupe under a bright light. If the stone will not seat, don't be tempted to continue burring past the mid-point of the ball burr; it will not cut any wider than its maximum diameter. If the stone and the burr measure exactly the same size to within 0.1 millimeter, then only a very small amount of metal is preventing the stone from being seated. Angle the burr 45 degrees from the vertical, at "north," "south," "east," and "west" while turning—the burr is not perfectly round and this will remove a little more metal. If this does not open the mount enough, then you will need a slightly larger burr. The risk of doing this is that distortion occurring around the bezel as it is set over the stone allows the stone to drop down much further than intended, and probably at an angle. If the stone sits at an angle, metal can be removed from the higher side of the seat with a spitstick, taking care not to damage the rim of the bezel.

Don't forget to polish the inside of the bezel before setting the stone. Set the stone using a flat-ended pusher, working at the points of the compass as previously described, and burnish it before giving the piece a final polish.

RIBBON RING
This organic ring by Joanne Gowan is made from 18-kt yellow gold and platinum. The diamond is set in a tapered bezel which has had portions filed away, exposing a greater area of the stone.

SETTING A FACETED STONE IN A TAPERED BEZEL
Ensure that the bezel is at exactly the right height before starting to seat the stone; the stone should sit on the top edge exactly halfway across the rim.

TOOLKIT
- Bezel (see page 96) and ring shank
- Binding wire
- Soldering equipment
- Pickle
- Emery paper and polishing materials
- Ball burr
- File and emery stick
- Flat-ended pusher

6 Fit the bezel to a ring shank by filing it. Good contact ensures a strong solder join, but check from every angle that the bezel is straight in relation to the shank once the two parts are held together with binding wire. Once soldered, remove the binding wire, and pickle and dry the ring.

7 Clean up the piece and remove any file marks with successively finer grades of emery paper, and polish the inside of the bezel. Check that the top of the bezel is the correct size for the stone, which should sit halfway across the top edge. Use a ball burr the same diameter as the stone to create a seat for the stone.

DANTE'S HELL RING
White and yellow gold have been used to create this ring by Elizaveta Gnatchenko. Moonstone and ruby cabochons have been set back to back in double sided bezels to form spheres.

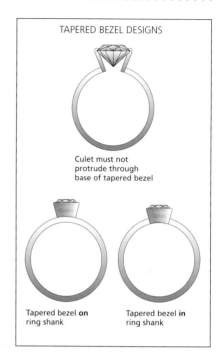

TAPERED BEZEL DESIGNS

Culet must not protrude through base of tapered bezel

Tapered bezel **on** ring shank

Tapered bezel **in** ring shank

ANGLES OF TAPERED BEZELS

17%   28%

8 Continue burring until the mid-point of the ball burr has just passed the top level of the bezel. The stone should sit in the bezel enough that there is a thin line of silver visible above the girdle. As a general rule, the table will be level with the top edge, but this can vary with stone proportions.

9 Thin the outer edge of the bezel wall with a file. The reduced thickness will make it easier to push the metal around the stone. Clean away the file marks with an emery stick.

10 Set the stone using a flat-ended pusher, working at opposite points until the metal is evenly compressed around the stone. Carefully remove any marks on the bezel with a fine emery stick before giving the piece a final polish.

Bezels with Corners

Making mounts for gemstones with shapes other than round or oval can be a challenge. Some simple methods for creating square, rectangular, trillion (triangular), and freeform bezel mounts are explored here.

skill level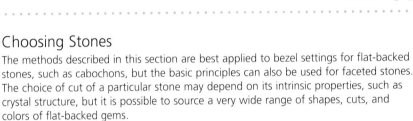

RUBELITE RING
A banded palladium shank is adorned with a striking red rubelite fancy cut in this ring by Nicholas Yiannarakis. The bezel was carefully constructed from 18-kt yellow gold to match the angles of the stone.

Choosing Stones

The methods described in this section are best applied to bezel settings for flat-backed stones, such as cabochons, but the basic principles can also be used for faceted stones. The choice of cut of a particular stone may depend on its intrinsic properties, such as crystal structure, but it is possible to source a very wide range of shapes, cuts, and colors of flat-backed gems.

Metals

Although fine metals are easier to set, and are especially appropriate if softer stones are being used, this must be balanced against the ease of construction with such malleable metal. If used, fine silver or gold sheet should be of a slightly thicker gauge than harder alloys or metals.

Construction Details

The shape or dimensions of square or rectangular bezels cannot be easily changed once they have been soldered closed, so it is best to make them from two L-shaped pieces of sheet metal. The corner of the L must be filed with a groove before it is folded so that the corner stays sharp. Once folded, it is important to ensure that the

---

CONSTRUCTING A SQUARE BEZEL FOR A SQUARE CABOCHON
Accurate measuring and soldering the bezel components in exactly the right position is absolutely crucial to the success of square bezels.

TOOLKIT
- Fine silver bezel strip
- File
- Parallel pliers
- Square cabochon stone
- Binding wire
- Soldering materials
- Ring shank
- Ring clamp
- Flat-ended pusher
- Burnisher

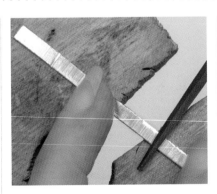

1 Determine the lengths of bezel strip required to make the mount. The bezel is made from two L-shaped strips and one side of each strip should be the same length as the side of the stone; the other side needs a little excess. File a groove in each strip so that it can be bent at a right angle.

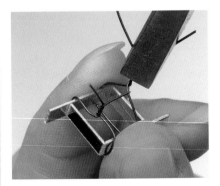

2 Bend the strips with parallel pliers and check that they are at right angles. Check that the bezel fits the stone, and file it to size if necessary. Use binding wire to secure the parts together—the two longer sides sit over the two shorter sides, creating a box with the correct dimensions. Bind the pieces with thin binding wire to hold them during soldering.

corners are exactly 90 degrees using an engineer's square, otherwise the setting will not be perfectly aligned. One side of each L should be a bit too long, so that the shorter side of the other L can butt up against it and be easily adjusted to the correct size.

Triangular settings can be made in a similar way to squares, with one folded piece soldered onto a flat strip of the same width—although the groove filed for the bend should have a more acute angle, made with a three-square needlefile. Navette settings should be made from two curved strips, and soldered closed with one end of each point against the inside of the opposite strip; the excess can be removed afterward.

This method allows for the most accurate internal angles on the bezel, ensuring that the stone will fit snugly inside the mount, with no obvious gaps once it has been set. Before setting the stone, file away the upper corners of the bezel. The degree to which you do this will depend on the exact profile of the stone, as well as being a matter of personal taste, but lowering any corners on a bezel is necessary to avoid flaps of metal being left after setting. The corners will not compress as much as necessary, so filing away the corners reduces the tendency for flaps of metal to be left. Use a flat-ended pusher to set the bezel over the stone, paying particular attention to the corners.

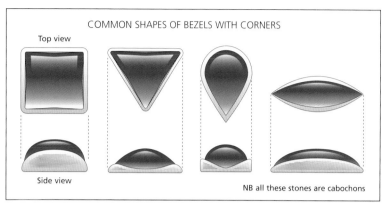

COMMON SHAPES OF BEZELS WITH CORNERS

Top view

Side view

NB all these stones are cabochons

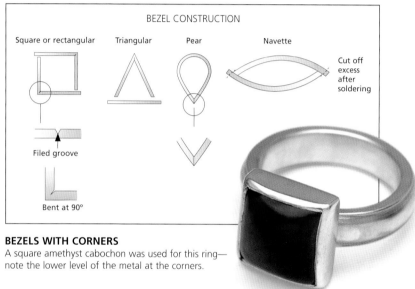

BEZEL CONSTRUCTION

Square or rectangular   Triangular   Pear   Navette

Cut off excess after soldering

Filed groove

Bent at 90°

BEZELS WITH CORNERS
A square amethyst cabochon was used for this ring—note the lower level of the metal at the corners.

3 Solder the bezel, then cut off the excess and file the corners true. Solder a base onto the bezel with medium solder, pierce off the excess metal edge, and clean up. You can then solder the bezel onto a ring shank. The corners of the bezel need to be filed down to match the curvature of the stone, and cleaned up before the stone is inserted.

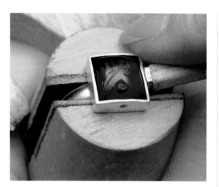

4 Secure the ring in a ring clamp and ensure the stone is properly inserted. The black marks visible on the stone and bezel indicate the best fitting sides; neither the stone nor the bezel are perfectly square. Use a flat-ended pusher to rub over the bezel.

5 Pay particular attention to setting the corners of the bezel, as they require much more compressing than the straight sides in order to sit against the stone. Ensure there are no gaps around the stone before burnishing and giving the piece its final finish.

Flush Setting

In a flush setting the stone is set level with the metal, just punctuating the surface of a piece. Flush settings are a comfortable and modern style of setting suitable for everyday wear.

skill level

OPEN SQUARE RING
Diamonds have been flush set around this simple eternity band by Lilly Hastedt. The white-gold ring slots into the gap in the double band which is bezel-set with a princess cut diamond.

Choosing Stones

Small, round faceted stones are generally used for this type of setting, with the actual size of the stone determined by the gauge of metal used and the design of the piece.

Metals

Standard alloys of any precious metal are suitable for flush settings, but fine silver or gold will be too soft. The surface being set into sheet needs to be at least 18 gauge (1 mm thick) to hold the stone, but may need to be thicker.

Construction Details

Although flush setting is most easily done on curved or domed metal surfaces, it is suitable for flat metal, too. This type of setting is often used with cast forms, but fabricated pieces are also suitable—the only requirement is that the metal is thick enough to hold the stone. Shallow curves will give better results than deep curves, which can cause the finished setting to distort and not be perfectly round. The culet of the stone must not protrude from the metal unless it sits in a recess, because it will either be uncomfortable to wear or be at risk of being chipped.

Stones can be evenly spaced around a polished band ring with the use of a circle divider, see page 193. Use a center punch to mark where the center of the stone will

FLUSH SETTING FACETED STONES ON A DOMED SURFACE
Pale sapphires of ⅒ in (3 mm) in diameter are used in this project, flush set into a domed pendant that has been decorated with hand-engraved lines.

TOOLKIT
- Metal with a domed surface
- Center punch, drill
- Ball burr
- Stones for setting
- Burnisher, polishing materials

1 Center punch and drill holes where the stones will be positioned. The size of drill bit used should be about two thirds of the diameter of the stone. When drilling on a curve, keep the angle of the drill bit perpendicular to the plane of the curve, otherwise the hole will be slightly oval.

2 Use a ball burr larger than the drill hole to tidy the underside of the hole, but do not burr too far. The purpose of this is to remove any sharp edges before the stones are in position.

A STAR IS BORN
A combination of flush and grain setting was used to set the tiny diamonds on the surface of this white-gold pendant by Paul Battes. The tip of each point of the star is set with a Tahitian pearl.

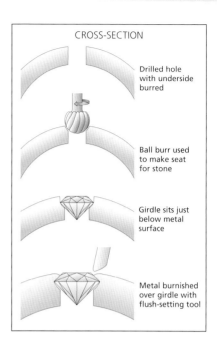

CROSS-SECTION

Drilled hole with underside burred

Ball burr used to make seat for stone

Girdle sits just below metal surface

Metal burnished over girdle with flush-setting tool

be, and start the drill holes off with a drill bit in a pin vise, before drilling right through the metal with a motorized drill. Use a burr smaller than the diameter of the stone to tidy up the back of the hole.

To seat the stone, use a ball burr exactly the same diameter as the stone and burr into the drilled hole. The first part can be done with a flexshaft motor for speed, but when the mid-point of the ball of the burr gets near the top of the hole, switch to using a pin vise. If the seat is burred down too far, the stone will sit too low in the setting and be obscured. With the stone in place, the girdle must sit just below the top edge of the hole and be absolutely level—check from all angles. Push the stone down firmly into the setting with a wooden object—the underneath of a bench pin is perfect for this. Use a flush setting tool to push the metal down at "north," "south," "east," and "west" before closing any gaps and ensuring the edge of the metal is in contact with the stone and the girdle is fully covered. Run a burnisher around the inside of the setting to tidy it up.

Top   Side   Underside

Handle
FLUSH SETTING TOOL

3 Open up the seat for the stone using a ball burr exactly the same size, or 0.1 mm larger than the diameter of the stone. When seated, the table of the stone should be flush with the surface of the silver. Carefully check the height of the stone at regular intervals when burring.

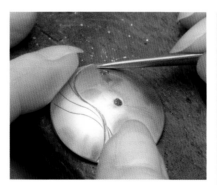

4 With the stone in position, use a burnisher to rub the edge of the metal down over the girdle of the stone. Set small areas at north, south, east, and west to begin with before rubbing down the remainder of the edge evenly.

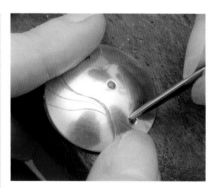

5 Burnish out the marks made on the surface of the metal by the burnisher. Run the tip of the burnisher around the inside edge of the flush setting to neaten and highlight it. Give the piece a final polish.

Channel Setting

Channel setting allows stones to be lined up along a channel, with no metal separating them, to create the appearance of an uninterrupted band of gems.

skill level

Choosing Stones

Faceted stones are most often channel set: square, baguette, or brilliant cut. Calibrated stones are essential for an even and level line of stones, although this will be less apparent with round stones set on a curve, as opposed to baguettes set on the flat.

Metals

Harder precious metals are more difficult to set in a uniform manner, but are far more durable and are therefore suitable for harder, valuable stones such as diamonds, rubies, and sapphires.

Construction Details

Commercially, it is common to cast the mounts for channel setting with the stones already in position in the wax. Special tools for cutting the groove in the wax to hold the stones in the wall of the piece are available, and CAD is used to aid the creation of accurate mounts.

True channel setting is a rub-over technique, with a seat cut for each stone, and the walls folded over once all the stones are seated. The seating can be problematic if using square or rectangular stones, because all of the stones need to be seated at precisely

PAGODA RING
Channel-set square black diamonds form a pleasing border around the ruby. A natural, untreated ruby is set with split prongs in this 18-kt gold ring by Ming.

CHANNEL SETTING IN AN ANTICLASTIC RING
This project looks deceptively simple, but forming the ring to exactly the right size for the stones is something of a technical challenge. Square-cut brilliants are most easily set using this technique, but you could use other shapes.

TOOLKIT
- 24-gauge (0.5-mm thick) silver sheet
- Dapping punch, mallet, steel rod
- Mandrel
- Stones for setting
- Flat steel block
- Soldering materials
- Silver rod (optional)
- Polishing materials, burnisher

1 Form an anticlastic ring from a band of 24-gauge (0.5-mm thick) silver sheet. The height of the strip should be roughly twice the width of the stone. Open up both sides of the band using a dapping punch to force the top edge out. Anneal the ring, and use a mallet to knock down the edges so that they form a flat-sided channel.

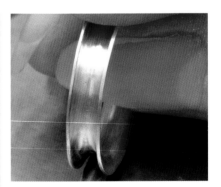

2 Force the channel to a perfectly even width by opening it up along a steel rod of the same width as the stones. Place the ring on a mandrel, and tap the rod into the groove. If the channel becomes too wide, mallet it narrower on a flat steel block.

UNDER THE SEA
This pendant by Ko Park was CAD designed and rapid prototyped before being cast in silver. The channel setting holds a single 80-ct London-blue topaz.

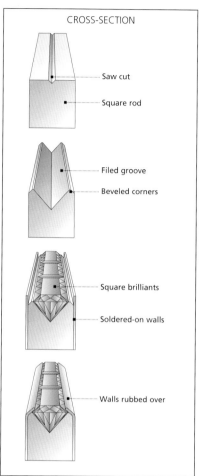

CROSS-SECTION

- Saw cut
- Square rod
- Filed groove
- Beveled corners
- Square brilliants
- Soldered-on walls
- Walls rubbed over

the same level or the piece will not look right. However, the term "channel setting" can be interpreted as any type of setting in which the stones are secured in a channel; if a groove is made along the inside edges of opposite walls, it is possible to slot the stones into position. The ends of the channel need to be secured somehow; whether plates are riveted or screwed into position to prevent the stones from moving, or grains are raised at the ends of the grooves, you can find plenty of ingenious solutions.

Another variation on channel setting is to have a wall on two sides, with the stones seated in the channel in between. The walls can then be rubbed over the ends of the stones to secure them. The wall should be a little thicker than is needed, so that it can be cleaned up to an even level after setting—though this will make rubbing over the walls harder work. For less malleable metals, keep the extra thickness to a minimum. You'll likely need to perform the setting with the use of a hammer-action burnisher in a flexshaft motor, because this provides more force than setting by hand or chasing the walls over.

3 If stones are not being channel set all the way around the ring, solder a piece of ⅛ in (3 mm) rod into the channel. Cut a groove in each end of the rod for the girdle of the stone to sit in—the rod must be exactly the correct length to allow no gaps between the stones.

4 Polish the inside of the channel. Position the first stone under the ledge in the end of the rod, and continue placing the stones in a row along the channel. The shape of the stones means they will support each other in the confined space. Use a burnisher to begin rubbing the edges of the channel over the stones' girdles.

5 Continue burnishing until the edge of the channel makes continuous contact with the stones and appears even and smooth. If necessary, clean up the ring with fine emery paper and polish it.

Prong Settings

Wires or sections of sheet are usually used to create prong settings, which often hold a faceted stone above the body of a piece and allow more of the stone to be visible.

There are many methods for constructing prongs with which to set stones, from carving a metal mount to make a crown setting, to lost-wax casting from a jeweler's wax model, or fabricating wire "baskets" to support the stone. Computer-aided design can be applied to this technique because it allows the creation of forms that would otherwise be very complex to construct. Prong settings may be complex, or relatively simple—wires soldered around the seat for a stone can be used to hold it.

CROWN SETTING
(see page 108)   skill level 👥

A fabricated tapered bezel was carved with a file to divide the bezel up into prongs, forming a crown setting in this silver and smoky quartz ring. Although a very traditional style of setting, handmade crown mounts can be adapted proportionally, and by the ways in which they are divided and carved made into uniquely crafted pieces.

BASKET SETTING
(see page 112)   skill level 👥

"Basket setting" usually refers to a style of prong setting constructed from wires to form an open structure. This ring by Philip Sajet featuring a large, faceted smoky quartz has been set between prongs in a white gold "scaffold." The hardness of the metal makes it strong enough to support such a large stone, which is held in place by grooves in the prongs as well as the internal tension of the structure.

CLOSED-BACK PRONG SETTING

(see page 114)　　　　　　　　skill level 💍

This ring by Regine Schwaizer is made from silver, with 22-kt gold prongs holding the faceted rubelite and rough quartz stones. Although the high-karat gold is relatively soft, the prongs are quite thick and will hold the stones securely. Closed-back settings are useful for intensifying the colors of pale stones, or for allowing foil to be used underneath the stone to enhance or alter its color.

CAM PRONG SETTING

(see page 116)　　　　　　　　skill level 💍💍

"Euclidean Pendant," by Lauren Elizabeth Tidd, was designed with the aid of Rhino and Matrix. The 18-kt white-gold overlapping linear forms are held together with bezel-set diamonds, which extend to form modified prongs for the 19.9-ct faceted rutilated quartz. CAM allows complex designs to be created for specific stones, ensuring that the resulting cast piece will be exactly the correct dimensions.

APPLIED PRONG SETTING

(see page 118)　　　　　　　　skill level 💍

This 22-kt gold ring by Leo Pieroni was fabricated with prominent prongs, to hold a 3.1-ct natural uncut diamond. The rich color of the metal and its texture complement the character of the stone, and give the piece an archaic feel. Prongs that are applied to a form rather than being an integral part of it can allow a greater freedom of choice over the shape of stone being set.

Crown Setting

Fabricated tapered bezels, made either from a template or from tubing, can be adapted to create individual prong settings, which will display larger faceted stones in style.

skill level ♂♂

KIMONO RING
The striking double spiral of the shank of this rose-gold ring by Ming opens up to form the prongs that hold a large cushion-cut pink tourmaline. The spirals are accentuated with a fine band of black enamel.

Choosing Stones

Hard stones, such as diamonds, rubies, sapphires, and spinels are most suitable for prong settings because they are resilient enough to cope with being under pressure, and the edges of the stones are resistant to knocks and bumps, which might chip softer or more brittle stones.

Metals

The design must account for the strength of the metal and its resistance to bending if caught, so prongs should be made in a hard metal such as white gold, palladium, or platinum, especially if they are holding a valuable gemstone. Silver can be used to make prong settings, but the gauge of the sheet used will need to be much thicker than that of harder metals.

Construction Details

This type of setting is often used to raise stones up so that the maximum amount of light can enter the stone and increase the internal reflections; as a result, this setting

---

MAKING A CROWN SETTING FROM A FABRICATED TAPERED BEZEL
Standard rub-over settings can be adapted in a number of ways. In this project, a tapered bezel is filed to make a crown prong setting.

TOOLKIT
- Tapered bezel (see page 96)
- Dividers
- Jeweler's saw
- Needlefiles
- Soldering equipment
- Jump ring
- File
- Ring shank

1 Make up a tapered bezel, as previously described (see page 96). The bezel needs to be taller to accommodate the prongs, so increase the top of the template by $\frac{1}{32}$–$\frac{1}{16}$ in (1–2 mm). Divide up the bezel using dividers, depending on the number of prongs that will be cut, and also mark for the depth of the cuts.

2 Starting with the top of the bezel, make small saw cuts for reference where the prong divisions are. Support the bezel as you file, and use a round or half-round needlefile to remove enough metal so that the prongs are clearly defined.

I PUT A SPELL ON YOU
This steel and silver ring by Dauvit Alexander is set with a richly coloured amethyst trillion held by tubes which are set with mandarin garnets. Grooves were cut into the tubes before they were levered around the amethyst to set it.

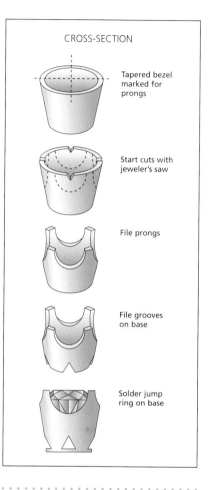

CROSS-SECTION

Tapered bezel marked for prongs

Start cuts with jeweler's saw

File prongs

File grooves on base

Solder jump ring on base

is commonly used to display large stones on ring shanks, but also for earrings. Prong settings are less suitable for bangles because the stone is not well protected from impact.

Tapered bezel settings can be adapted to form prong settings by filing V-shaped sections out of the bezel at regular intervals on its top and bottom edges; these must be evenly spaced otherwise the width of the prongs will not be equal—the number of prongs should be three or more, and is determined by the number of filed areas on the bezel. The underside of the bezel is also filed, and a jump ring is soldered to the base of the filed bezel to close it, giving the effect that the setting has been pierced. You can create a variety of designs using this method, or adapt the basic idea further for even greater variety—holes could be drilled into the bezel before or after it is formed, or if thicker-gauge metal is used to form the bezel, files can be used to carve the metal to a greater degree than would be possible with thinner sheet.

It is possible to buy prefabricated prong settings, but these lack the charm of handmade settings. The bezel is formed in the same way as described on page 96, using either the formula to calculate the template for the stone, or a piece of tubing

3 File the base of the bezel to make divisions—this will give the appearance of a pierced bezel and will allow more light to enter the stone. These cuts made with a round needlefile can be angled to create an attractive pattern, but other shapes of needlefile, such as three-square, can be used.

4 Clean up the filed areas of the base of the bezel and ensure that the base is flat. Solder a jump ring to the base and, once pickled, file it level with the bezel so that it appears to join seamlessly.

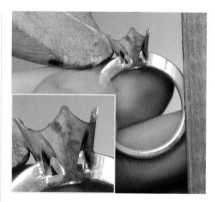

5 Solder the bezel into a ring shank, taking care to position it carefully so that it is aligned from all sides. The ring shank needs to make good contact with the mount; the base of the bezel will need to be filed to fit the curve of the inside of the ring, so set it a little low in the shank. Clean up the ring.

Continued over

GOLD RINGS
This pair of gold rings by Karl Karter use extensions of the architectural shanks to form flat prongs which hold the large oval stones securely.

COUPÉ EN DEUX
This colourful ring by Philip Sajet is prong set with a replica of the Hope diamond cut from blue glass. The gold shank of the ring is embellished on its outer surface with shades of green enamel.

shaped in a bezel block. The top and bottom surfaces of the bezel must be absolutely flat and true before you mark out where the grooves will be, otherwise the results will not be even. Mark the centers of the points between the prongs, rather than the prongs themselves, before starting the grooves with a jeweler's saw. Methodically carve the grooves with a three-square, square, or round needlefile, depending on the design. Work down to a mark around the circumference of the bezel—which should be just lower than the level of the stone's girdle—taking care to keep the spacing of the prongs even; if some grooves are filed too deeply then the prongs on either side will be thinner than the others. Repeat this process on the lower part of the bezel, though here the grooves are purely decorative and need not be so deep. A suitably sized jump ring made from square-section wire can then be soldered to the base. Complete all work, including cleaning up, on the mount before soldering it to the piece of jewelry.

SETTING A FACETED STONE IN A CROWN MOUNT
The smoky quartz brilliant used in this ring must be seated at exactly the correct height for the prongs to be left at the correct length; mark the position carefully before cutting the seat.

TOOLKIT
- Ring shank, bezel, stone (see page 108)
- Dividers
- Jeweler's saw
- Needlefile
- Polishing materials
- Flat-ended pusher
- Burnisher

6 When the stone is placed in the bezel, it should sit inside the prongs. Mark on the inside of the prongs just below where the girdle of the stone sits, using dividers.

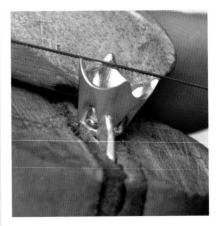

7 Starting with a precise saw cut, file a groove on the inside of each of the prongs. The groove should not be too deep—just enough for the stone to click firmly into position. The groove should match the profile of the girdle; some stones have wider girdles than others. Polish the inside of the mount before inserting the stone.

"MARGARET" RING
A brilliant-cut citrine is prong set in this ring by Katherine Agnew. The entire ring, including the prongs, was pierced from sheet silver before being scored and folded to create the open cluster.

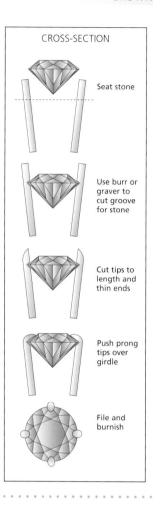

CROSS-SECTION

Seat stone

Use burr or graver to cut groove for stone

Cut tips to length and thin ends

Push prong tips over girdle

File and burnish

Accurate seating of the stone is crucial, so the construction of the setting needs to be carried out with a high degree of accuracy. The stone must sit evenly within the setting: if the girdle is not touching each prong, then the angle of the prongs should be adjusted until it does—make sure that the prongs look even overall. The prongs are then marked inside at the level at which the stone will finally sit—it is crucial that the marks are all at the same height, otherwise the stone will not be level once set. You can then use a graver or hart burr to remove a small amount of metal from the inside of the prong for the stone to sit in. The stone should click into position, and be held level while it is set. It is often necessary to thin the tips of the prongs with a file before setting, otherwise the thickness of the metal prevents it from moving easily.

8 Thin the outside of the prongs to make them easier to set. The inner surface of the prongs above the stone may also need filing a little so that they sit flat against the stone. Take care not to thin the metal too much. You can also adjust the height of the prongs at this stage.

9 Push the tips of the prongs over the girdle. A flat-ended pusher is used for this ring, but if the prongs are narrower or more rounded, a prong pusher may be more appropriate because it will not slip out of position.

10 File the tips of the prongs to shape with a file that has a "blind" side so that it does not scratch the stone. Burnish the prongs so that their edges are flush with the stone, ensuring there are no areas that could snag on clothes. Give the ring a final polish.

Basket Setting

Wire structures can be used as the basis for fabricating pronged mounts that use minimal metal to secure the stone, allowing it to be clearly viewed.

OFFSET RING
The basket setting has been attached sideways to the silver shank in this ring by Thomas Smith. The base of the basket tapers into a solid rod which intersects with an extension of the shank.

skill level 👥

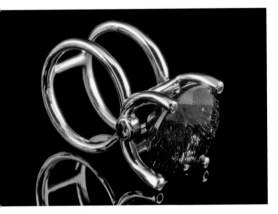

QUARTZ COCKTAIL RING
Jayce Wong's ring features a cut rutilated and tourmilated quartz stone displayed in open basket-set gold shanks. The tips of the prongs and intersections with the shanks are tube-set with diamonds and sapphires.

Choosing Stones

Stones that are hard but not brittle are most suitable for this type of setting because they will be held under pressure. Pronged wire mounts are often used to make a feature of valuable stones, allowing the maximum amount of light to enter.

Metals

Most wire prong mounts are made from high-karat golds and platinum, and the thinner the gauge of wire used, the harder the metal should be. The use of silver for this type of setting should be restricted to trial runs and test pieces and will need to be a thick gauge. For final pieces, silver should only be used with inexpensive stones because the resulting mount is unlikely to be strong enough for a long life.

Construction Details

Traditionally, basket setting consists of pairs of wires soldered onto two rings smaller

BASKET SETTING A BUFF-TOP CUT
Getting the proportions and angles of the prongs of the basket correct is vital to a strong and secure setting. While silver is good for practicing the technique, it is too soft a metal to make strong wire settings for larger stones.

TOOLKIT
- Silver wire for jump rings and prongs
- Soldering equipment
- Stone for setting
- Needlefile
- Jeweler's saw, reverse-action tweezers
- Ring shank
- Chain-nose pliers
- Prong pusher, graining tool

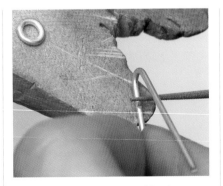

1 Make two jump rings and solder them closed. One ring should be a bit smaller than the diameter of the stone, and the other much smaller—the difference between the two jump rings and their spacing determines the angles of the prongs. Bend sections of straight wire to make the prongs, and file a groove to fit the small jump ring first.

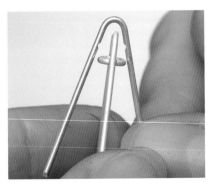

2 Solder the small jump ring into the grooves in the first pair of prongs. Cut out a section at the base of the prongs to allow the second pair of prongs to be positioned. Check the alignment carefully before soldering, and support the prongs that have already been soldered using reverse-action tweezers.

STYLES OF PRONG TIPS

Rounded

Pointed

Flat

Split/double

than the diameter of the stone; the proportions of the two rings and the distance between them determines the angle of the wire prongs, and how high or low the stone sits within the mount.

There are many variations that can be made on this basic premise, as well as plenty of other methods for constructing settings from wire, and both offer far more design possibilities than mounts formed from tapered bezels.

Individually positioning wires to form prongs can be troublesome—it is far easier to use one wire to form an opposing pair of prongs, either by bending the wire into a U-shape or by forming a cross from two wires before continuing with construction. The wires for the prongs can be soldered onto a supporting form, directly onto a ring shank, or into drilled holes, which will give them greater strength.

It is a design decision as to whether the stone rests on a seat, and will also depend on the size of the stone, its height in the setting, and the thickness of the prongs. Thick prongs will support the stone better than thin ones. Adaptations to this setting could include two wires soldered together to make a wider prong with a "split" in it, or the use of different sections of wire, such as square or triangular. The shape of the prong tips can also be adapted to suit a particular design, with the most commonly used being flat, pointed, rounded, or split.

Accurate marking and filing is required to evenly space the prongs around the mount, with notches filed into the ring rather than the U-shaped wire before the prongs are soldered into position. The finished mount can then be applied to a range of different pieces before the stone is seated and the prong tips pushed over to secure the stone.

CROSS-SECTION

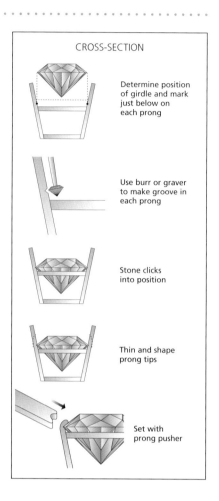

Determine position of girdle and mark just below on each prong

Use burr or graver to make groove in each prong

Stone clicks into position

Thin and shape prong tips

Set with prong pusher

3 Mark the height of the groove for the larger jump ring a bit below where it sits between the prongs. File grooves and solder the jump ring in place. Fit the basket mount to a ring shank and solder in position. Clean up the ring and file grooves for the stone to click into, ensuring it sits level within the basket. Cut the prongs to length.

4 Thin the prongs so that they can be more easily set. Use chain-nose pliers to push over the tips of the prongs—align one side of the pliers down a prong and close the pliers to push over the opposite prong tip. File the tips to adjust the length, if necessary, and shape them.

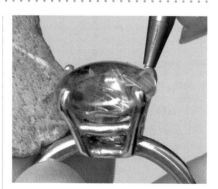

5 Finish setting the prongs with a prong pusher, so that they sit securely against the stone. Rounded tips can be burnished with a suitably sized graining tool that has a polished concave recess at the tip.

Closed-back Prong Setting

Pale stones can be enhanced with the use of a closed-back setting to increase the internal reflections, making colors appear more intense.

skill level

CITRINE RING
A marquise-cut citrine has been set in this silver ring by Chris and Joy Poupazis. Four prongs extend from the body of the flat-topped shank to hold the stone close to its tips.

Choosing Stones

This type of setting is often used to intensify light-colored stones. It is not often used with intensely colored stones because it darkens the color too much—they would usually be mounted in an open setting. Faceted stones are often used, but many cuts and shapes can be mounted in this way.

Metals

Mixed precious metals can be used if prongs or tabs are being applied to an existing form; harder precious metals should be used for more valuable stones to ensure their security.

Construction Details

Closed-back settings may be less suitable for jewelry items such as rings, which will be exposed to water and other substances that may get trapped behind the stone. It is impossible to clean the stone without removing it from the mount, unlike open settings, which are accessible from behind.

Wires can be soldered around the appropriate area of a form to create a custom prong setting—the prongs do not have to be evenly spaced, or even made from the same metal or diameter of wire. Small sections of sheet can be used instead of wire, if it is more appropriate that tabs, rather than prongs, are used to set the stone; the only necessity is that the stone is securely held.

USING FOIL WITH A CLOSED-BACK PRONG SETTING
Closed-back settings will intensify the colors of paler stones, but can also be used to trap gold or colored metallic foil behind a stone to alter its color.

TOOLKIT
- Cast silver ring (see page 78)
- Files, abrasive and polishing materials
- Stone for setting
- Burr
- Soldering materials
- Gold wire
- Pickle
- Top cutter
- Gold foil, gold size
- Prong pusher, burnisher

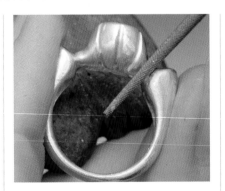

1 This project continues on from Wax Carving (see page 78). The silver cast of the wax model needs to be cleaned up—cut the sprue off with saw, and file the area. The surface of the ring can be refined with files to adjust the shape or remove marks and scratches. Remove file marks with abrasives—a flexshaft motor will greatly speed up this process—before polishing.

2 A small amount of shrinkage is caused as a result of the casting process—check that the stone will still sit at the correct level and burr the seat if necessary.

INLAID NECKLACE
The prongs that hold the faceted square stone in this necklace by Jānis Vilks were constructed as part of the box setting that holds it.

Wax carving can also be used to fabricate closed-back prong settings, either separately or as an integral part of a jewelry piece. Wax wires may be useful for creating the "wire" parts of the setting, but it is often preferable to solder wires on after the piece has been cast because it is easier to clean up the form without them in place. When wax carving for pieces that will be cast in gold or platinum, it is useful to make a master in silver with wire prongs soldered in position, which is then reproduced in the more expensive precious metal with the use of a mold and lost wax casting. The casting must be cleaned up and polished before the stone is set. The seat may need burring again, as the casting process reduces the volume of the piece slightly and the stone may no longer fit perfectly.

One of the benefits of a closed-back setting—and this applies to other forms of closed-back setting including grain and bezel—is that the appearance of the stone can be enhanced with the use of foil or other reflective materials. This is a practice that has been used for centuries to improve the intensity of paler stones, or to create the appearance of a greater amount of light within colorless stones, particularly paste or synthetics. Any thin reflective material that will not tarnish, including gold foil and colored candy wrappers, can be used to intensify the color of stones or create contrasting effects.

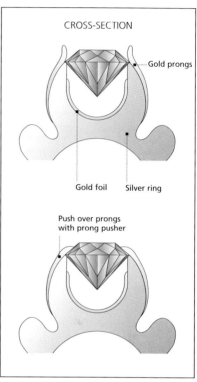

CROSS-SECTION

Gold prongs

Gold foil   Silver ring

Push over prongs
with prong pusher

3 The grooves around the seat for the stone were carved in the wax and designed to receive wires to make a prong setting. Solder U-shaped lengths of gold wire into position, using silver solder. Once pickled, clean up and polish the ring again before trimming the wires to length.

4 Cover the inside of the closed-back setting with gold foil, which will show through the stone and affect the appearance of its color. Paint the inside of the setting with gold size, wait for it to go tacky, and apply the foil. Shape the tips of the prongs with a cup burr.

5 Insert the stone, ensuring it sits level, and push the prongs over the girdle with a prong pusher. The tips should be burnished down against the surface of the stone so that they are flush and feel smooth to the touch.

CAM Prong Setting

Building a virtual model of your setting eliminates many of the problems associated with the complex fabrication required for pronged mounts; the design can then be rendered in wax and lost-wax cast.

skill level

Choosing Stones

The choice of stone may be dependent on the type of metal being used and the exact design of the metal mount. However, it is likely that the piece will be designed around the stones which are going to be used, or standard cuts will be used—mounts for these often come as templates in jewelry-specific CAD software, but you can also create custom mounts for different cuts.

Metals

As with other forms of prong setting, precious metals are most suitable for this type of mount. Silver is less suitable due to its malleability, but will be fine to use at a thicker gauge and for less valuable or softer stones.

Construction Details

The process of building a three-dimensional model is discussed in detail on pages 80–85. Unless you are using a service that provides design, rendering, and casting on-site, it will be necessary to source companies to print or mill the model of the piece as well as cast it. Prototypes can also be made in acrylic or resin, which may be more appropriate for certain forms.

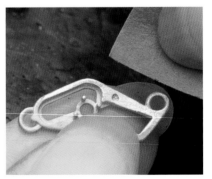

3E EARRINGS
These long, chain-link earrings by Anastasia Young are set with graduated rose-cut garnets. The sections were built virtually so that the scale could easily be altered to create different sizes of links, as well as mirror the forms.

CAM PRONG-SET EARRINGS
The crucial stages in this project are tackled when designing the piece; the form must be the correct size for the stones being used, and the tolerances sufficient to allow successful casting.

TOOLKIT
- Wax models rendered from CAD files
- Abrasive materials
- Soldering materials
- Earring posts
- Polishing materials
- Cup burr
- Wood for support

1 Wax models are rendered from CAD files using a 3D printer. The waxes are incredibly fragile and no cleaning up should be attempted before they have been cast into metal.

2 Clean up the castings to remove the texture of the printed wax from the pieces. If multiple components are produced using CAD/CAM, you can adapt the pieces to make various jewelry forms.

CROCUS RINGS
This pair of rings by Zoe Marie were designed using CAD to fit specific shapes of stone. A round blue topaz is held by five tapered prongs set with diamonds, and a pink tourmaline trillion is set with three prongs to complement its shape.

The prongs that form the mount for the stone should be made a little longer than required and are likely to be thin and fragile, but they can be cross-linked with "wires" that are cut away once the piece has been cast into metal. The prototyped wax models are so fragile that it is not advisable to attempt any cleaning up of build-lines or marks from milling; cleaning up must instead be done on the metal cast.

Intricate areas of the form may be problematic, but many small abrasive attachments are available for flexshaft motors, which are useful in situations like these. Abrasive cord and tape are also useful for cleaning pierced areas, and thrumming can be used to polish hard to reach areas. If multiples are being created from the first cast "master," this should be cleaned up well so that the subsequent copies will not require so much finishing time.

When the piece is ready for the stones to be mounted, check that the prongs are all evenly spaced and mark the positions of the areas that need filing or burring to seat the stone. Mark the correct height of the prongs with the stone in position, before trimming away the excess with flush cutters. Depending on the style of the prong tips, clean up the cut ends so that they are not sharp, and push them over the stones with a suitable prong pusher. Burnish the tips so that they are flush with the stone, taking care if it is a softer or more brittle stone.

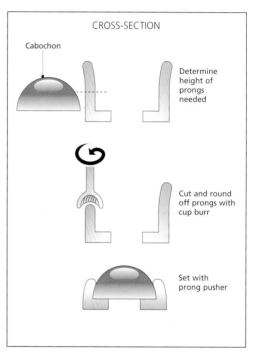

CROSS-SECTION

Cabochon

Determine height of prongs needed

Cut and round off prongs with cup burr

Set with prong pusher

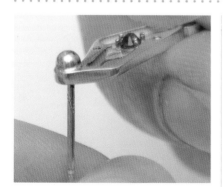

3 Solder a large granule and earring post through the hole at one end of the component. Give the piece a final polish at this stage, paying particular attention to the area around the prongs, which will be inaccessible once the stone is set.

4 Check the height of the prongs with the stone in position, but remove it to trim the prongs. Use a cup burr to reshape the ends of the prongs once they are at the correct length. Insert the earring post into a drilled hole in a secured piece of wood to support the piece during mounting and setting.

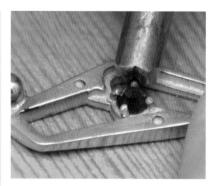

5 Use a prong pusher to set the prongs around the stone. Set two opposing prongs first, and check that the stone is still level before pushing over the second pair of prongs.

Applied Prong Setting

Many metal forms can be adapted to take stones simply by the addition of wire prongs, allowing unusual-shaped stones to be secured without using a complex mount.

skill level

OWL RING
A carved topaz intaglio is set in this gold ring by Whitney Abrams. Although the stone is supported by a textured bezel, it is set by four prongs with balled ends which echo the beaded bands that form the ring shank.

Choosing Stones

Flat-backed stones, such as cabochons or rose cuts, are the easiest to set using this method, as they require little or no seating. The same is true of uncut crystals if they have large, flat facets. Faceted and spherical stones will need to be seated to some degree, so that they are stable and held securely.

Metals

Longer wire prongs should be made from harder metals so that they are strong enough, but larger gauges of fine silver or gold wire can be used and are especially appropriate for setting fragile stones. Mixed metals can be used within the same piece. For example, where the main body of the piece is silver, you could use gold wire to make the prongs, creating a color contrast and increasing the strength of the prongs.

Construction Details

Applied prongs or tabs are a popular choice for mounting uncut crystals because the placement of the prongs is not restricted to a specific formation. They are also used for securing mixed-media elements to a metal structure, often a supporting wire framework.

SETTING NATURAL CRYSTALS WITH PRONGS
Prongs can be applied to a base or form in a pattern dictated by a specific stone, choosing positions where the prongs will provide most structural support and can be set against the stone.

TOOLKIT
- Natural crystals for setting, metal base
- Center punch, drill
- Ball burr
- Wire for prongs
- Soldering equipment
- Top cutters
- File
- Pliers
- Cup burr
- Prong pusher, burnisher

1 Position the crystals on a metal base and decide on the best positions for the prongs to be. Mark as closely as possible to the stones the positions of the holes that will hold the wire prongs. Center punch and drill holes the same diameter as the wire that will be used.

2 Use a small ball burr to clean the front and back of the holes. Insert U-shaped wires into the holes, ensuring that the prongs they form will be long enough to hold the stones. Solder the wires into place.

ROYAL JEWELS
The uncut stones set with blanched silver prongs are chabazite in basalt, rubies, apatites, and garnets in this set of earrings and a ring by Regine Schwaizer.

The strongest method for soldering wires to a form, whether sheet or thick rod, is to drill a hole into which the wire can be inserted before it is soldered. The top and underside of the hole can be lightly countersunk to reduce the meniscus of solder around the base of the wire if this will interfere with the seating of the stone. Where the base is too narrow to drill through, you could file grooves to increase the contact of the wire, making a stronger solder join—but any method which will increase the surface area of the points being soldered will help to make the join stronger.

Wires are more easily soldered in pairs—bend a length of wire into a U-shape and insert the ends through the drilled holes in the base of the piece. This increases the stability of the wires during soldering and will keep them more accurately placed, so that they do not move when heated. If you are using wires with balled ends, it may not be possible to bend the wire into a U shape. To keep the balls at a regulated height, cut the wires to a specific length, longer than the final length, and allow the ends of the wires to come out through the holes underneath. If the main piece is then propped up to raise it above the level of the heat brick, the wires will all sit down against the brick and stay in position and at the correct height. Take care not to overheat the wires when soldering; this should ideally be the final soldering performed on the piece so that easy solder can be used. Aim to heat the thicker and larger areas of the piece first—it is likely that the wires will reach temperature without being heated directly themselves.

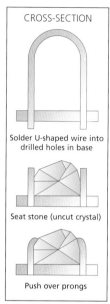

CROSS-SECTION

Solder U-shaped wire into drilled holes in base

Seat stone (uncut crystal)

Push over prongs

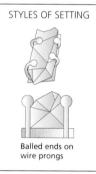

STYLES OF SETTING

Balled ends on wire prongs

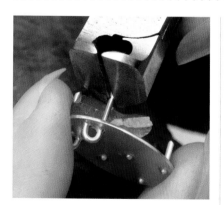

3 Trim the wires roughly to length with top cutters. Clean up the back of the base sheet—file the ends of the wires flush or file them short and round with a cup burr. Bend the ends of two of the wires with pliers to make loops to hold a chain.

4 Use a suitably sized cup burr to shape and shorten the prongs accurately. The prongs need to be long enough to bend around a facet of the crystal, but not so long that they cover too much of the surface or can easily be pulled away if caught.

5 Use a prong pusher to push the prongs over the crystals with firm, even pressure. Burnish the prongs to polish and further work-harden them. Ensure that all the prong tips are burnished flush against the surface of the crystal.

Grain Settings

Tiny beads of metal hold the stones in their seats for grain settings. Most common is the pavé technique, in which the surface of a piece is carpeted in small faceted stones.

The mount for grain-set stones is a metal surface with sufficient area and depth to receive the stones. The variations in this style of setting are mainly derived from the pattern of the stones and their spacing—five-grain setting places an extra, decorative grain between stones so that they sit farther apart from one another, whereas in standard grain setting, each grain holds two stones because they are so closely positioned.

GRAIN SETTING
(see page 122)   skill level 💍💍💍

This diamond ring by Ming follows the classic combination of diamonds and white-rhodium-plated, high-karat white gold. The brightness of the metal adds more light to the stones to dazzling effect. The outer surfaces of the split bands that hold the larger stones have been grain set with small diamonds; this technique is perfect for placing small stones in a linear formation. The grain-set diamonds in this ring are all of the same size, but graduated stones can be used to decorate bands that increase in width.

SQUARE-GRAIN SETTING
(see page 128)   skill level 💍💍💍

Square- or box-grain setting is used to set a single stone within an engraved border, usually to accentuate a particular area of a piece. Round brilliant-cut stones are most often set in this manner, but cabochons or other cuts of brilliant may also be used. The tips of the prongs of this citrine and white-gold ring by Natasha Heaslip have been square-grain set with small diamonds.

FIVE-GRAIN SETTING

(see page 126)   skill level ♂♂♂

Five-grain setting is a variation of grain setting, with the position
of the grains in relation to the stones determining whether or
not a "fifth" decorative grain is required. The shoulders of this
pearl ring by Joanne Gowan are set with sapphire-covered leaf
forms. Extra grains are used where the shape of the metal will
not allow for another stone and the metal would otherwise be
bare—the grain tricks the eye with another small polished surface
to maintain the texture of the setting overall.

PAVÉ SETTING

(see page 130)   skill level ♂♂♂

Pavé setting is used to cover part, or all, of a surface
with small brilliant-cut stones; the stones are carefully
arranged to fit the space available, with any areas too
small to receive stones being disguised with decorative
metal grains. This cast silver pendant by Ishbel Watson
was designed using CAD, creating a concave stepped
surface on five sides of the cube, with the sixth
decorated by a square formation of pavé-set brilliants
bounded by a polished border of metal.

MICRO-PAVÉ SETTING

(see page 132)   skill level ♂♂♂

Blue diamonds and sapphires have been set over
the entire front surface of these Peacock Earrings
by Annoushka. Micro-pavé setting is done with
stereo binocular lenses, allowing tiny stones to
be pavé set with a very high degree of accuracy.
The colors of the stones used in this piece are
complemented by the colors of metal used—rose-
gold prongs hold the pink tourmaline drops, and
the gold has been black rhodium-plated around the
micro-pavé.

Grain Setting

Small metal beads appear to hold the stone in this elegant style of setting, which can be used to set stones individually or in rows.

skill level

Choosing Stones

Small, brilliant-cut calibrated (machine-cut) stones are usually used for grain setting, but flat-backed stones, such as cabochons and rose cuts, can also be used, as can half- or three-quarter-cut pearls. Take care when setting softer stones.

Metals

Most metals can be grain set, including refractory metals such as tantalum. Beginners should practice with copper or silver as they are relatively soft and grains will be more easily raised. Harder precious metals will provide more secure settings for more valuable stones, but are more difficult to work.

Construction Details

The simplicity of the mount for grain setting means that it can be performed on a wide range of surfaces, including domed, concave, flat sheet, and cast forms. Grain and pavé setting is suitable for most jewelry forms.

Grain-set brilliants are used often in contemporary jewelry pieces to provide highlights and draw the eye to a particular area of a piece. It is a very skilled method of stone setting, so jewelers will often send the work out to specialist setters. The high

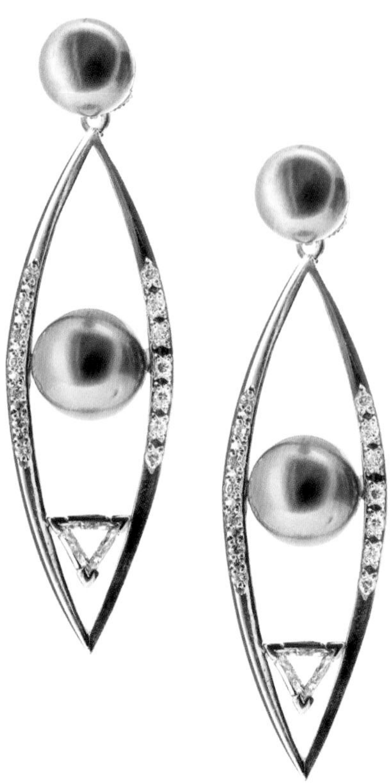

GRAIN-SET EARRINGS
Grain-set diamonds accentuate the linear navette form of these platinum earrings by Joanne Gowan, which are also set with Tahitian pearls and prong-set triangular brilliant-cut diamonds.

GRAIN SETTING A ROW OF BRILLIANTS

Small beads of metal are raised either side of the row of stones to hold them in position once they have been seated. Hours of practice with a graver is the only to way to produce even and regularly spaced cuts.

TOOLKIT

- Strip of silver, stones for setting
- Bezel-setting punch
- Ball burr, drill, flexshaft motor
- Setter's wax
- Wax stick
- Half-round and flat scorpers
- Graver, spitstick
- Grain tool
- Acetone

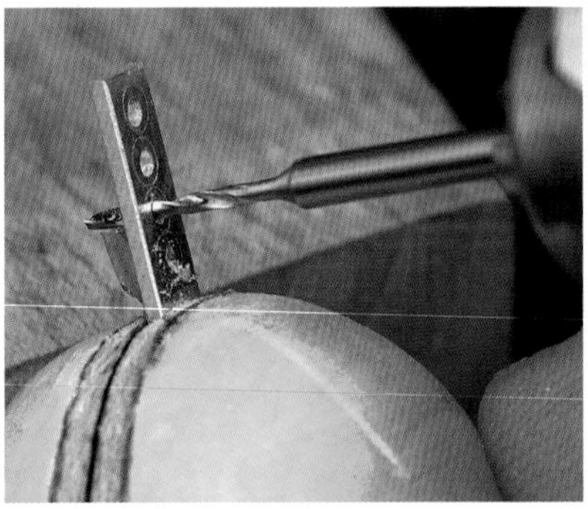

1 Mark out the metal with the positions of the stones—once seated, the girdles of the stones should almost be touching—so using a bezel-setting punch of the same diameter as the stones will mark the outlines. Use a small ball burr to start off the hole rather than a center punch, and then drill the holes.

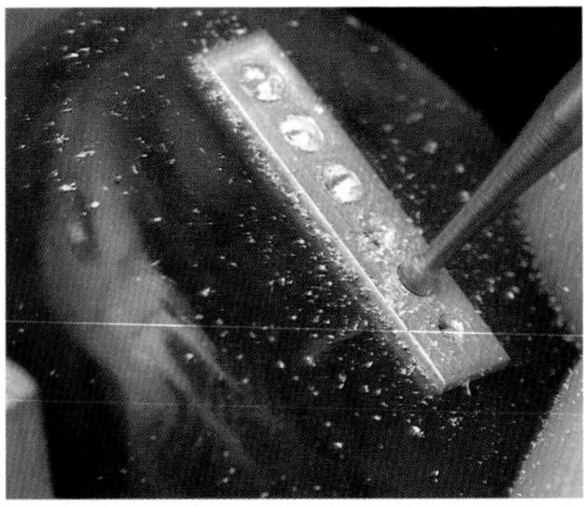

2 Mount the silver into setter's wax. Wax that pushes up into the drilled hole can be drilled out with an old drill bit. Use a 1.6 mm ball burr in a flexshaft motor to open up the drill holes—burr down a bit further than the widest part of the burr.

cost of the setting often means that it is a technique cost-effective only for high-end jewelry made in platinum or gold.

Using a bezel-setting stake of the same diameter as the stones, mark where the stones will be positioned on the metal; the girdles of the stones should almost be touching. Center punch the holes, or use a ball burr in a flexshaft motor to start the holes off before drilling with a drill bit half the diameter of the stone. Secure the piece in a clamp or setter's wax that has been melted onto a length of wooden doweling. Warm the wax using a spirit lamp or a torch with a soft yellow flame, taking care not to overheat it. Roll the warmed wax on a flat steel surface to create a suitable surface in which to set the piece. Using tweezers, push the metal into the wax far enough for it to be held, but take care that no wax comes over the surface. The wax can be cooled in cold water to harden it again.

The wax must be removed from the drill holes using an old drill bit; otherwise the burrs will get clogged with wax. Burr the drilled holes to create the seat: first, using a ball burr smaller

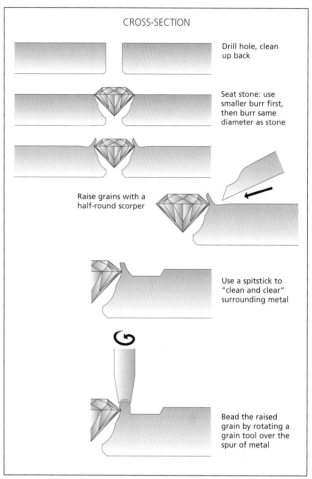

CROSS-SECTION

Drill hole, clean up back

Seat stone: use smaller burr first, then burr same diameter as stone

Raise grains with a half-round scorper

Use a spitstick to "clean and clear" surrounding metal

Bead the raised grain by rotating a grain tool over the spur of metal

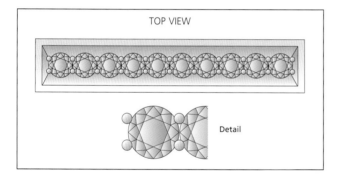

TOP VIEW

Detail

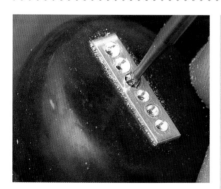

3 Use a ball burr 0.1 mm larger than the diameter of the stone to seat the stones. Burr down just enough so that the table of the stone is level with the surface. Having used a smaller burr first ensures that the seat grips the stone so it will not move during setting.

4 Place the stones into position, ensuring that they are all at the correct height and firmly seated. A "wax stick" is very useful for handling such small stones and allows greater accuracy than fingers or tweezers.

5 Use a small half-round scorper to raise grains along one side of the stones—this ensures that all the cuts are at the same angle. Force the graver into the metal and push forward with a slight side-to-side movement that will help raise the spur. Raise the angle of the graver as it nears the stone, to push the spur upright.

Continued over

LOVE RING
Rows of grain-set diamonds and pink sapphires
are set around the three shanks of this playful
set of rings by Ben Day, spelling out the
word "Love." The larger central stone is a
demantoid garnet, held in a rub-over setting.

than the stone, and to a depth greater than the girdle will sit, then using a burr
0.1 mm larger than the diameter of the stone. Deepen the seat with the burr until
the stone's table is level with the surface of the metal. Seat all of the stones.

Use a small half-round scorper to raise grains between the stones. Work along one
side first, and then the other—each grain holds two stones. This technique requires
confidence and force from the wrist—start the cut a couple of millimeters from where
it will end and push forward with the scorper at an angle of 10 to 15 degrees. A slight
rocking motion from the wrist will help force the metal up, and it is crucial that the
raised spur is not cut off with the graver. When the cut is almost the correct length,
raise the angle of the graver to lift the spur. There will be a bulge of metal at the front
of the spur; it is this that holds the stones firmly in position. Raise an extra grain at
each corner of the end of the lines of stones.

Use a spitstick to cut a line (a thread) along the edge of the stones. This should
be positioned just outside the edge of the grain cuts, joining them up to make a box
framing the stones. Engrave the backs of the cuts, so that an angled surface leads
from the surface of the metal down to the base of the grains; take care not to knock
off the spurs. The thread around the edge of the frame will need to be tidied again
with a flat scorper.

Choose a graining tool of an appropriate size to ball the ends of the raised slivers
of metal over the edges of the stones. If the tool is too big it is likely to chip the stones,
but if it is too small, it will make unsightly slivers of metal around the base of the grain,
which will catch on fabric and are difficult to remove. Ideally, the same size of graining
tool should be used for all the grains on a piece, but it may be necessary to use several
different sizes if the slivers are not of a uniform size. Place the graining tool over the
raised spurs and, applying firm and even pressure, begin to move it in a circular motion,
with the tool rotating at an angle of around 15 degrees from an imagined vertical axis.
This will round off the spur, press it against the stone, and harden and burnish it,
leaving a shiny little bead.

As with gravers, grain tools must be kept sharp, otherwise they will not work
efficiently. At regular intervals, roll the tip of the tool at an angle over emery paper
to reshape it.

6 Raise the grains along the other side of the
stones—one grain between two stones and
with the cuts started at the same distance from
the stones. The grains for the four corners can
then be raised, two at each end and with the
graver in line with the corners.

7 Cut a line, or thread, around the stones
with a spitstick. This is to make a neat
border around the stones. The thread should
join up the cuts that were made to raise the
grains, leaving a border of unmarked metal
around the outside.

8 Use a flat scorper to cut inside the thread.
This will tidy the thread and create an
angled edge to the frame—angle the scorper
away from the stones while cutting. The inside
corners of the frame should also be neatened
at this stage.

RUBELLITE PENDANT
This hand-engraved and enameled white-gold pendant by Henn of London is bezel set with a 9.79-ct rubellite, with a row of graduated, grain-set diamonds on either side, accentuating the form.

TWIST DROP EARRINGS
The brushed gold surfaces contrast with the glitter of tiny grain-set diamonds to accentuate the edges of these elegant twisted earrings by Jessica Poole.

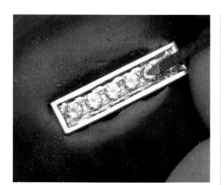

9 Clean and clear the metal around the grains and stones with a spitstick, taking care not to accidentally cut off the grains, which should appear as neat "islands" protruding from the engraved ground.

10 Form the grains using a grain tool of exactly the right size, otherwise the stone may be chipped or spurs of metal formed where they are not wanted. Firmly rotate the tool over each raised spur to compress it into a shiny grain.

Gently warm the setter's wax to remove the piece—wax residue can be removed by soaking the piece in acetone.

Five-grain Setting

In this technique, four grains hold the stone and the fifth grain is purely decorative. It is raised between the stones, allowing them to be spaced more widely.

skill level 👁👁👁

Choosing Stones
Small brilliant-cut stones of 7 Mohs or more are most suitable for this style of setting, but other cuts can be accommodated.

Metals
Five-grain setting is most often used to set gems into high-karat gold, platinum, and palladium, but silver and many base metals can also be used.

Construction Details
This is a variation of the basic grain-setting technique (see page 122); so much of the process is the same. The crucial difference is in the spacing of the stones; there must be sufficient space between the girdles to accommodate the fifth grain—they must not be touching. Leave a gap of about a millimeter between the stones when marking out; the gap can be proportionally larger for bigger stones, and the grain will be larger, too. Drill, burr, and seat the stones as described for grain setting; however, the position of the grains is slightly different, too. Instead of the grain between the stones holding the stones either side, the extra gap means that each stone needs its own grains—a total of four—to set it.

EARTH TREASURES RING
The lip of this ring by Chris and Joy Poupazis is embellished with fishtail setting—a variation of grain setting. The concave inner surface of the ring is dotted with three grain-set diamonds without an engraved border.

SETTING A ROW OF BRILLIANTS WITH FIVE GRAINS
The addition of a fifth, decorative grain allows the row of stones to be more widely spaced. The positions of the stones will be dictated by the space available to set them on.

TOOLKIT
- Strip of silver, stones for setting
- Bezel-setting punch
- Ball burr, drill, flexshaft motor
- Setter's wax
- Wax stick
- Half-round and flat scorpers
- Graver, spitstick
- Grain tool

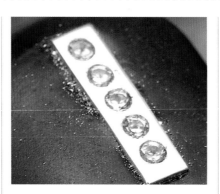

1 Mark out, drill, and seat the stones into a piece of silver (see page 122). The spacing of the stones must allow for a grain to sit between the girdles of the stones, so they should not be as close together as for standard grain setting.

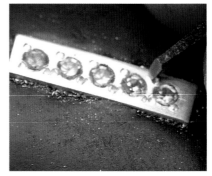

2 Each stone is held by four grains, cut in diagonally with a half-round scorper. Cut one grain per stone on one side of the row of stones in order to maintain the same angle for each cut, before doing the same on the other side. Then cut the second grain for each stone along each side.

Use a small half-round scorper and, working along one side of the line of stones, raise one grain for each stone. The cut should be angled so that it approaches the stone straight on; cutting all the grains in one direction first will help to keep the cuts more even and at the same angle. Next, cut all the grains in the same direction along the other side so that each stone has diagonally opposing grains; this will help to keep them level. Then cut the grains along both sides in the other direction—each stone should have four grains.

Make diagonal cuts from the back of one grain toward the girdle of the next stone; this leaves a central island of metal between the two girdles which will form the fifth grain. First, clean and clear the metal surrounding the grains, using a spitstick to cut a thread around the stone, and then engrave out the cuts at the back of the grains with a small flat scorper. Use a suitable size of graining tool to form the grains, including the fifth grain between the stones.

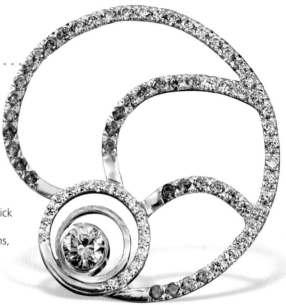

STARBURST PENDANT
This fabricated silver pendant by Fiona McCulloch is grain set with brightly coloured cubic zirconia, radiating out from a larger, tube-set brilliant. The spacing of the grain-set stones in such a piece requires careful planning before the stones are seated.

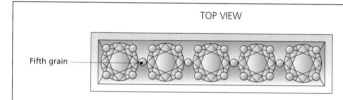

TOP VIEW

Fifth grain ....

The stones are spaced farther apart to accommodate the fifth, decorative grain.

3 Make diagonal cuts between the stones to create an island for the decorative fifth grain. Use a spitstick to cut from the back of one grain diagonally across to the center of the girdle of the next stone.

4 Cut a thread and angled frame around the stones to neaten the appearance of the setting, and clean up the metal surrounding the stones and raised grains with a spitstick.

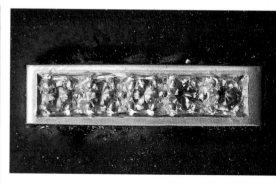

5 Use a grain tool of the correct size to burnish and shape the grains. The fifth grain fills up the extra space between the stones, and creates the illusion that it helps to secure the stones.

Square-grain Setting

This type of grain setting is used to frame a single stone within a square engraved border, with the stone held in position by four grains, one in each corner.

skill level

BASKET RING
Diamond tipped prongs surround the faceted citrine in this complex basket ring by Annoushka. Each diamond is grain set and bounded by a perfect engraved box to match the shape of the prong tips.

Choosing Stones
Brilliant-cut, round gemstones are traditionally used in this style of setting, and it is best to use harder stones, which are not brittle or prone to fracture. Larger diameters of stone can be used than for the grain setting techniques previously described.

Metals
Because there is a significant amount of engraving required to complete this setting, silver is the easiest metal to work with, but other precious metals are commonly used.

Construction Details
The area into which the stone will be set should be prepared in the same way as for grain setting. Marking out for a single stone is straightforward, but you need to leave enough space around the stone for the box to be engraved. Center punch and drill a hole before securing the piece in a clamp or with setter's wax. Burr out the seat for the stone, using a burr smaller than the diameter of the stone first, going a little deeper than the widest part of the ball burr, and then use a ball burr 0.1 mm larger than the stone size to open up the hole to the point where the table of the stone sits level with the surface of the metal. Remove the stone and put it to one side.

Using a square graver, cut an inverted "V" at each corner of the setting, with the widest part of the "V" next to the stone. This creates an island of metal that will

**SQUARE-GRAIN SETTING
A SINGLE STONE**
This technique is used to grain set single stones, enclosing them in an engraved box. Accurate positioning of the grains at the four corners of the square is crucial for the setting to work visually.

TOOLKIT
- Strip of metal
- Setter's wax
- Drill, burr
- Square graver
- Spitstick
- Small flat graver
- Half-round and small flat scorpers
- Graining tool

1 Mount the metal in setter's wax so that it is secure and can be more easily held. Drill and burr the metal to seat the stone, then remove the stone. Use a square graver to make two cuts at each corner of the stone—the cuts form two sides of a triangle and leave an island of metal next to the stone that will form the grains.

2 Cut a square thread around the stone using a spitstick, before straightening up the sides of the box with a small flat graver. These cuts should join up the triangles in the corners, leaving the islands untouched.

GRAIN-SET PENDANT
Several styles of setting have been used to set the rubies in this pendant by Jayce Wong. The small rubies on the top section are grain-set in a square box.

SQUARE-GRAIN SETTING: TOP VIEW

Use square graver to cut away surrounding metal, leaving four triangles

Use flat graver to cut straight edges of "square"

Raise grains

Bead grains and tidy square with a flat scorper

become the grain that holds the stone. Next, use a small flat graver to join up the "V"-shaped cuts, and straighten the sides of the box, taking care not to cut into the islands of metal at the corners.

The seat for the stone will need to be burred again, as the engraving will have pushed some metal over the edge of the hole. You can then put the stone in place and raise the grains using a small half-round scorper. Use a flat scorper to recut the corners of the box, and tidy up any areas that need it, before forming the grains at the four corners. It is possible to create a line of set stones using this technique, but each one should have its own engraved frame.

3 Re-burr the seat for the stone, as the graver cuts will have pushed metal into the seat, and put the stone into position. Raise the grains with a half-round scorper diagonally toward the stone.

4 The corners of the box will need recutting to neaten them and create the correct angles, using a small flat scorper. A graining tool is then used on the four grains.

TRIANGULAR GRAIN SETTING: TOP VIEW

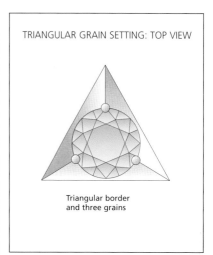

Triangular border and three grains

Pavé Setting

With grain-set brilliants fitted neatly in rows to create a ground of stones, and the bright-cut engraving between the stones, this setting reflects light and creates an overall effect of opulent glamour.

skill level

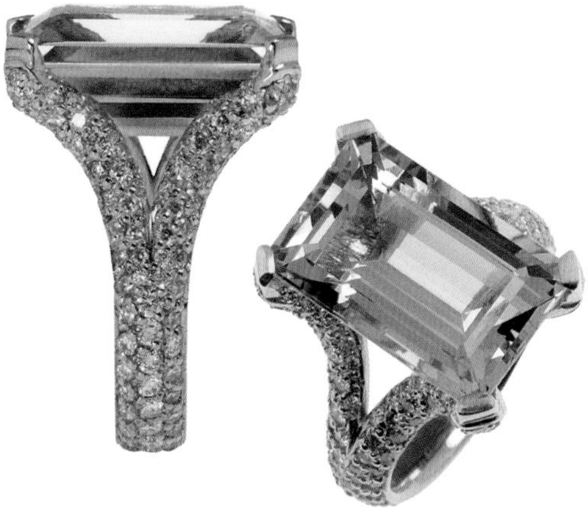

PAVÉ AQUAMARINE RING
Two views of "Aquamarine Lake Ring" by Ming show how pavé-set diamonds encrust the shank of the white-gold ring to create a bold form that splits into the prongs that hold the large aquamarine.

Choosing Stones

Choose small, hard, calibrated brilliant-cut stones of 7 Mohs or above. Often the same diameter of stones is used throughout a piece, but this will depend on the design—if the pavé tapers or follows a form you may have to use smaller stones in some areas to keep the spacing even. Colored stones can also be used successfully; use cubic zirconia as practice stones.

Metals

Gold, palladium, and platinum are most commonly used for this technique. This style of setting can be applied to mixed-metal pieces, and to a range of forms, from flat sheet to curved shapes. Recessed areas can be pavé set, but this may affect the sequence of construction, with some portions being cold-joined or laser-welded together once the stones have been set.

Construction Details

Marking the positions of the stones accurately for pavé setting is crucial, because if the spacing of the stones is wrong, the technique will not work. If the stones are too closely set, the girdles will clash, but if they are too far apart, the grains will not be properly spaced. Smaller stones should be set slightly closer together and with smaller grains than larger stones, so, if a piece contains stones that graduate in size, very

PAVÉ SETTING AN AREA OF SHEET SILVER
While the pavé technique is often used to cover an area of a piece with small round brilliants, when starting out it is best to practice on a smaller area.

TOOLKIT
- Sheet of silver
- Stones for setting
- Bezel-setting punch
- Drill, burr
- Half-round scorper
- Spitstick
- Graining tool

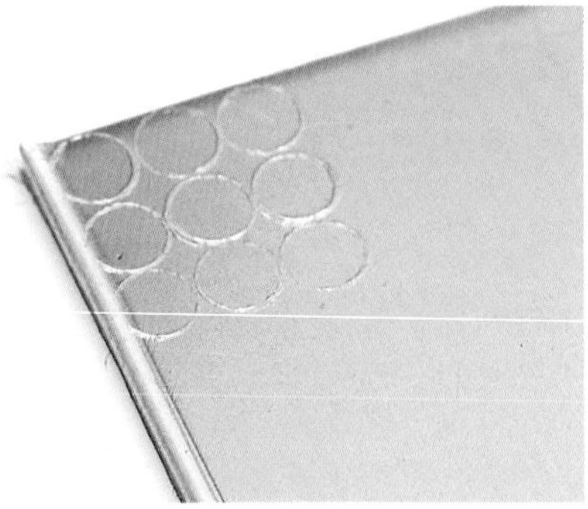

1 Mark out a grid for the positions of the stones using a bezel-setting punch exactly the same diameter as the stones that will be set. The girdles of the stones should almost be touching. Drill, burr, and seat all the stones.

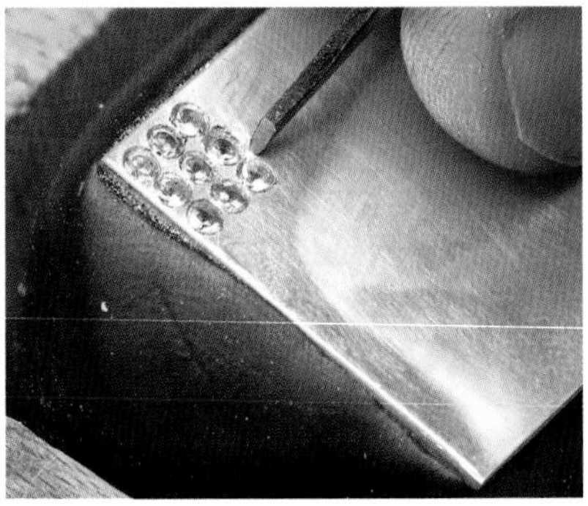

2 Raise grains between the stones in rows, using a half-round scorper, performing all the cuts in one direction on each row as described for Five-grain Setting (see page 126).

PAVÉ SAPPHIRE PENDANT
Pavé-set sapphires extend right into
the inner corners of this geometric
"Rift" pendant by Paul Battes.

careful planning of the area to be set is necessary. Drill holes for the stones and seat
them so that the tables are flush with the metal's surface. Raise the grains around the
stones, four for each, in rows as described in "Five-grain Setting," page 126. It is
important to be methodical, working along the rows one at a time and cutting all the
grains in one direction first, so that the stones stay in position and all the cuts are of
an even size. The grains at the outer corners of the area of pavé are raised last.

Cut an "X" between the stones to leave an island of metal to form the fifth grain.
This grain is purely decorative and is used to disguise the areas of metal left between
the stones by mirroring the grains that surround the stones. Clean up the metal
around each grain with a graver, removing the back of the cut and taking care not to
knock off any grains. Cut a thread around the outside of the pavé to create a neat
border to the engraved metal.

Ideally, the same size of graining tool should be used throughout the piece, but in
practice this depends on the exact size of the spur raised, and a variation of one or
two sizes is unlikely to be noticeable. The fifth grain may require a different size of
graining tool—this will depend on the spacing of the stones and the amount of metal
left between them after the cleaning and clearing has been completed. Cutting deeper
"X"s between the stones will leave less metal remaining and will therefore produce a
smaller grain.

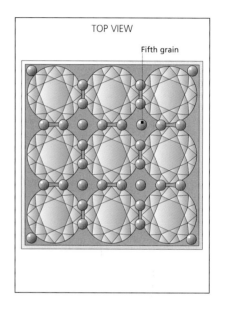

TOP VIEW

Fifth grain

3 Once all these grains have been raised,
cut the grains at the four corners of the
pavé area. When applying pavé to a shaped
area, disguise any spaces at the edges that are
not large enough to take a stone with
decorative grains.

4 Use a spitstick to make diagonal cuts
between the stones, creating islands for
decorative grains. The island should yield grains
that are of a similar size to those that secure
the stones.

5 Clean up the metal from around the grains
using a spitstick, and then cut the thread
that borders the outer edge of the group of
stones. Shape the grains with a graining tool.

Micro-pavé Setting

Tiny brilliants are used to create a uniform carpet of stones on a miniature scale—the stones are almost too small to identify individually with the naked eye, scattering light deceptively.

skill level

Construction Details

This style of setting is usually done with the aid of stereo binocular lenses; because the stones used are so small it would be difficult to accurately place them and raise grains with the naked eye. The miniature scale of micro-pavé means that the technique is different to pavé—the main difference being the sequence in which the steps are performed.

Mark out and seat the stones so that one row is offset against the next, allowing the stones to be closely spaced. Remove the stones and use a small bud burr in a flexshaft motor to grind out metal from between the stones, leaving raised areas or "castellations"; this is first done from top to bottom, then from left to right, and finally diagonally. Burr the seats again with the correct size of ball burr to seat the stones. The stones can only be placed one at a time, otherwise they will get in the way of the grains being raised, so start in the center of the pavéd area. The limited areas of metal available for raising grains means that when raising the grains, the graver must twist the spur around so that it is in the correct position for a particular stone. The grains for each stone must be raised before the next stone is seated. Once all the stones are set and the grains made, the outer thread can be cut, and any areas that require it cleaned up.

SWAN EARRINGS
The surface of these stylized white-gold hoop earrings by Ming is encrusted with 18-ct micro-pavé-set white diamonds. Micro-pavé setting is surprisingly smooth to the touch.

MICRO-PAVÉ SETTING
Small stones can be used to coat a surface, but the smaller scale of the setting means that fewer grains can be raised than for other types of grain setting; a binocular microscope is used to magnify the area being worked on.

TOOLKIT
- Sheet of silver
- Stones for setting
- Drill
- Bud burr
- Small flat scorper
- Half-round scorper
- Graining tool
- Spitstick

1 Marking out is crucial for successful micro-pavé; for this technique, the stones' girdles should be almost touching and the rows of stones are offset so that they are tessellated. Drill, burr, and seat the stones before removing them from the metal.

2 Using a 0.6 mm bud burr, carve grooves between the seats to remove sections of the raised areas. The grooves should go from top to bottom and then from left to right between the stones. Cut diagonals so that "castellations" are left around the seat for each stone. The outer areas should be left untouched.

MICRO-PAVÉ-SET RINGS
This set of white, yellow, and black rhodium-plated gold rings by Annoushka is micro-pavé set with matching colors of diamonds—white, brown, and black. This technique completely covers the surfaces of the rings and the metal is barely visible.

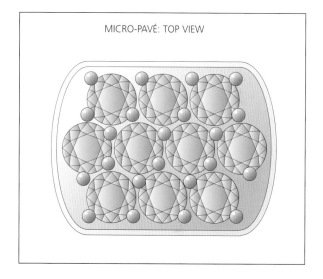

MICRO-PAVÉ: TOP VIEW

3 The stones will need to be seated again to remove burrs from the inside edges of the seats; position the stones one at a time, otherwise it will be difficult to raise grains. Use a small flat scorper to lift and push a diagonal castellation against the stone. The scorper needs to be twisted as the grain is raised so that it ends up in the correct position.

4 Work from both sides of the first row of stones, keeping track of which grains are going where. You can then start the next row and work it in a similar way—the grains on the outside of the area of stones are raised in the usual way, with a half-round scorper.

5 Once all the grains have been shaped with the graining tool, cut a thread around the stones with a spitstick to neaten the overall effect; there will be little space between the stones to clean up, and at such a small scale it is unlikely to be necessary.

Fancy Settings

The term "fancy" covers "everything else," both in cuts of stone and styles of setting. Variations of standard techniques can be combined, as in combination setting, or experimental processes such as sand casting may be used to set stones.

Innovative ways of setting stones can be devised using metals and other materials such as wood or plastics; less traditional techniques, such as laser welding or precious metal clay can also be employed. Mounts can be hidden—when stones are set from behind, mounts can swivel, or allow the stone to be loose. Cold-joining techniques including riveting, wire wrapping, and spectacle setting are an alternative to traditional setting methods and are particularly useful for fragile stones.

COMBINATION SETTING

(see page 136)   skill level

This white-gold ring by Ming displays an array of precious and semiprecious marquise-cut gemstones extending from the stylized wing that curls out from the shank.
The stones are secured under the ledge of feathers at one end and the tips are set with prongs at the other. Combination settings can utilize two or more styles of setting to hold a single stone, although many stones and types of mount can be used within the same piece of jewelry.

TENSION SETTING

(see page 142)   skill level

Tension setting relies on the forces within a metal form to hold the stone in place, so it is crucial that both the stone and metal are suitably tough. This stainless steel ring by Kara Daniel holds a princess-cut green sapphire in place securely; the steel was recessed to hold the stone, supporting it at four points along its straight sides, and was given a brushed finish to contrast with the reflective surfaces of the sapphire.

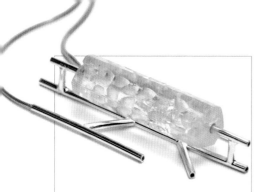

SWIVELING SETTING

(see page 148) skill level 👁👁

This pendant by Annie Cracknell is constructed from silver tubing, and holds a quartz crystal. The stone is part-drilled at either end and held under tension by the inserted tubes, allowing it to swivel in the setting. Any part of a piece that is fabricated to pivot along an axis can be used as a swiveling stone or setting; this is a way of making double-sided elements that can be turned around within a frame.

SETTING FROM BEHIND

(see page 154) skill level 👁👁

Stones are usually set from behind to prevent the texture or form of a surface form becoming distorted or altered during setting, or to disguise the method of setting. In this brooch by Barbara Christie, the shell cameo and emerald are set from behind to leave the delicately textured surface of the gold intact. Decorative rivets have been used to secure the brooch fitting, which is entirely concealed from the front of the piece.

CASTING

(see page 160) skill level 👁

Rubies were cast directly into this 18-kt yellow-gold ring by Kelvin J Birk, creating an experimental form. Processes such as sand or cuttlefish casting allow molten metal to be poured into a shaped void that has stones positioned within—the metal flows around the stones and secures them in position. It is important that the stones being used are able to survive the high temperatures involved in working with molten precious metals.

UPSIDE-DOWN SETTING

(see page 156) skill level 👁

Many different styles of setting can be used to set stones upside down. The inverted intense blue sapphire in this ring by Whitney Abrams contrasts beautifully with the rich color of the 22-kt gold shank that holds the stone in a bezel setting; much more of the stone is visible because it has been set upside down. Cabochon stones can also be inverted, but it is the flat base that will then be uppermost, and the mount must be able to accommodate the curved face of the stone and support it so that it does not move out of position during setting.

Combination Setting

As long as the stone is adequately held, almost any combination of setting styles in one piece is theoretically possible—part prong, part rub-over, or part grain-set.

COMBINATION-SET PENDANT
This pear-shaped cubic zirconia was set into a silver mount using both rub-over and prong settings.

skill level 👁👁

TOURMALINE RING
A fantasy-cut vivid green tourmaline is seated against the body of this ring by David Fowkes. A brace holds the tip of the stone and a strap secures the wide end.

Choosing Stones

Unusual cuts of stone may be more easily set with this method than standard cuts because the angles may lend themselves to differing setting styles. The methods of setting can be adapted to suit softer stones, so hardness need not be an issue.

Metals

The choice of metal will depend on the types of setting used and the hardness of the stone, but this technique provides scope for experimenting with mixed metals within one piece.

Construction Details

There are a number of ways of approaching the fabrication of a combination setting, but they will depend on the styles of setting and the particular cut of stone used. Tapered bezels and basic bezels can be made to fit a stone; areas can be cut or filed out and parts of different tapered bezels can be soldered together to make a single mount. Cast forms can be adapted to receive a stone by soldering wires into positions that can be used for prong or peg settings, and ledges can be constructed for the edge of the stone to sit under. It's important that the basic mount fits the stone well—any

COMBINATION SETTING A PEAR-CUT BRILLIANT
Non-standard cuts, such as pear-shaped are ideal for combination settings because the tip and back of the stone can have different styles of setting used without it looking out of place.

TOOLKIT
- Strip of silver for bezel (see page 88)
- Soldering equipment
- Needlefile
- 8-gauge (3-mm) tapered silver wire
- Gallery strip
- Jett Sett
- Pusher, flush setting tool
- Burnisher

1 Make a bezel the same size as the stone—this pear-shaped bezel was formed from a strip of silver and soldered closed at the point. File an angled ledge on the inside of the bezel so that the girdle sits on top. Form a pendant frame from 8-gauge (3-mm) tapered silver wire.

2 The tip of the large curl of the pendant will form the rub-over portion of the mount, holding the stone's point. File a groove in the flattened end and bend it to match the profile of the bezel. Fit the pendant frame to the bezel, ensuring it sits higher. Solder a section of gallery strip at the back of the bezel to form prongs.

10 RING
The emerald-cut rhodolite in this ring by Anastasia Young has been secured with a silver tab along its top edge, and two 18-kt yellow-gold prongs on its lower corner facets.

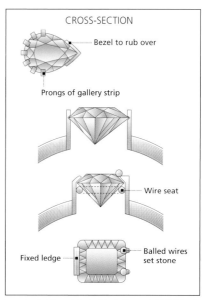

CROSS-SECTION

Bezel to rub over

Prongs of gallery strip

Wire seat

Fixed ledge — Balled wires set stone

room for movement may become exaggerated over time, causing the stone to become loose. Ensure that the stone is properly seated, carving the correct-shaped groove with a graver until the stone is level and stable. If one part of the stone is being held under a ledge, the engraving of the seat may be more of a challenge. If the mount is first made up in wax with the seat carved before casting it may be more easily accomplished. Any refining of prongs, such as cutting them to the correct length, using a cup burr on the ends of the wires to round them, and thinning the wires, should also be completed at this stage.

Once the stone is seated in the mount, and the piece is secured so that it can be accurately set, a small amount of setting should be done on the different parts of the mount. Pressure can be applied with the setting tool without too much risk of the stone moving out of position. Make sure each part of the mount securing the stone is making good contact with it by carefully burnishing the metal against the stone until the edges can no longer be felt. This will ensure that parts of the setting are not easily caught on clothing and loosened, and will also polish and work-harden the metal.

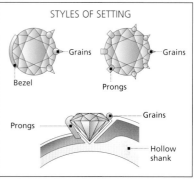

STYLES OF SETTING

Grains

Grains

Bezel

Prongs

Prongs

Grains

Hollow shank

3 Solder the bezel into position in the pendant frame, having filed an area inside the large curve to make more contact between the bezel and the frame, and thus a stronger solder join. File the prongs and bezel tip to thin them so that they will be more easily set.

4 Pour boiling water over some Jett Sett granules (see page 65) and, once they have gone clear, embed the pendant in the plastic. Make sure that the parts that will be set are still fully accessible, and push the Jett Sett down inside the bezel so that the stone will sit correctly. Allow the plastic to cool and turn white again.

5 Set the point of the stone using a pusher (flat-ended or prong)—a flush setting tool with a curved face will aid setting on the concave curve. Make sure that the tip is adequately compressed and looks neat. Use the pusher to push down the prongs and remove any marks. Adjust the shape with a needlefile, clean up, and then burnish both parts of the combination setting.

Multiple and Cluster Setting

Using more than one stone in a piece adds more scope for combining color and contrasting cuts but can affect the design and construction of the piece.

skill level

Choosing Stones

Because this type of setting commonly uses different cuts of stone, it is likely that the choice of stone will be made during the design process.

Metals

The mount must be reasonably durable and able to withstand the setting of multiple stones without distortion, so this might mean that the main structure of the piece is made from a harder metal than the prongs or tabs if setting more fragile stones. It is also possible to use three-dimensional shapes that will offer integral strength to a structure made from a softer precious metal. Use less malleable metals for longevity and durability, especially if more valuable gems are being mounted.

Construction Details

As the name suggests, "cluster" setting involves a group of stones set closely together on a piece. Tapered bezels are often used to seat the stones, with prongs holding them in place. This means that the prongs can be placed where there is access for the setting tool, unlike bezels, which are placed all the way around the stone. The positioning of the mounts must allow access for each stone to be set, but it is possible to have one metal element securing more than one stone at a time.

STONE CLUSTER RING
Crushed amethyst, tourmaline, and quartz have been formed into a cluster and applied to a blanched silver ring using glue, in this piece by Kelvin J Birk.

CLUSTER-SET SILVER RING

This project uses a marquise- or navette-cut stone, clustered with several sizes of round brilliant. Plan ahead and work out the best positions for the prongs; these prongs are made from palladium wire, which is harder than silver.

TOOLKIT

- Silver strips and tube, stones for setting
- Needlefile, ball burr
- Soldering materials
- Jeweler's saw, drill
- Wire for prongs
- Prong pusher
- Mallet and hardwood
- Cup burr
- Burnisher, polishing materials

1 Make bezels for all the stones that will be set in the cluster—the bezels should have the same outer dimensions as the stones. Sections of tube can be used for round stones, but you will have to construct walls for stones of other shapes.

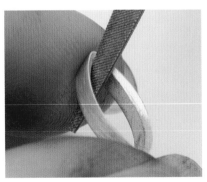

2 Create a bevel on the inside of the constructed mount with a needlefile, to enable the girdle of the stone to sit level with the top of the mount. Use a ball burr the same size as the stone to bevel the inside edges of the tubing for the round stones.

THAI PRINCESS RING
This opulent ring by Ming displays tiers of rubies set in 18-kt yellow gold. The central ruby is prong set, with the smaller surrounding stones half pavé-set, and half bezel-set.

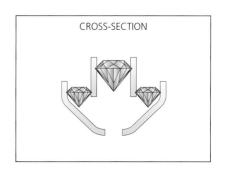

CROSS-SECTION

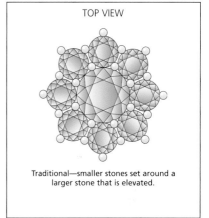

TOP VIEW

Traditional—smaller stones set around a larger stone that is elevated.

Combination settings (see page 136) are sometimes used to create cluster settings, with a sheet-built element holding one end of several radially positioned stones. Historically, this type of setting was arranged in a tiered construction, with the stones radiating out from the center, and often gradated in size; similar formations are still used today.

The design and construction of the piece as a whole has a great impact on how the stones will be set, potentially, even down to the order in which they are set. The easiest production method in terms of construction would be to cast from a printed or milled wax model (see page 78). An expert can render designs from drawings, with detailed specifications for the stones, but the use of standard stone sizes and cuts may well be necessary. Using this method will allow the piece to be cast in one or more

3 Solder the bezels onto a base, and then pierce out the base sheet from inside. Mark the positions of the prongs for each stone and drill holes for them. Solder wire in to make the prongs, ensuring that the solder not only seals them to the base sheet, but also runs up to hold the wires against the bezels. Clean up the ring.

4 Check that all the stones are seated well and sit level—burr the bezels again if necessary, having bent the prongs out of the way if they are obstructing access. Trim the prongs to length and file the tips thinner before starting to set the stones.

5 The construction of the piece may dictate which stones are set first—mount any stones that will get in the way of others being set last. It is also important to remember which prongs are allocated to which particular stones. Use a prong pusher to lever the prongs into place.

Continued over

PRIMROSE RING
Five Polki diamonds are prong set as petals on this ring by Annoushka, surrounded by borders of micro-pavé set diamonds. The center of the flower is set with rose-cut diamonds and pink sapphires in white gold.

sections, avoiding all the fiddly construction, but the nature of the software can often lead to rather traditional formations of stones.

It is possible to fabricate a cluster of mounts attached to a jewelry piece without too much complexity. It will take time, and careful design and planning, but the mounts themselves may benefit from being simplified, both in terms of design and ease of construction. Elements of one mount may form parts of the mount for another stone, allowing less metal to be used and possibly simplifying the construction process. This may be aided by the cut of the stone, because certain shapes can be more easily spaced or tessellated.

The simplest method for creating multiple seats for stones within one piece of metal is to drill or pierce recesses slightly smaller than the stone's girdle into a thick gauge of sheet—18 gauge (1 mm) or more. The sheet can be formed so that it is not flat, and the degree of forming determines whether the holes should be made before or after forming; holes in heavily formed pieces will distort, but certain areas may be less accessible on a three-dimensional form, so should be made first. The prongs can then be applied relative to these. Solder prongs into drilled holes to make the solder join stronger. You can use many variations of the prong, including balled ends to the wire, to create more visual interest.

If you are using bezels or partial bezels, it may be more appropriate to solder these onto the sheet first, before piercing out the sheet from inside. The bezels can then be shaped and adapted further to accommodate the stones.

It is advisable to make a model for complex pieces of this type to discover any flaws in the design before you start; if the model is successful it can even be used as a master for lost wax casting, which will allow the piece to be reproduced in a variety of metals.

CLUSTER SETTING: SETTING THE PRONGS
Keeping track of which prongs are allocated to which stone is important during the setting process. Take it slowly, making sure every prong is properly pushed over and burnished.

6 Use a custom setting tool to push over prongs that are obstructed by other bezels or prongs—this tool has a narrow, flat taper at the end to allow it into tighter spaces.

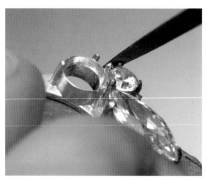

7 During setting, thin the prongs with a file if necessary. This will help neaten the appearance of the piece as a whole. At this stage, the prongs should be only partly pushed over the stones to hold them in position so you can still make adjustments to their height.

AMETHYST AND DIAMOND RING

This stylish ring by Zoe Marie features an optix-cut trillion amethyst tension set between prongs which hold rub-over set diamonds. The concave facets on the amethyst are cut with a laser, and produce an unusual lensing effect in the reflections of the pavilion facets.

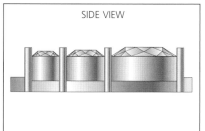

SIDE VIEW

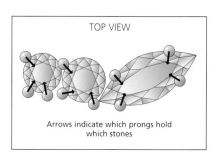

TOP VIEW

Arrows indicate which prongs hold which stones

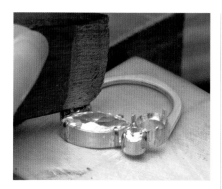

8 If a stone slips out of alignment slightly, tap it back into position with a mallet and a piece of hardwood. This will not damage harder stones, and will force the stone level with the top of the bezel if the higher side is tapped.

9 Continue setting the stones in position until they are all held in place. Using a suitably sized cup burr, shape and shorten the all of the prongs to a similar length.

10 Burnish down the tips of the prongs so that they are flush with the surface of the stones and will not catch or snag on hair or clothing. The surface should feel smooth to the touch, with no sharp areas. Give the piece a final polish.

Tension Setting

Tension settings are arguably the most minimal type of mount, relying on the pressure created when a single piece of metal is forced open to hold a stone permanently in position.

skill level

TENSION-SET AQUAMARINE
An unusual method of tension setting was used for this ring by Teena Ramsay. Wire loops hold the prongs under tension, securing the stone in place.

TAHITIAN PEARL RING
This intriguing ring by Danila Tarcinale displays a large Tahitian pearl tension set into a sculptural 18-kt yellow-gold ring. Caps allow greater contact with the pearl, which is further secured with epoxy, and grain-set brilliants embellish one band of the shank.

Choosing Stones

This type of setting exerts a great deal of pressure on the stone, so only very hard stones such as diamonds, rubies, and sapphires can be used, but even then, any internal flaws in the stones may cause problems.

Metals

Only very hard metals, such as white gold, steel, titanium, or platinum should be used for tension settings, and special alloys of these metals are available that are particularly effective. The metal used must be capable of retaining its work-hardened state and maintaining the pressure on the stone, otherwise it will eventually become loose.

Construction Details

Because the ring shank for a tension setting needs to be made from a hard metal, which is thicker than the height of the stone—so that the culet does not protrude inside—forming the shank itself may be a challenge. The ring cannot be easily resized once the stone is set, so if a particular size is required, then this must be resolved before the stone is put in place. If the ring is to be formed from metal rod or wire, it is easier to work with a longer length of metal than is needed in order to create enough

---

TENSION SETTING A DIAMOND IN A WHITE-GOLD BAND
Tension setting relies on the force of the ring shank alone to hold a stone, so use a hard metal such as white gold to form the ring shank.

TOOLKIT
- Metal for ring shank
- Hammer, vise
- Soldering equipment
- Ring stretcher
- Jeweler's saw, file
- Stone for setting
- Ring clamp
- Hart burr
- Polishing materials

1 Form a ring from a thick-gauge hard metal, such as 9-kt white gold. Use a combination of hammering and squashing in the vise to shape the wire, and use a longer piece than necessary to increase the amount of leverage. Tack solder the ends of the ring together, and use a ring stretcher to make it perfectly round. Cut out the solder join and file the gap.

2 The gap between the two ends of the ring shank needs to be shorter than the diameter of the stone that will be set. Use a ring clamp to force the shank open slightly—this style of clamp tightens from the base, forcing the top wider.

leverage to curve it. The rod can be formed around a mandrel with the help of a vise. Using the protective jaws on a vise to squash the rod into shape allows much more force to be applied than with a hammer alone. Once the ring is circular and the correct size, the excess metal can be cut away and a gap cut in the ring, which is smaller than the diameter or width of the stone—the metal is held apart by the stone and it is this tension that keeps the stone in position.

Casting allows more room for design details and also makes the construction much easier, but the piece must be cast in a hard alloy in order for the tension setting to have longevity. It will be necessary to use a burr smaller than the diameter of the stone to carve the seat. A fraise burr that slips easily into the gap should be used with a flexshaft motor to carve grooves in the same position on both sides of the gap. It is very important that the grooves are even, level, and deep enough so that the stone cannot move at all—try to match the profile of the edge of the stone as perfectly as possible. All work on the ring should be finished before the stone is set, including polishing.

To set the stone, stretch the shank open either with a ring stretcher or by forcing it up a mandrel, just enough to slip the stone into place. Be careful not to overstretch or the ring will not close enough to hold the stone, and the shape may be distorted. When the ring is released, the shank will contract and hold the stone.

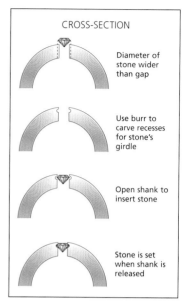

CROSS-SECTION

Diameter of stone wider than gap

Use burr to carve recesses for stone's girdle

Open shank to insert stone

Stone is set when shank is released

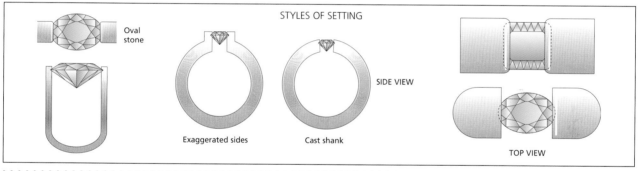

STYLES OF SETTING

Oval stone

Exaggerated sides

Cast shank

SIDE VIEW

TOP VIEW

3 Begin to cut a groove for the stone to sit in, using a hart burr smaller than the diameter of the stone. The groove should be deeper in the center to accommodate the girdle of a round stone, and must be level on both sides so that the stone sits straight.

4 The groove must be close enough to the top of the shank so that the culet does not protrude underneath. Clean up and polish the ring. Open up the ring enough to slip the stone into position—if the metal cannot be opened that far on the clamp, force the ring up a mandrel, or use a ring stretcher.

5 Release the ring from the tension and the gap will close again, trapping the stone. The stone should sit level and be held so firmly by the shank that it does not move.

Caged Setting

Caged setting allows stones to be permanently secured within a structure.
It can be used to create an openwork showcase for individual stones or to
trap contrasting stones together in groups.

skill level

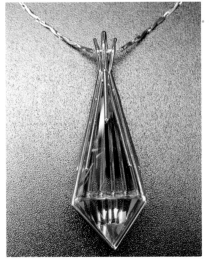

TOPAZ PENDANT
Platinum wires have been laser welded to form
a cage for this topaz drop pendant by Cathy
Stephens. The platinum wires accentuate the
shape of the stone.

Choosing Stones

The choice of stone is likely to be influenced by the design and construction of the
piece. If laser welding will be used, no heat is required to finish the mount, so more
vulnerable stones such as pearls can be used. Cubic zirconia and other heat-resistant
gems will allow the soldering of elements with the stone in its final position.

Metals

Because caged settings are often constructed from thin wire, it is advisable to use less
malleable metals, which will not be accidentally bent out of shape; however, you can
use thicker gauges of softer metals to counteract the problem. If the cage is to be
soldered closed, silver—which has the lowest soldering temperature of the precious
metals—is the most suitable choice because there is less potential for damage to the
stone from heat exposure. If you are welding the cage, the options for metal choices
are far greater and include stainless steel and the refractory metals.

Construction Details

Caged settings can provide an attractive way of displaying stones in the round,
but can cause technical problems in terms of securing metal parts. Technology such
as laser welding is very useful for permanently joining metal elements in order to trap
stones securely inside.

**CAGE SETTING A MOSS
AGATE CYLINDER**
There are a number of construction
techniques that can be used to create
caged settings; in this project, wire rivets
are used to hold the top on a form
constructed from wire and fine tubing.

TOOLKIT
- Wire for jump rings
- Cylinder-shaped stone
- Soldering materials
- Round needlefile
- Binding wire
- Pickle
- File
- Jeweler's saw
- Steel block and hammer

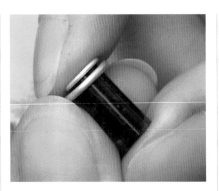

1 Make four jump rings, two of which should
be just large enough to fit around the
cylinder-shaped stone. The other two jump
rings should be smaller, but should not be able
to pass through the first two and should be
smaller than the diameter of the stone.

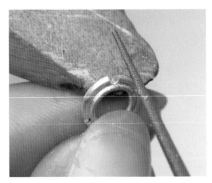

2 Solder the small jump rings into the larger
ones to form a pair of double rings. Divide
the outer rings into three, and file a groove
with a round needlefile at each of the points.
The groove needs to be deep enough to hold
a piece of thin tube, but not so deep that the
tube would stop the stone from sitting on the
inner ring.

CAGE-SET NECKLACE AND EARRINGS

This set of jewelry by Daphne Krinos is made from oxidized silver. It holds crystal-cut citrines on wires that were laser welded at each end to secure them within the cages.

STYLES OF SETTING

Simple cages

Silver is one of the most difficult metals to laser weld because it is so reflective, but it can be dulled with the use of a marker pen. Silver wire is sometimes used to "stick feed" into the welded joins. It is advisable to check the minimum gauge of wire or sheet metal that can be used, because if the metal is too thin the laser pulse may cause it to vaporize. There are specific problems associated with particular alloys of certain metals, including white gold and titanium, so do check before beginning construction of the piece.

As when making prongs, it is far easier to construct a cage using one piece of wire that is bent to form two prongs that can be joined to the piece at the same time. Pierced sheet can also be used to form caged structures but it will need to be carefully formed once pierced, so that the design does not distort. Placing a thin sheet of copper underneath the form will help to prevent thinner areas warping. It is important to decide how and in which order you'll carry out the construction of the cage—especially which portion of the mount will be left unattached so that the stone can be put in, or how easily the stone can be inserted without distorting the shape of the cage. All component parts should be assembled, cleaned up, and ready to be joined before handing the pieces over to the laser welder, along with clear instructions.

CROSS-SECTION

Stone put into soldered frame

Laser- or TIG-welded cage closed

3 Cut three lengths of tube to form the cage around the rings. Use binding wire to hold them in position for soldering. Ensure that the gap between the rings is large enough for the stone to sit in. Remove the binding wire before pickling the piece and, once clean, dry thoroughly.

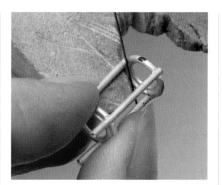

4 File the ends of the tubes flush with the outer rings. Mark corresponding points on both rings so that they can be matched up again, and use a jeweler's saw to cut through the tubes on the inner side of one of the rings. File the ends of the tube flat, taking care not to bend them out of position.

5 Insert riveted wires into all three tubes and put the stone in position. The lid should slip onto the wires so that it is touching the stone—if the tubes are too long, file them some more. Working on a steel block, rivet the ends of the wires to secure the cage.

Wobbly Stones

Settings that allow stones to wobble can add playfulness to a piece of jewelry, and many different cuts and colors of gemstone can be used.

skill level 👥

WOBBLE ROSE RING
A wobbly setting is used in this white-gold ring by Zoe Marie. A ball and socket joint has been made to allow the mount for the natural pink diamond to move freely.

Choosing Stones

Because little or no pressure is exerted during setting, soft stones can be used for this technique; however, if the stone is likely to receive wear from rubbing or moving around inside the setting, then it may be advisable to use a harder stone. Because the stones are not fitted tightly within the mount, many cuts can be used which would be problematic to seat in the usual way. "Wobbly" mounts require stones with properties suitable for the particular type of setting that will be used.

Metals

Because the stones are not being set in the traditional manner—and because it is likely that cold-joining will be necessary in some form—mixed materials or metals with surface effects that cannot be heated can be incorporated into the piece without too much extra design work. Most precious metals are suitable for this technique, as are many base metals.

Construction Details

The design of the mount is crucial and will determine much of the construction process; this is an opportunity to explore ideas around a theme, or create a piece that is materials-led. Creating a mount that allows the stone to wobble inside can also be used for interchangeable stones, see page 166, if the mount is not permanently fixed shut and can be opened and closed.

AVENTURINE SPHERE WOBBLY PENDANT
Screw threads are a useful method for cold-joining components, but do a trial run first to ensure that all the measurements are accurate in order for all parts to function properly.

TOOLKIT
- Soldering equipment
- Jump rings
- Dapping block and punches
- Sheet of silver
- Drill
- Rod
- Tap-and-die set
- Jeweler's saw
- Watchmaker's screwdriver

1 Solder together enough jump rings to make a domed form large enough to hold a spherical stone. The excessive use of hard solder will give the form greater strength and, as more soldering will be done on the piece, also help prevent problems later on. Dome the form in a dapping block, and solder a large jump ring onto the base.

2 Solder a jump ring onto either side of the dome, large enough for the size of screw being used. Trace around the outline of the domed form onto a base sheet, which must be at least 16 gauge (1.2 mm thick) to take a screw thread. Drill holes in this sheet which align perfectly with the jump rings.

CAGED EARRINGS

Free-moving rhodochrosite spheres in caged forms are the feature of these earrings by Chris and Joy Poupazis. The forms were constructed from sterling silver.

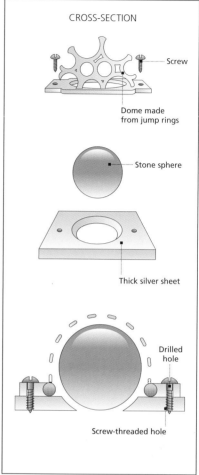

CROSS-SECTION

Screw

Dome made from jump rings

Stone sphere

Thick silver sheet

Drilled hole

Screw-threaded hole

STYLES OF SETTING

Rub over

Ball and socket = wobbly mount

Because they usually rely on metal exerting pressure against the stone to hold it in position, it is unlikely that the usual methods for stone setting can be used for a wobbly setting. This means that the mechanism for setting a stone that can move will require cold-joining techniques; these could include riveting, screws, tabs, staples, or a bezel used to set a metal element that traps a stone. Whichever method you choose, accurate construction of the parts so that they fit together well and function correctly is very important. The mount must be secure and designed so that even if slightly bent out of shape, the stone cannot come out of the mount.

All the component parts should be completed, cleaned up, and be given their final finish before the piece is assembled. If cold-joining is used, effects such as patinas or gold leaf can be used on the inside of the setting to create interesting effects and color contrasts.

3 Cut a screw thread on a piece of rod, and in one of the drilled holes. The starting diameters of the rod and drilled hole will be determined by the size of tap and die being used, as well as the system—BA, metric, or ISO. Cut the threaded section of rod off, leaving a small amount of uncut rod to form the screw head.

4 Check that all the component parts fit together and function properly, cleaning them up and polishing, or applying the final finish. The inside surfaces should be polished, but the outside can be made matte with an abrasive to create a contrast to the stone.

5 Attach the dome to the base with a jump ring at one end that doubles as a bail, insert the stone, and use a watchmaker's screwdriver to tighten the screw into the base plate. Trim the screw shorter if necessary.

Swiveling Setting

Swiveling settings can be set with one stone or with two different stones. The settings can be turned around, for a more versatile piece, whether for different colors or cuts of stones, or contrasting designs.

skill level 💍💍

Choosing Stones

The best type of stone to use for a swiveling setting depends on the exact type of setting used to hold the stone, as well as what the final piece will be—ring, pendant, or earrings for example. Other considerations include how often the piece will be worn, and whether one or both of the stones will touch the skin; some stones are susceptible to oil and may become dull over time.

Metals

Softer metals are suitable for bezels in this type of setting, but for moving parts hard metals should be used for longevity.

Construction Details

This type of mount is commonly set into a U-shaped frame, or between two ends of a ring, but other shapes and forms of frame can be devised. When designing for this type of setting, always consider the height and comfort of the finished piece.

It is possible to weight the mount on one side so that the setting tends to sit with a particular side uppermost. The mount can be made to rotate freely within its frame, or be held more tightly, so that it has to be turned to change side. The construction can

INSIDE-OUT RING
The outer band of this ring swivels away from the pavé-set inner band of the ring by Anna Molinari, allowing the dark rubies to be viewed more clearly. Black rhodium plate has been used around the stones over the 18-kt yellow-gold band.

DOUBLE-SIDED SWIVELING PENDANT
A section of tube soldered between two back-to-back bezels forms the pivot for the bezels to swivel inside the frame of this pendant.

TOOLKIT
- Silver for making bezels (see page 88)
- Cabochon stones for setting
- Needlefiles
- Soldering equipment, pickle
- Drill
- Polishing materials
- Flat pusher
- Rivet, hammer

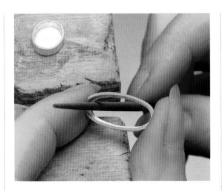

1 Make up bezels for a pair of cabochon stones that have the same width. Use fine silver for the walls and sterling silver for the bases. One or both of the backs may be pierced out to leave a ledge, allowing light to pass through the stones. Clean up the bezels.

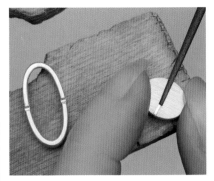

2 Use a round needlefile to create a fine groove along the central line of each bezel. Continue filing the groove until a thin section of tube can be held between the backs of the bezels, with the backs making good contact.

be as simple or as complex as you like, but you'll need at least a pivot and a frame in which the mount can turn. The simplest form consists of two wires soldered to either side of the mount, which are riveted into place in the frame. More complex constructions can feature tubing, screw threads, and washers, with the working parts hidden inside the mount.

When making double-sided mounts, the two stones do not have to be the same size or shape, but if they are then it will be much easier to construct the bezel and solder a dividing wall to support the stones so that they do not touch. If you make two separate bezel cups, they can be soldered together with a mechanism between them to allow pivoting—a piece of narrow-gauge tubing is perfect.

Because it is the stones that will dictate the dimensions of the piece, and because the construction will need to be very accurately fitted, the bezels should be constructed before the frame. The frame can then be made to fit the mount. The rivet or screw should be made of a hard metal, such as white gold, so that it has greater longevity, especially if it is for a piece that will be worn often.

All metalwork construction, including the frame, should be completed before the stones are set, but the cold-joining of the mount and the frame should be left until afterward, unless there is a reason not to, such as very fragile stones or mechanisms that are hidden under the stones. The mount will need to be supported while the stones are set, and in this case setter's wax will be the most useful medium, because it will prevent the unset mount on the underside from becoming damaged while the first stone is set.

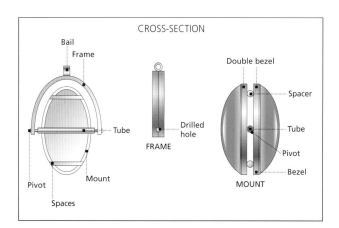

CROSS-SECTION

FRAME

MOUNT

STYLES OF SETTING

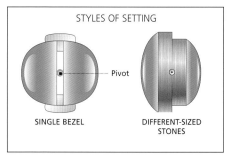

SINGLE BEZEL

DIFFERENT-SIZED STONES

3 Solder the section of tube into position between the two bezel cups. Once pickled, file the tube so that it is flush with the sides of the bezels, and clean up the form, inside and out.

4 Make a frame for the setting to swivel within, and drill holes the same diameter as the inside of the tube at either end. Check that the holes line up on either side of the tube by carefully inserting a drill bit. Solder a bail on top, and clean and polish the frame.

5 Set the stones in the bezels, rubbing over the fine silver walls with a flat-ended pusher. Insert a rivet made from half-hard wire of the same diameter as the inside of the tube, and rivet the setting into the frame.

Built-up Setting

Built-up settings raise the level of the stone above the main piece, and can be pierced to allow more light to enter a stone without compromising the strength of the setting.

skill level

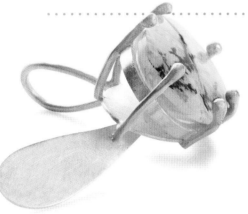

POETICS PENDANT
This abstract pendant piece by Michelle Xianou Ni uses balled prongs to hold the agate stone above the body of the piece.

Choosing Stones

Most types of stones are suitable for built-up settings, but they will need to be of an appropriate cut and hardness for the specific setting used. Raised, pierced mounts help to show off faceted stones by allowing more light to enter the stone.

Metals

Metal should be chosen with both the construction method and the properties of the stone in mind. If you are making a thin wire structure, silver is fine to practice with, but is unlikely to be durable enough to use for the finished piece. Store-bought, manufactured gallery strips and settings can be used, but they are limiting in terms of both the range of metals available and the choice of design. However, they can be adapted or enhanced and will save fabrication time.

Construction Details

Fabricated galleries can be as complicated as your skill levels will allow. Pierced designs can be used to great effect, to apply figurative or abstract designs around the mount. Granules or other soldered-on elements can also be applied to add visual interest, but do ensure that the design does not compromise the strength of the gallery, or the amount of light that can enter the stone.

BUILT-UP SETTING FOR A PENDANT
This project utilizes stamped gallery strip to raise the large cubic zirconia above the level of the piece, allowing more light to enter.

TOOLKIT
- Stamped gallery strip
- Stone for setting
- Soldering equipment
- Jump ring
- File
- Wire or ring shank
- Pickle, emery stick
- Jig
- Flat-ended pusher, mallet, burnisher

1 Construct a pierced mount for a stone from gallery strip—the stone should fit inside the wall. Make a jump ring to form a ledge for the stone to fit on—the jump ring needs to be a tight fit inside the mount so that it can be soldered accurately in the right position.

2 Check the height of the wall around the stone when it is in position in the mount, and reduce the wall height by filing if necessary. Construct a frame from wire to hold the mount to make a pendant, or solder the mount onto a ring shank.

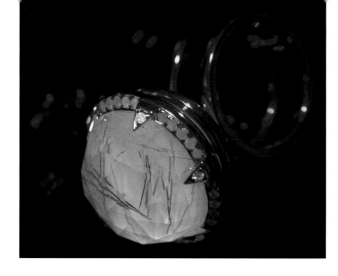

FLUORESCENT SPIRAL RING
Layers of stones have been built up to create the stunning effects visible under UV light in this ring by Jayce Wong. A ruby disk sits under the large tourmalated quartz, making it glow in the right conditions.

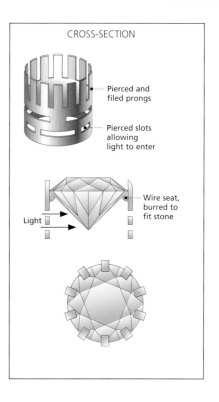

CROSS-SECTION

Pierced and filed prongs

Pierced slots allowing light to enter

Wire seat, burred to fit stone

Light

Wire constructions can also be used to make galleries. The section of the wire will greatly influence the design and fabrication of the mount; consider round, square, triangular, or D-section wires. Sheet metal can also be used to make gallery settings. While gallery mounts usually form the base for prong settings and their variations, exaggerated prongs or tabs of sheet metal could be used to form a rub-over setting, and these do not have to be evenly spaced.

Solder paste in a syringe may offer a neater and more convenient soldering process, but the resultant joins may be more brittle than those produced by traditional pallion and flux soldering. Take care not to overheat any wires when working with thin forms—position the join so that it is at the back of the piece and the rest of the mount is effectively behind the flame during heating. A small, intense flame will also help with accuracy.

Once all soldering and construction has been completed, finish mounts in the usual way. The exact method of setting will depend on the design. Bought gallery strips should be made up in the same way as a bezel, so that the stone fits inside. A supporting seat will need to be soldered into position or, alternatively, the bezel can be made a little too small and a groove carved into the base of the prongs with a hart burr—the stone then clicks into the groove.

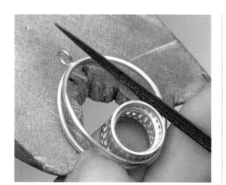

3 Pickle the piece, then clean it up and thin the edge of the wall so that can be more easily rubbed over the stone. Remove the file marks with an emery stick and polish the piece.

4 Support the piece in a jig to set the stone. Use a flat-ended pusher to force the wall over the edge of the stone evenly; make sure the piece is adequately supported, hold the pusher in one hand, and tap it with the mallet.

5 Use the tip of a burnisher to smooth and highlight the inside of the setting, which will help to reflect more light inside the stone. The pierced wall of the mount that holds the stone will also allow light in.

Protective Setting

Spacers, barriers, cages, and raised walls can all be used to create settings in which a stone is protected from accidental knocks and everyday wear.

skill level 👁👁

SHERRY TOPAZ RING
Two bands of pavé-set diamonds make a physical barrier to protect the fragile sherry topaz in this ring by Boodles, which is elegantly prong set in yellow gold.

Choosing Stones

The protective nature of this type of setting means it is ideal for soft, brittle, or otherwise fragile stones, such as pearls, amber, and turquoise. It's also good for other materials that may be set in place of stones including shell, bone, and jet.

Metals

As with other types of setting, use softer metals for bezels and harder metals for prongs. The raised or protective areas of the setting should be made from a harder metal so that there is less risk of movement, which could expose the stone to damage.

Construction Details

Constructing an area of metal that is more prominent than the stone makes it less likely that the stone will be rubbed or knocked and damaged by accident. The higher protective area of metal must either allow space for the stone to be set, or it must be possible to securely attach the mount to the interior of the raised area after the stone has already been set. Certain forms of setting will be more easily performed under these circumstances—peg or prong settings, for example. Wires can be soldered into the base of a dome or press form that will hold the stone below the level of its top edge and therefore protect it.

Bezel setting is also suitable for protective mounts, but can be trickier to put together if a continuous raised section or wall surrounds the stone. Cut-out areas can

---

PROTECTIVE BEZEL SETTING
The stone used for this project is a form of "goldstone," which is a type of glass and therefore relatively vulnerable to wear. The raised edge of the setting will help to protect softer stones.

TOOLKIT
- Fine silver for bezel (see page 88)
- Cabochon stone for setting
- Silver sheet, dapping block and punches
- Wire for jump ring
- Soldering equipment
- Square-section wire for ring shank
- File, polishing materials
- Burnisher

1 Make a bezel from 28-gauge (0.3-mm thick) fine silver to fit a stone. This cabochon is synthetic and relatively soft, so the very thin bezel will prevent the stone from being damaged as it is set. Ensure that the bezel is not too tall, because the stone will be sitting deeper than it would in a flat-based bezel.

2 Form a dome that is roughly twice the diameter of the stone—the stone will sit down inside the dome and be prevented from accidental knocks and scuffing. Form a wire ring to sit on the top edge of the dome and solder it in place. Solder the bezel centrally in the base of the dome.

TURQUOISE RING

This 18-kt yellow-gold ring by Lilly Hastedt, set with a Persian turquoise cabochon, has not only protective "petals" surrounding the main stone, but also tube-set diamonds raised up around the turquoise, which is a relatively soft stone.

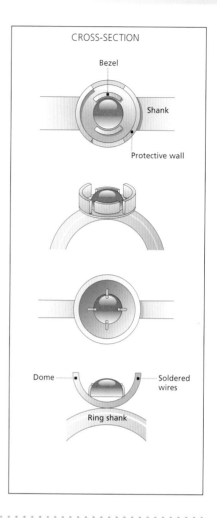

CROSS-SECTION

Bezel

Shank

Protective wall

Dome

Soldered wires

Ring shank

be filed into both the outer wall and the bezel, but you will need to ensure that enough of the bezel is left to hold the stone securely. Any gaps in the outer wall should correspond with the areas of the bezel that require setting, so that access is not inhibited during assembly.

The access allowed by the protective raised sections may dictate exactly how a stone is set. Bezels may need to be pushed over the stone at a higher angle than is ideal due to lack of access. If this is the case then it is important that the bezel is exactly the right height for a stone, and not too tall, otherwise it may wobble in the setting. Under certain circumstances it may be necessary to make or modify tools so that the setting can be performed in a restricted space. Old burrs can be adapted to make small setting tools and burnishers; snap off the blunt head and grind the end of the burr to a suitable shape with an oilstone before polishing the tool. Angles can be bent into the shaft of the tool so that it can access places more easily and without damaging the surrounding metal.

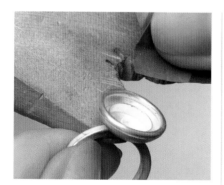

3 Using square-section wire, construct a ring shank. After soldering and cleaning up, file a curve in the top of the shank for the dome to sit on, and solder the two parts together. Clean up the ring.

4 For setting in a restricted space such as this, it is often necessary to make a custom setting tool. File one end of a thin piece of steel rod to a flat taper, and polish it. The inner edge of the top ring provides leverage and very little force is needed to push the thin bezel around the stone.

5 Finish setting the bezel with the custom pusher, before smoothing the bezel with a burnisher. Carefully clean up the inner surface of the dome with wire wool to impart a shine—cover the stone with masking tape so that it does not get scratched.

Setting from Behind

Securing the stone on the back of the piece allows more intricate detail to be applied around the stone with no risk of it being damaged during setting.

SETTING FROM BEHIND
A large, black onyx cabochon was set into a press-formed pierced frame from behind using an applied fine silver bezel.

skill level ♉♉

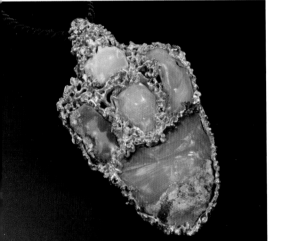

CRUISE ON THE LAKE TANA
Ornella Iannuzzi's pendant holds 102.5 kt of Welo opals in 22-kt gold, rub-over set from behind. Diamonds, sapphires, and tsavorites punctuate the gold borders.

Choosing Stones

This style of setting can accommodate any type of stone, and most shapes, too; however, your choice of stone may depend on the exact method of setting, in terms of the hardness of the metal required.

Metals

The choice of metal will depend on the style of setting, and type and shape of stone—select a metal based on your knowledge of setting and stone properties.

Construction Details

Many different methods of stone setting can be adapted so that stones can be set from behind, including rub-over, prong, and grain. However, you'll need to adapt the design of the mount so that it is worthwhile setting the stone from underneath. Decorative elements or other factors should dictate that it is necessary to form the front of the mount first, otherwise there is little point in going to the trouble of setting a stone in this manner.

There are many construction variations to consider for this type of setting, such as riveting components together, or using an unsoldered sprung ring of hard metal which

SETTING A CABOCHON IN A PIERCED PRESS FORM

Setting a stone from the back allows intricate designs to be applied to the front, which might otherwise be distorted during setting. Fitting a form to the contours of a stone can be a challenge, however.

TOOLKIT
- Stone for setting
- Pencil, acrylic sheet, silver sheet
- Jeweler's saw
- Copper sheet, rubber sheet
- Vise or hydraulic press
- Chasing hammer, steel block
- Fine silver for bezel (see page 88)
- Soldering equipment
- Sandbag, flat-ended pusher, burnisher

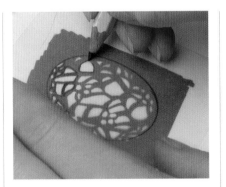

1 Draw around the stone to make a template to cut a hole in a piece of acrylic sheet, adding on at least ¹⁄₃₂ in (1 mm) all the way around to accommodate the metal. Draw out and transfer a design onto 24-gauge (0.5-mm thick) silver sheet, and pierce it out.

2 Do a few test-run press forms with copper sheet first to check that the stone fits. Layer up the acrylic die, copper base sheet, pierced silver, and rubber sheet and compress it in a vise or hydraulic press to force the metal into the hole in the acrylic. Anneal the copper and silver between rounds of pressing.

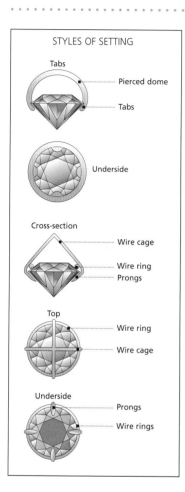

STYLES OF SETTING

Tabs

Pierced dome

Tabs

Underside

Cross-section

Wire cage

Wire ring
Prongs

Top

Wire ring

Wire cage

Underside

Prongs

Wire rings

slips into a groove in the bezel behind the stone, or tabs of metal that are folded down over the stone once it is in place. As long as the stone sits hard up against the inside of the setting and is held there securely, there is no right or wrong way to design the mount.

When setting the stone, the front of the setting, including the mount, must be protected from damage—the face of the stone is likely to be the highest point and it may not survive direct contact with certain surfaces. Cover the stone with masking tape, and work on a surface covered by leather—hardwood or rubber blocks are ideal. A sandbag can be used if the piece is large enough to hold steady while setting and does not require too much force to set the stone. Setter's wax or a reusable thermoplastic fixturing compound such as Jett Sett can also be used to support the piece during setting, especially if the stone is a cabochon and will not sit flat on a surface, or if the method of setting requires a larger amount of force. The setter's wax can be applied to a wooden block, making it possible to secure the piece in a vise during setting; this leaves both hands free should the bezel need chasing around the stone with a hammer and pusher.

HAWTHORN NECKLACE
The focal point of this piece by Lucy Sylvester is a labradorite cabochon, set from behind to preserve the replica-gold decoration of the hawthorn leaves.

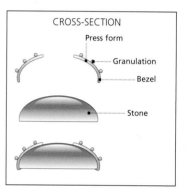

CROSS-SECTION

Press form

Granulation

Bezel

Stone

3 Once the press form is deep enough to hold the stone, chase the edge of the oval flat on a steel block. Make a bezel from fine silver to fit the stone. Pierce out around the base of the press form and sand down the base on a large flat surface until it is the same size as the bezel.

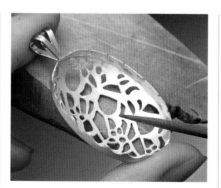

4 Solder the bezel onto the press form, and then file the edges so that they appear as one piece of metal. Divide up the bezel into sections, and use these as a guide to file a scalloped edge with a half-round needlefile. Clean up the edges and the form and solder on a bail.

5 Working on a sandbag so that the front of the piece does not get damaged or distort, set the scalloped bezel over the back of the stone with a flat-ended pusher. Burnish the edges down further and ensure the bezel is smooth around the stone.

Upside-down Setting

Setting stones in an unexpected manner adds another layer of interest and curiosity to a piece of jewelry. Inverted stones are perfect for design-led jewelry, because many variations can be explored.

skill level

ECLIPSE PORCUPINE RING
This statement ring by Annoushka is upside-down set with tiny diamonds. The pavé-set stones are set table-side up further down the shank so that the ring is comfortable to wear.

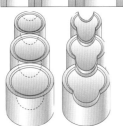
CROSS-SECTION

Stone is same diameter as mid-point of tube wall

Seats for stones burred to correct depth

File a groove with round needlefile

Remaining wall set with pusher

Choosing Stones

It could be argued that only stones that will obviously look like they are upside-down should be used for this technique, but in fact, any cut can be used. The hardness of the stones used will depend on the setting method and the type of piece being made.

Metals

The choice of metal will depend on the type of setting, but harder metals can be used for harder stones where strength is required, and softer metals for softer stones.

Construction Details

In theory, many of the standard setting types—tapered bezel, prong, and grain—could be performed with the stones upside-down, with few or no extra adjustments needed to the mount. Mounts or bezels for flat-backed stones and cabochons will need to be adapted to accommodate the shape of the stone so that it stays level during setting.

You should consider the implications of setting a stone upside-down, with the culet sticking out, in relation to the type of stone and the piece of jewelry itself. Sharp points are not appropriate for rings, because they may cause damage to the wearer and to the stone, but earrings, pendants, and brooches are more suited to this kind of setting. Hard stones such as diamonds are less likely to be chipped; the culet of softer stones is likely to be damaged as a result of wear.

INVERTED-STONE EAR STUDS
Faceted stones can be set upside-down with the culet uppermost, but should only be applied to pieces where the sharp points won't be too uncomfortable!

TOOLKIT
- Fine silver for bezel (see page 88)
- Soldering materials
- Silver sheet, earring posts
- File, ball burr, stones for setting
- Flat-ended pusher, burnisher

1 Construct a bezel for the stone in the usual way (see page 88), and solder a base and an earring post onto the base. File the top of the bezel to shape if you like. Use a ball burr the same diameter as the stone to create a seat for the stone.

2 Place the earring post in a hole in a block of wood while you set the stone with a flat-ended pusher. Burnish around the edge of the bezel before giving the piece a final polish.

Capping

Capping is a method of suspending top or side-drilled gemstones, often drops and briolettes. The metal fitting can take a variety of forms, but should always complement the stone.

WEEKDAY EARRINGS
The stones in these earrings by Nicholas Yiannarakis have been laser-riveted into the gold caps that hold them.

skill level

Choosing Stones
Briolettes are inexpensive when cut from stones such as quartz. Any price range can be catered for—ruby or diamond drops will cost much more. Stones are part-drilled from the top, fully drilled horizontally across the top, or vertically from end to end.

Metals
The choice of metal can be determined by the design rather than by functionality. The only necessity is that a narrow-gauge wire passes through the drilled hole in the stone, so a harder metal can be used to ensure durability.

Construction Details
The construction of the cap does not need to be complicated—the basic form can be fabricated or cast in wax, and a range of decorative elements applied. The only requirement is that the drilled portion of the stone fits neatly inside the cap.

For top-drilled stones, a flat wire should be soldered into the cap in the correct position. Once pickled and cleaned up, the wire can be twisted and cut to length. The twisting helps the adhesive make a stronger bond with the metal.

Side-drilled gems can be secured in a similar manner, but the ends of the wire must be adequately resolved. For soft wire they can be carefully riveted or screw threaded; for hard wire, they can be used to construct a bail that slips into the drill hole in the stone from either side.

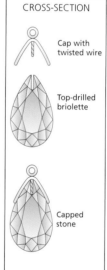

CROSS-SECTION

Cap with twisted wire

Top-drilled briolette

Capped stone

STYLES OF SETTING

Hard wire inserted from either side

CAPPING A TOP-DRILLED GREEN QUARTZ DROP
A simple cap for a briolette or drop can be secured with the use of a twisted wire and epoxy adhesive.

TOOLKIT
- Hammer, scribe
- Annealed silver tube, jump ring
- Soldering equipment, wire
- Briolette stone for setting
- Epoxy adhesive

1 Construct a long cone by hammering a scribe into a length of annealed tube. Solder a jump ring on the wider base, and a shallow dome on the top. A drilled hole in the top will allow a wire to be inserted—form a loop at the top and leave a long end until you have soldered in the wire.

2 The wire must be thin enough to fit the hole in the briolette and should be twisted at the end. Apply a small amount of epoxy adhesive to the tip of the wire and insert it into the briolette. Allow to dry. The length of the cap will hide the wire and the drilled hole in the bead.

Precious Metal Clay

Synthetic gemstones can be fired into precious metal clay, allowing scope for experimental forms of setting, and the use of unusual cuts of stone for which mount construction would otherwise be difficult.

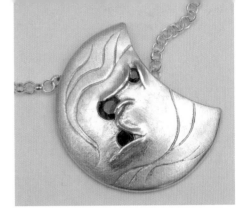

GARNET PENDANT
To set the stones in this pendant by Anastasia Young, the main body of clay was allowed to dry and seats for the garnets cut with ball burrs. Rolled-out slivers of clay were applied to the form to hold the stones, before the piece was fired.

skill level

RUBY RINGS
This pair of precious metal clay rings by Pat Waddington use a modified carved bezel to hold the large stone in the wider band. The thinner band displays a row of smaller, flush-set rubies which were set into the clay.

Choosing Stones

Stones must be able to survive the firing temperatures required for precious metal clay, so there are a limited number of options. Diamonds, rubies, and sapphires are heat-resistant enough, but if they have been heat-treated to improve their color, it may change during the firing process. Clear cubic zirconia will be fine, but colored ones may change color—try to find heat-resistant synthetic gems. Dichroic glass and garnets are also possible options for setting in precious metal clay.

Metals

There are several brands of precious metal clay available, in silver, copper, and gold. Once fired, the clay becomes fine metal. Several different forms of clay are available, including sheet, lump clay, and slip, which can be extruded from a syringe.

Construction Details

Once you have decided on a design and chosen stones, there are a number of methods for making a form in precious metal clay. You can make a mold from an object or

SETTING STONES IN PRECIOUS METAL CLAY
Elements of metal clay can be combined with slip once they are dry and at the "greenware" stage. Make sure enough metal clay is used to counter the shrinkage that occurs during firing; exaggerate the bezel walls and push the stones quite deeply into the clay.

TOOLKIT
- Olive oil
- Precious metal clay
- Cubic zirconia
- Old file
- Acrylic rod
- Polishing materials

1 Working on a lightly oiled surface, and with oiled fingers, roll small amounts of clay into balls and push in the cubic zirconia, which are heat resistant. The stones should be pushed in quite deep because the clay will shrink during firing.

2 Allow the clay to dry, and then clean up the outsides of the balls using an old file or other abrasive. The forms can be altered at this stage, and any unwanted marks on the clay removed. Even up the border of clay around the stones and ensure no clay is left on the surface of the stones.

BAND RING
Precious metal clay has been used to create a stylish bezel setting for a trillion-cut stone, applied to an anticlastic band in this pair of rings by Emma Baird.

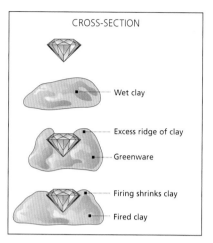

CROSS-SECTION

- Wet clay
- Excess ridge of clay
- Greenware
- Firing shrinks clay
- Fired clay

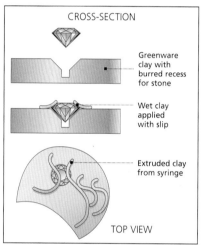

CROSS-SECTION

- Greenware clay with burred recess for stone
- Wet clay applied with slip
- Extruded clay from syringe

TOP VIEW

texture and push the clay into it so that it takes on its shape. Silicone putty is ideal for making this kind of open mold. The clay can be left to dry in the mold, or carefully removed while still damp.

Other, more sculptural techniques are ideal for metal clay. Working on an oiled surface, you can roll the clay out and cut it to a basic outline. Shaped pieces of clay can then be applied to the outline, bonded in place with a little water. You can add accurate detail and further shaping with small steel carving tools; impressed textures can be very effective. If the clay begins to dry out while you work on it, apply water using a spray or paintbrush.

Clay can also be molded around an existing metal frame or structure, but the clay must enclose parts of the frame otherwise it may come apart; steel mesh is useful for supporting large flat forms, as the clay will penetrate the weave of the mesh.

You can push stones straight into the clay when it is damp, so that the table of the stone is below the surface of the clay with a raised ridge surrounding it—alternatively, build pieces of clay up around the stone to form a setting. The stone must be mounted with enough clay to hold it securely at strategic points. The clay will shrink and contract during firing by as much as 25 percent, so it's better to have too much clay than too little.

Dry the clay in a domestic oven for 30 minutes at 300°F (150°C) and allow it to cool. At this "greenware" stage, further refining and cleaning up can be done. Ensure that the clay around the stone is neat and smooth using fine steel tools and emery paper.

The exact method of firing the clay varies by brand, but most can be fired either with a torch or in a kiln. Read the manufacturer's instructions for the exact temperatures and times required. Allow the piece to air cool, before working on the surface with a fine steel brush to remove the blanching. You can then polish the piece as if it were metal.

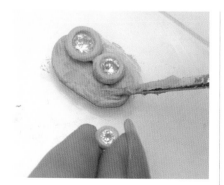

3 Roll out flat shapes of clay on the oiled surface, using a piece of acrylic rod as a rolling pin. Apply the "stone settings" to the base using slip, which can be made from watered-down clay or by adding water to clay dust. Once they are dry, clean up the forms again.

4 Fire the clay at the lowest recommended temperature for the amount of time specified in the clay's information sheet. Place the pieces in the kiln while it is cold and allow it to come up to temperature before starting a timer. When the time is up, let the pieces cool down with the kiln to prevent the stones cracking.

5 Clean up the forms with a wire brush in a flexshaft motor. Pieces can be barrel polished—this will help to work-harden the fine silver clay form, as well as polishing it. Run the tip of a burnisher around the inside edge of the settings to give them a highlight.

Casting

Stones can be cast directly into place using either lost wax or sand casting techniques, allowing for an experimental approach to mounting and setting gemstones.

skill level

CRYSTAL RINGS
This series of rings by Mabel Hasel was created using the lost wax casting technique. The rough crystals of ruby, sapphire, emerald, and aquamarine were embedded in wax models before being cast into silver forms.

USING CASTS
The cast silver form on the left forms a perfect, stone-set copy of the bronze original on the right, once cleaned up.

Choosing Stones

Stones used for casting must be able to survive the temperature of the molten metal, but this is the only limiting factor, so colorless cubic zirconia, heat-resistant synthetic gems, diamonds, rubies, sapphires, and garnets are all suitable.

Metals

Any of the metals commonly used for casting can be used—bronze; sterling silver; yellow, red, and white gold; palladium; or platinum. For sand casting, scrap metal can be melted down and used, but it must be clean and free of solder.

Construction Details

If you are having the piece commercially cast, you will need to discuss construction with your caster. It is crucial that the casting is not quenched because this will cause the stone to fracture. Different types of wax can be used to create the jewelry form—sticky wax wires can be added to carved wax, and may help to hold a stone better than welded-on or melted additions. See page 78 for more information on wax carving.

Sand or clay casting requires a form with which to make an impression. Models can be made from acrylic, metal, or wood, or a suitable found object with no undercuts—

CASTING STONES IN PLACE USING "DELFT CLAY" SAND CASTING
Synthetic or heat-resistant gems can be cast directly into metal forms using the sand casting technique. Use smaller stones because larger ones will crack with the shock of the molten metal hitting them.

TOOLKIT
- Delft clay and aluminum frame
- Steel ruler, hammer
- Model for casting
- Talcum powder
- Stones for setting
- Silver for casting, borax, crucible
- Pickle
- Jeweler's saw
- Polishing materials

1 Prepare the Delft Clay by chopping it finely with a ruler. Pack it into the bottom half of the aluminum frame and compact it with a hammer. Scrape the surface with the steel ruler to make it level with the rim of the frame. Push the model halfway into the clay, and dust the surface with talcum powder.

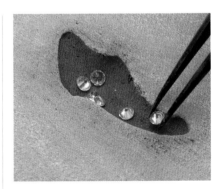

2 Place the top part of the aluminum frame in position with the registration mark lined up. Pack in more clay and compact it with a hammer. Carefully separate the two halves and remove the model. Place the stones into the recess left by the model, pushing them down lightly. Cut a ¼ in (6 mm) hole to make a sprue in the top half that connects directly to the recess.

otherwise it cannot be removed cleanly from the sand. The form shouldn't be too complex or delicate—not less than ¹⁄₁₆ in (2 mm) thick— and you need to consider the flow of the molten metal throughout the form.

The stone can either be incorporated into the model so that its position is dictated—when the model is removed the stone will need to be placed back in position before the molten metal is poured in—or the stone can be pushed into the clay once an impression has been made. The clay must cover enough of the stone to hold it in position during casting, but likewise, enough of the stone must be left exposed so that the metal will secure it. Remember that the empty space will be filled with metal.

Once the smaller half of the aluminum mold has been packed with sand, you can push the object in. Place the second ring on top with the registration marks lined up, and pack more sand in. When the two halves have been separated again and the object removed, cut a sprue hole in the upper half, and poke several air holes through the clay at strategic points with a thin steel rod. Realign the two halves before the molten metal is poured in through the sprue hole.

The weight of the model should give an indication of how much metal will be needed—silver is 10.4 times heavier than wax and acrylic, and an extra 5–10 grams of metal should be added to account for the sprue. Casting grain is not suitable to use because of its additives. Melt the correct amount of metal in a crucible with some borax powder, and pour it quickly, with the torch keeping it hot until the very last second. Allow the mold to air cool before opening it and retrieving the piece, which will need pickling before you can cut the sprue away. You can then clean up and polish the piece.

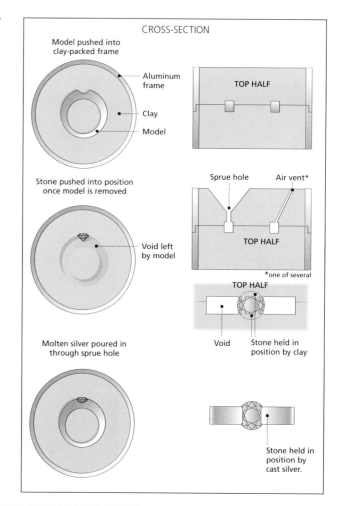

CROSS-SECTION

Model pushed into clay-packed frame

Aluminum frame
Clay
Model

TOP HALF

Stone pushed into position once model is removed

Void left by model

Sprue hole — Air vent*
TOP HALF
*one of several

TOP HALF
Void — Stone held in position by clay

Molten silver poured in through sprue hole

Stone held in position by cast silver.

3 Push thin holes through the top half as well to allow air to escape. Replace the top part of the frame, making sure the registration marks are lined up. Weigh the model and calculate how much scrap silver will be needed, adding on 10 grams for the sprue. Melt the silver with plenty of borax powder in a crucible.

4 When the silver forms a liquid mass, pour it into the sprue hole. Keep the torch on the silver for as long as possible, and pour very quickly, with the crucible on the edge of the frame so that the silver does not cool too much before it fills the mold. Allow the mold to cool.

5 Pickle the cast silver form to remove the oxides. Cut off the sprue with a jeweler's saw and file the area to shape. You can then clean up and polish the piece, taking care not to scratch the stones.

Soldering Stones into Place

When a design requires stones to be soldered into position between metal components, accuracy is often the key to success, creating interesting construction challenges.

skill level 👌👌

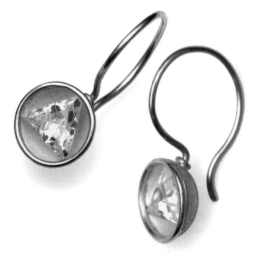

CZ EARRINGS
A groove was filed for the tips of each stone in a silver dome before a jump ring was soldered in place to hold the stone.

Choosing Stones

Cubic zirconia and heat-resistant synthetic gemstones are the most suitable stones for this technique. There are other stones that will survive the temperatures reached during soldering, but it is not worth taking the risk with valuable stones.

Metals

For soldered-in stones, the lower the soldering temperature the better, so use easy solder wherever possible. Because silver has the lowest soldering temperature of the precious metals, it is the safest metal to use until you gain confidence with this technique. Where silver and gold are used in the same piece, silver solder should be used, making the combination of these metals ideal for this process.

Construction Details

Stones can be secured in recesses with soldered-on elements; the stone can fit tightly into a space, or be loosely held, as long as there is no way for it to work free. All fabrication and finishing should be completed before soldering in the stone.

Points to be joined with solder must make good contact and should be held securely in position with binding wire so they don't move during heating. Build a box around

CUBIC ZIRCONIA SOLDER-SET EAR STUDS
Heat-resistant and synthetic stones can be soldered into position, trapped between metal elements. Do ensure that the components are close-fitting, otherwise the solder joins will be weak.

TOOLKIT
- Sheet silver, jeweler's saw
- Rectangular stone for setting
- Dapping block and punches
- Earring post
- Wire for jump rings
- Soldering equipment
- Reverse-action tweezers
- Pickle, burnisher

1 Pierce out a disk with cut-outs to accommodate the corners of a rectangular stone. Dome the disk using a dapping block and punch so that the stone fits inside, and solder an earring post to the back of the dome.

2 Make a large jump ring that fits the top edge of the dome, to hold the stone in position. The ring can sit directly on top of the edge, or just inside it, depending on how deep you want it within the domed form.

DELUXE FREEFORM RINGS
Sapphire and garnet were used for these sand-cast rings by Kelvin J Birk. Techniques that require the metal to be heated to set the stone must use heat-resistant stones to ensure that they survive the process.

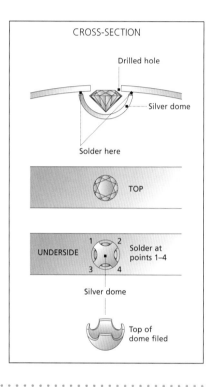

CROSS-SECTION

Drilled hole

Silver dome

Solder here

TOP

UNDERSIDE
1 2
3 4
Solder at points 1–4

Silver dome

Top of dome filed

the piece with fire bricks before starting. This will allow the piece to be heated much more efficiently, and will stop any drafts from affecting it as it is cooling. Use the lowest melting point solder available for the particular metal; in some cases it may be appropriate to use syringe solder so that there is no risk of solder running into difficult-to-clean areas. Heat the piece slowly at first to dry out the flux, and to bring the thickest areas of metal holding the stone up to temperature. Never heat the stone directly, even when soldering very close to it. Do not quench the piece—allow it to air cool very slowly, and do not move it until it has completely cooled.

It is possible to solder pieces that already have stones set in them—for example, if a ring needs resizing—but if the stones are valuable it is advisable to take the piece to a professional repairer. Heat-resistant paste is very useful for protecting stones—always follow the manufacturer's instructions, but a layer of paste around ½ in (1 cm) thick is usually effective. The stone and surrounding metal should be packed with paste, and reverse-action tweezers applied to the ring shank either side of the solder join to act as a heat sink. A very small intense flame is required to get metal hot enough under these circumstances.

3 Support the earring post in a pair of reverse-action tweezers and place the stone and jump ring in position. Apply flux with a fine brush to the edge of the form and place pallions of easy solder so that they are touching both the edge and the ring.

4 Gently heat the piece to dry out the flux and then bring the parts up to soldering temperature quickly, trying not to heat the stone directly. As soon as the solder melts and runs across the join, remove the flame. Allow the piece to cool completely before moving it.

5 Pickle the piece until it is thoroughly clean and rinse well to remove pickle residue. The area underneath the stone cannot easily be cleaned, so make sure it is evenly blanched by the pickle. Clean up the outside of the form, burnish the jump ring, and ensure that the earring post is straight.

Setting Odd-shaped Stones

Uncut or unusually shaped stones can be a challenge to make mounts for, but there are several methods that provide adaptable solutions to securely setting this type of stone.

skill level ♂♂

NATURAL DIAMOND RING
A 22-kt gold bezel was used to rub-over set the rough diamond in this textured ring by Leo Pieroni. The high-karat gold is quite soft and forms a deep bezel that follows the form of the uncut stone.

Choosing Stones
This type of setting is suitable for any stone that is not a conventional shape, such as beach stones, pebbles, drusy, polished stone slices, and uncut crystals.

Metals
Because irregularly shaped stones are likely to be softer or more fragile it is better to use fine silver or gold for the setting; these metals are very malleable, allowing bezels to be fitted snugly around the stone. Make wire mounts from harder metals.

Construction Details
When making a simple bezel for an irregularly shaped stone, the bezel needs to follow the contours of the stone. If you are using fine silver, it should be possible to push the silver around the stone accurately enough, but ensure that the wall stays perpendicular to the base all the way around. Harder metals will probably need to be shaped with pliers to get a good match with the stone's profile. The shape can be adjusted further once the ends are soldered closed, and it is easier to accurately shape closed forms, but once the bezel has been soldered to a base this will be difficult.

SETTING AN AMETHYST SLICE
Fine silver bezel strip, sold off-the-reel, is ideal for setting odd-shaped stones because it is so thin and malleable. This allows the metal to be burnished closely to the contours of an uncut edge.

TOOLKIT
- Fine silver bezel strip (see page 88)
- Amethyst slice
- Burnisher
- Pliers
- Soldering materials, jump ring
- File
- Flat-ended pusher

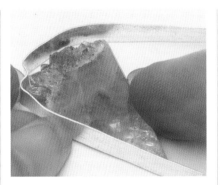

1 Working with fine bezel strip, which is very thin and soft, fit the bezel roughly around the stone. Try to fit the bezel more closely to any areas of the stone that protrude so that the bezel does not end up being too big—it can be easily pushed into recesses with a burnisher, or bent with pliers to shape it more accurately.

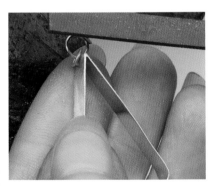

2 Solder the bezel closed and solder on a jump ring from which to hang the piece. The pointed end of the stone is tapered and beveled, so the bezel needs to be reduced in height with a file from both sides. It would otherwise be difficult to compress it over the point.

The height of the bezel may need to be lowered at certain points; lower areas of the stone will require a reduced bezel height, otherwise too much of the stone may be obscured. The bezel should be set around the stone in a similar manner to a normal bezel—pushing in at opposing points until all of the bezel is flush with the stone; however, tight curves may be problematic and you'll have to take care to compress the metal slowly and methodically. If the stone is not level on its base, it may move while being set, so at first, push the bezel around areas which will keep it level.

Wire forms, similar to caged constructions (see page 144) can also be used to hold irregularly shaped stones and are perhaps most suitable for rounded pebble shapes. The cage can be left with an opening that can be closed using one of a number of different methods, such as riveting, screwing, laser or TIG welding, or wire wrapping. Whichever method you choose, it must be both secure and in keeping with the design.

Another way to set uncut stones is using prongs attached to a frame or base which the stone sits on. A slightly thicker gauge of wire can be used to make the prongs if silver is being used; this will ensure that the prongs are strong enough. This type of prong is also a bit longer than the traditional style and the ends of the wire can be "balled" to make an exaggerated terminus.

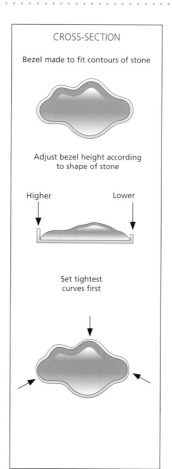

CROSS-SECTION

Bezel made to fit contours of stone

Adjust bezel height according to shape of stone

Higher   Lower

Set tightest curves first

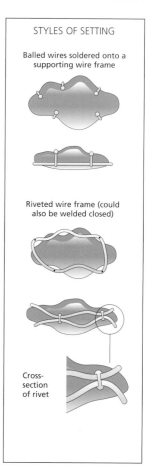

STYLES OF SETTING

Balled wires soldered onto a supporting wire frame

Riveted wire frame (could also be welded closed)

Cross-section of rivet

3 Insert the stone in the bezel and use a flat-ended pusher to begin working the bezel over the edge of the stone at key points. Work from both sides until the stone is held in place.

4 Continue rubbing over the bezel with the pusher, paying particular attention to any areas of the bezel that will need to compress more than others, such as protrusions or corners. The bezel will begin to fit the contours of the stone more closely.

5 Use a burnisher the force the fine silver over the edge of the stone, smoothing and polishing it. Burnish out any sharp edges and ensure that the stone is firmly secured within the bezel.

Settings for Interchangeable Stones

Simple mechanisms can be used to allow a setting to be opened and closed so that the stone can be changed, allowing the wearer greater choice over the color or cut of stone.

skill level

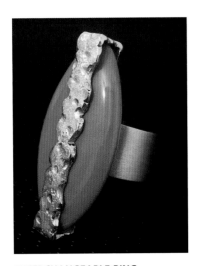

INTERCHANGEABLE RING
A hammered and reticulated band holds the marquise cabochon in this ring by Donna Russell. The setting can be removed from the ring to allow other stones to be attached.

Choosing Stones

To keep the mount reasonably simple, use different stones of the same cut in contrasting colors. It is not advisable to use very valuable gemstones because there is the potential for the loss of stones as they are being changed over. With this in mind, standard cuts and sizes are the easiest to source and replace if necessary.

Metals

Working parts of mechanisms should be made from hard, and therefore more durable precious metals that will not wear or distort with use. But these are the only functional restrictions, and the choice of the main metal for the piece may be influenced by design.

Construction Details

It is the function of the mechanism, rather than the mount itself, which poses the greatest construction challenge for this type of setting. This needs to be uncomplicated and easy to use, with no risk of it coming open by accident—unless a complex mechanism is a design feature of the piece and written instructions are perhaps provided. Giving the wearer the choice of color of stone to wear in the piece on a particular day adds another dimension to a piece, but if the mechanism is too difficult to use, then it may prevent the owner from changing the stones.

BAYONET FITTING FOR INTERCHANGEABLE STONES
Simple mechanisms can be used to allow different mounts to be changed on a piece. For this project, tube settings are altered to make a bayonet fitting for a ring.

TOOLKIT
- Tube, chenier cutter
- Drill
- Soldering equipment
- Jeweler's saw
- Ring shank
- Pickle
- Files and burrs
- Stones for setting
- Pliers

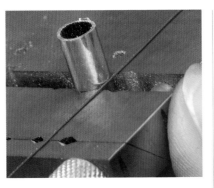

1 Cut sections of tube using a chenier cutter—the longer pieces will form tube settings for several stones. The shorter piece must fit around the longer pieces, forming the bayonet fitting.

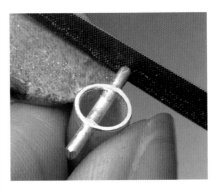

2 Drill a 16-gauge (1.3-mm) hole close to the base of each piece of longer tube and solder a wire of that diameter through the hole. Trim the wires so that they protrude further than the base tube that forms the fitting.

The design of the piece, and its mechanism, is crucial to its success: a number of technical devices can be used to effect this, from screw threads, bayonet fittings, or hinges to catches or springs, and more than one device may be used in combination. The piece can be designed so that either loose or mounted stones are interchangeable. Stones that are already mounted may offer more versatility, because the mount itself can be adapted to be attached to the main piece of jewelry—loose stones will require the opening of the mount itself, which may be limiting in terms of function. However, you can always find ingenious solutions to a technical challenge.

It's a good idea to make test pieces and models of the mechanism you decide on in base metals. This will provide a clearer idea of metal gauges and proportions, and will reveal any pitfalls of the design—it is unlikely that the first attempt will work perfectly.

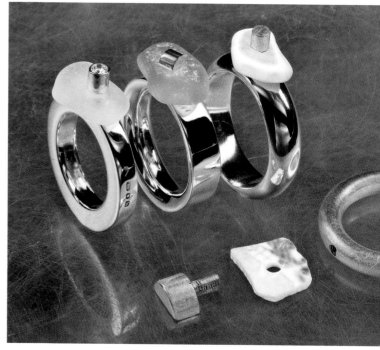

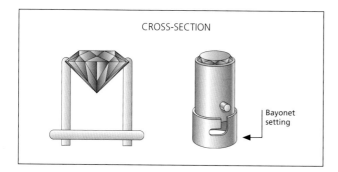

CROSS-SECTION

Bayonet setting

SCREW RINGS
Drilled beach glass and ceramics are interchangeable on this set of silver rings by Melissa Hunt. The screws that hold the glass are made from white and yellow gold for durability, with yellow-gold tube-set diamonds.

3 Solder the base tube onto a ring shank, pickle, and clean up. Mark the position of the wires from one of the long tubes, drawing a mark as wide as the wire; the mark goes straight down for a distance and turns at a right angle as it reaches the base.

4 Use files and burrs to carve the gap on both sides of the tube, checking the fit of the wire in the gap at regular intervals until the bayonet fitting functions well. Set the stones in the longer sections of tube as described in Tube Settings (see page 92).

5 The stone settings should slip easily into the ring, and are secured with a quarter twist. The base tube can be adjusted carefully with pliers to tighten the gap if necessary.

Spectacle Setting

This technique for setting is often used for fitting spectacle lenses, but it can also be used to great effect in jewelry designs to hold fragile stones, as it applies so little pressure to them.

skill level 👥

DONNA RING
The amethyst cameo in this silver and gold ring by Barbara Christie is spectacle set by a gold band slipped over the ends of the extended bezel.

Choosing Stones

In theory, many shapes of stone can be set in this way—round or oval being the easiest—but in practice, it is most suited to flattened forms.

Metals

Any of the standard alloys of gold and silver can be used, as well as other metals. The level of construction required means that softer metals are not suitable.

Construction Details

This type of setting uses a band of metal to secure the stone—the band is closed either with a rivet or a screw thread. Looking at old pairs of spectacles, it is apparent that the settings for the lenses are often formed from a U-shaped piece of metal, thereby using the least amount of metal possible. This is very difficult to do without specialist equipment and is rather time consuming. It is far easier to fabricate a wall with a groove or recess on the inside that will hold the stone. This type of form could either be carved in wax and cast, or constructed in the following way.

Make two rings very slightly smaller than the diameter of the stone from round-section wire, and solder them closed. True them on a mandrel, clean up the solder

SPECTACLE SETTING AN OVAL ROSE QUARTZ CABOCHON
Although spectacle setting is often used to set very fragile stones or enamels, it makes an interesting alternative setting for less brittle stones too.

TOOLKIT
- Silver wire
- Soldering equipment
- Oval mandrel, mallet
- Tube
- Ball burr, jeweler's saw
- Stone for setting
- Scribe, steel block

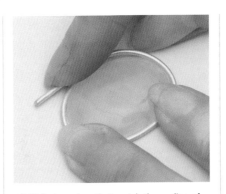

1 Make two rings that match the outline of the stone; they need to be a bit smaller than the circumference of the stone so that it does not quite fit inside. Solder the rings closed and true the ovals on a mandrel with a mallet. Solder the two rings together, one on top of the other.

2 Solder two sections of tube onto the rings—one thinner, longer piece that will form the closure of the spectacle setting, and a larger piece to act as a bail. Use a ball burr with the same profile as the edge of the stone to carve a groove on the inside of the mount, between the two wire rings.

DRUSY THREE-ROW NECKLACE
Fragile onyx drusy ovals have been spectacle
set in gold and suspended between chains to
create this necklace by Annoushka.

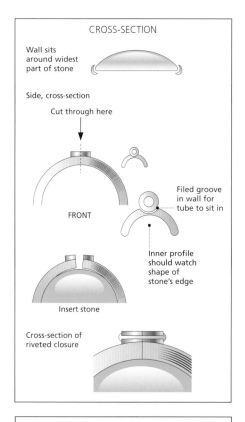

CROSS-SECTION

Wall sits
around widest
part of stone

Side, cross-section

Cut through here

FRONT

Filed groove
in wall for
tube to sit in

Inner profile
should watch
shape of
stone's edge

Insert stone

Cross-section of
riveted closure

STYLES OF SETTING

Two round wires
soldered together,
groove burred on
inside for stone

Wire rings
soldered on
either end of
sheet ring

seams, and ensure that they are flat. Solder them together, one on top of the
other, making sure that they are perfectly aligned. Use a burr to reshape the inner
intersection of the two rings to conform to the edge of the stone—if there is a
rounded edge on the stone, use a ball burr of a similar diameter to carve out an
even groove all the way around.

Solder a section of small-diameter tube over the first solder seams—file a
groove for it first, so that there is greater contact. Any fittings, such as a bail,
should also be soldered on at this stage, before cleaning up and polishing.

Cut through the rings and the tube at its mid-point—the form will spring
open a little, enough for the stone to be slipped into position. If the stone is loose
when the setting is closed, file the cut ends of the setting to make it shorter and
test it with the stone in place again. You can then rivet the tube shut or, if you
prefer and the tube is thick enough to take it, cut a screw thread in one half of
the tube, and make a small screw to go through the blind tube, screwing into
the other half and pulling the setting closed. The screw should be made from a
hard metal such as white gold, and will need a head that cannot pass through
the blind tube. The screw end of the wire may be riveted lightly to prevent it from
coming undone, but if there is likely to be any change or adjustment needed this
should not be done.

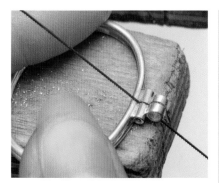

3 Once the groove is deep enough to
securely hold the stone evenly along its
length, cut through the central point of both
pieces of tube with a jeweler's saw to open up
the form.

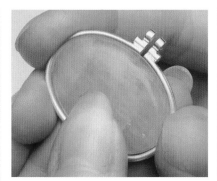

4 Fit the stone into the mount and squeeze
it closed. If the stone is loose, file the cut
ends to reduce the length of the metal
surrounding the stone. Ideally the stone should
be held under slight pressure, so there should
be a very fine gap when the ends of the mount
are pushed together.

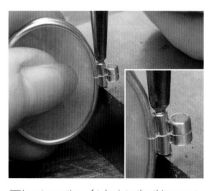

5 Insert a section of tube into the thinner cut
tube. Spread one end of the inserted tube
with the tip of a scribe and then do the same
for the other end. Support the tube on the
edge of a steel block while working—firm
pressure on the scribe should be enough to
open up the ends of the thin tube and hold the
join closed.

Wrapping

Wire wrapping can be a simple way of securing gemstone beads, but this cold-joining technique can also be used to mount undrilled stones, using a combination of wire wrapping and textile techniques.

skill level

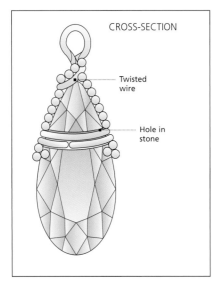

CROSS-SECTION

Twisted wire

Hole in stone

Choosing Stones

Most types of gems are suitable for this style of mounting; the shape of the stone will directly influence the way the wire is used, whether the stone is drilled or not. Larger stones are easier to handle, and smaller gemstone beads can be incorporated within wrapped wire pieces (see also Wired Beads, page 188).

On more unusual cuts, you can use the shape of the stone to facilitate the wrapping, catching the wire at various edges and points, and the shape of some types of stone can be adapted with carved grooves to aid the process.

Metals

Wire for wrapping pearls and beads needs to be malleable enough to be manipulated, but strong enough to hold its position and not snap easily. Fine silver or gold wire of 26–28 gauge (0.3–0.4 mm) is ideal and is very versatile. Colored copper wires can also be used, but they cannot be soldered.

WIRE WRAPPING A SIDE-DRILLED BEAD DROP
Wrapping is a useful solution for combining drilled semiprecious gemstones with enameled copper wire because neither can be heated or soldered.

TOOLKIT
- 18-gauge (1-mm) enameled copper wire
- Former
- Chain-nose pliers
- 28-gauge (0.3-mm) wire
- Drilled briolette stone
- Tweezers

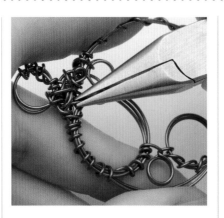

1 Make a wire-frame pendant to support the stone using 18-gauge (1-mm) enameled copper craft wire. To make loops, wrap the wire around a former a few times, remove the former, and wrap more wire around and through the loop to hold it firm. Tuck the ends into the form so that they do not stick out using a pair of chain-nose pliers.

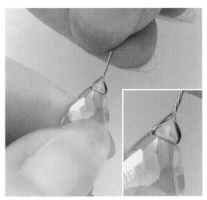

2 Thread thinner 28-gauge (0.3-mm) wire through the drilled hole in a briolette drop. The wire may be of the same color, or a contrasting one. Pass the wire along the center of the section of wire and twist both ends of the wire together.

WRAPPED WIRE BRACELET
This wire Swarovski Rivoli crystal bangle by Huan Pham was constructed with solid silver and gold-fill wire. The central stone has been framed by the wires to form the bracelet and enhance its beauty.

Construction Details

There are two main considerations when securing loose stones with wire: that the stone is adequately mounted and that the ends of the wire are dealt with in an aesthetically pleasing and comfortable way. Stones with drilled holes allow the ends of the wire to be secured inside the hole with adhesive, but you'll need to find other solutions for undrilled stones. If the bulk of the piece that will hold the gem is constructed from wire before the stone is included, it should be possible to solder one wire end into the form to prevent it from poking out. Tubes and crimps can be used to hold ends, but may not be as visually satisfying as a solution, especially if they are used as an afterthought. Knitted or woven wire structures may have enough thickness to allow wire ends to be tucked carefully inside the form.

Pliers will help with wire wrapping, but take care not to damage the wire when bending or shaping it—always choose the appropriate pair of pliers for the shape you are making. Wires may be wrapped around themselves, or around a former or jig, to create specific shapes that can then be adapted or worked around. Half-hard wire can be used to form a structural basis for the piece, with thinner-gauge, softer wire used to create the wrapped mount. The weight of the stone may influence the gauge of wire and type of structure you create, which must be able to withstand wear and bear the weight of the stone.

COLORED RING
Tourmaline and aquamarine crystals have been wrapped around a gold ring with wire in this piece by Kika Alvarenga. The pieces are held in place with transparent resin so the stones are less precarious than they appear.

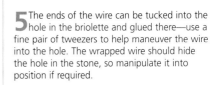

3 Thread the thinner wire around a loop on the frame and wrap it around this loop a few times, allowing a little length for the stone to hang.

4 Work the thinner wire around itself at the top of the stone, and if the drilled hole in the stone is large enough to allow it, pass the wire back through to increase the strength of the structure. Continue wrapping the top of the stone onto the frame until the join looks well made.

5 The ends of the wire can be tucked into the hole in the briolette and glued there—use a fine pair of tweezers to help maneuver the wire into the hole. The wrapped wire should hide the hole in the stone, so manipulate it into position if required.

Settings as Functional Devices

Gemstones can be used as an integral part of devices such as catches, as well as forming decorative rivet heads that can be used to join metal and mixed media components.

skill level

EMBOSSED ARMOUR FINN CUFFS
Stone settings form the closing mechanism for these leather cuffs by William Vinicombe.

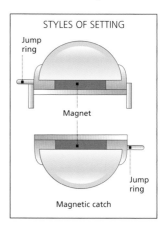

STYLES OF SETTING
Jump ring
Magnet
Jump ring
Magnetic catch

Choosing Stones

The choice of stone really depends on the design of the mechanism and the functional requirements of the piece—for particular forms, flat cabochons will be appropriate because the piece as a whole will be less bulky. When making catches, a large interesting stone can be used as a decorative centerpiece. If it is necessary to hammer on the reverse of the setting, as for tube riveting, choose hard stones that are unlikely to fracture or cleave easily.

Materials

The choice of metal for the stone mount is dictated by the design and function of the piece. The devices discussed here include methods for joining or linking elements of mixed materials, and decorative rivets are particularly suited to flexible materials such as leather, soft plastics, or textiles. Magnets can also be used within mounts to make magnetic clasps.

Construction Details

Many types of stone setting can be used to decorate catches and clasps, but large bezel-set stones are particularly effective when used to conceal the inner workings of

DECORATIVE RIVETS FOR SECURING FLEXIBLE MATERIALS

Flat-based bezel cups can easily be converted into decorative stone-set rivets. The difference between the diameter of the bezel and that of the tube rivet makes it ideal for holding flexible materials, especially with the addition of a washer on the underside.

TOOLKIT

- Fine silver for bezel (see page 88)
- Soldering equipment, sheet silver, tube
- Shagreen, washer
- Jeweler's saw, file
- Steel rod
- Stone for setting
- Dapping punch, mallet
- Burnisher

1 To make a decorative stone-set rivet to secure fittings to shagreen, first make a fine silver bezel for the stone. Solder a base onto the bezel, and a piece of tube to the underside. The tube must be long enough to pass through two layers of shagreen and a washer, with enough length left to spread the end.

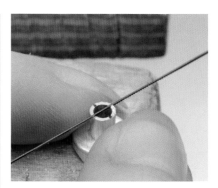

2 File the top of the bezel to shape it into "petals," and use a jeweler's saw to cut four slits in the tube. File the cut sections of the tube to divide them further—this will help the rivet spread more easily and neatly.

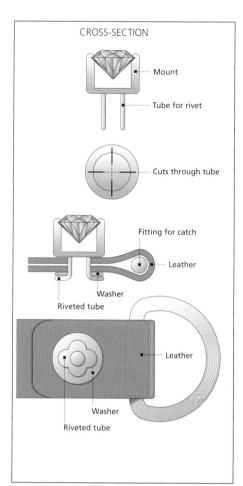

CROSS-SECTION

Mount

Tube for rivet

Cuts through tube

Fitting for catch

Leather

Washer

Riveted tube

Leather

Washer

Riveted tube

mechanisms, providing a decorative and functional solution to fitting elements and then concealing them from view. Magnets are a great example of this. Very small and powerful magnets that have enough power to work through sheet metal can be secured in the base of a mount before the stone is set; this is useful for magnetic catches, but do make sure the magnet is placed the right way around, so that it pulls rather than pushes away.

Rivets are very good for securing flexible materials, especially when combined with functional metal elements such as catches. Decorative rivets can be made by soldering wire or tube to the base of the bezel cup prior to setting the stone.

Tube settings (see page 92) are ideal for making rivet heads because they are reasonably quick to make up. A base disk can be soldered onto the underside before a second, smaller diameter of tube is soldered to the other side of the disk; for very soft materials it's best to use an oversized stone and a washer on the underside to prevent the rivet from slipping out. The length of the rivet must be greater than the thickness of the materials it will join, and two saw cuts should be made through the end of the tube so that it spreads more easily when hit. A hole just a fraction smaller than the tube rivet should be punched into the material, and the rivet slipped into place. Working stone side down, on a surface protected with leather, use a punch to spread the cut tube end evenly. Use a mallet to flatten the ends of the cut tube against the washer so they are not sharp.

FUNCTIONAL DEVICES

A hematite cabochon forms the front of this decorative rivet, which is used to secure a fitting to a shagreen cuff.

3 Punch two holes the same size as the tube through the shagreen, and thread it through the silver fitting before inserting the rivet. Place a washer over the back of the tube rivet to make the tube rivet stronger—the flexible shagreen will be less likely to come away from the rivet.

4 Place the bezel cup on a steel rod the same diameter as the stone—this is to prevent the bezel from distorting during setting. Use a dapping punch to spread the ends of the tube rivet over the washer by tapping it with a mallet. Use the mallet to ensure that the petals of the tube rivet are knocked down flush.

5 Working on a steel block, insert the stone into the bezel cup and use a bezel setting punch to close the bezel around the stone. The metal parts of the piece can be carefully cleaned up and burnished to finish the piece.

Mixed Materials and Other Metals

From wood, acrylic, and resin to niobium and aluminum, mixed materials are very useful for adding more color and visual texture to a piece than is possible with precious metals alone.

skill level 👁👁

ACRYLIC AND WOOD

Choosing Stones
These relatively soft materials can be used to make mounts, so it is possible to use very soft or fragile stones with them, as long the fabrication methods used will allow it. However, the contrast between very hard, well-cut expensive stones and nonprecious materials can provide an interesting design feature.

Metals
Cold-joining methods, such as riveting, require metal to be used with mixed materials to aid construction. Harder metals, including half-hard silver, are best for wire rivets and screws. Metal mounts for stones can also be combined with mixed materials to great effect.

Construction Details
Acrylic and close-grained hardwoods can be worked in a similar way to one another. They should be cut with a spiral saw blade and refined with a rough file (cut 0) before being cleaned up with wet-and-dry paper. Plastics should always be sanded with water to prevent harmful dust from being released, but some woods will absorb too much

HYACINTH RING
Silver has been combined with an experimental plastic technique to create this outlandish ring by Alidra Alic. A faceted strawberry quartz nestles between the petals of one of the hyacinth flowers.

SANDWICH SETTING WITH WOOD AND ACRYLIC
Mixed materials can be riveted together to trap a stone in a carved recess between the two halves. For this project, mopani wood and ⅛ in (3 mm) ivory acrylic sheet are used to make a cold-joined ring.

TOOLKIT
- Wood and acrylic sheet
- Spiral saw blade, file
- Wire for rivets
- Drill
- File, small burr
- Hammer, steel block

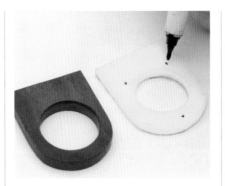

1 Cut out two identical ring blanks from wood and acrylic sheet using a spiral saw blade, and file them to shape. The thickness of the two sheets needs to be greater than the diameter of the stone being set. Mark the positions of drill holes for the rivets that will hold the two pieces together.

2 Drill holes in the acrylic first with a drill bit the same gauge as the rivet wire. Holding the wood and the acrylic firmly together in the correct position, use the drill bit to mark through one drilled hole onto the wood. Separate the pieces and drill this hole. Pass a wire through both parts to hold them in position and mark and drill the remaining two holes.

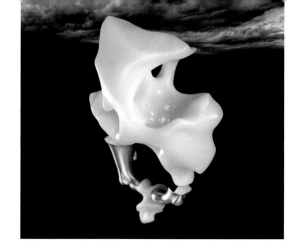

WEATHER RING
Diamonds have been set directly into sculpturally carved white jade to form this ring by Xin Ran Lu. The jade is held in white-gold mounts.

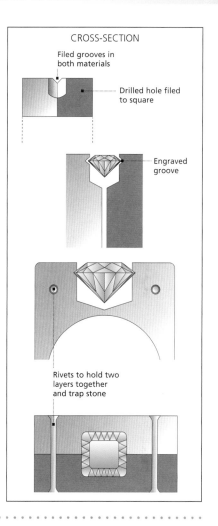

CROSS-SECTION

Filed grooves in both materials

Drilled hole filed to square

Engraved groove

Rivets to hold two layers together and trap stone

water to make this feasible, so always wear a suitable dust mask when working with dry wood. Both materials can be polished in the usual manner; use Vonax or other polishing compounds for plastics. Acrylic and hardwood can also be carved with engraving tools, burrs, and files to produce intricate three-dimensional forms.

In order to incorporate stones into pieces made with wood and acrylic without using metal mounts, it is necessary to use cold-joining techniques such as rivets, screws, or adhesive. Stones can be trapped in recesses between layers of sheet material before being permanently secured, in effect making a flush setting; for round stones, file a small, short groove at corresponding points on the inside edges of two sheets to be joined. When the materials are clamped together, the groove forms the starting point into which you can burr a seat for the stone—but the seat size should be smaller than required for a particular stone. With the two sheets separated, use a graver to cut a line about 1/32 in (1 mm) from the top of the seat into which the girdle of the stone will be trapped once the two halves are joined.

The layers of sheet material can either be riveted together, or bonded using a suitable adhesive (taking care not to let the adhesive come into contact with the stone). Two-part epoxy resin adhesives form a very strong bond between mixed materials; however, if just wood is being used, then wood glue is the best option because it is absorbed into the surface of the wood and forms a very strong bond.

3 Mark the center of the front of the top of the ring on both materials, and file a groove. Use a flat-faced file to create a rectangular recess at the front of the ring, but do not file away any material from the inside of the finger hole. At the top, the recess must be smaller than the dimensions of the stone.

4 Use a small burr to carve a groove inside the filed recess in both the wood and the acrylic. This will create a lip to hold the stone in place once the two halves of the ring are put together, with the groove accommodating the stone's girdle.

5 Make three rivets. Put the two halves of the ring together, with the stone trapped in the recess and push the rivets through so that the heads are on the wood side. Working on a steel block, trim the wires, file them flat, and rivet the ends.

HIDDEN RING
The texture for the cast resin elements of this ring by Kika Alvarenga were molded from the black tourmaline crystal which forms its focal point. The gemstone and resin parts of the ring are attached to a silver liner with resin.

RESIN

Choosing Stones

Some stones, including quartz, have a very similar optical refraction qualities to resin, and as a result of this their edges appear indistinct when they are embedded in it—only a hint of color gives away their presence and all sparkle is gone. Cubic zirconia and other synthetic stones are fine, but foil-backed stones will also lose their sparkle.

Resin Types

Resins are liquid plastics that harden when mixed with a chemical catalyst. This allows them to be easily colored with dyes and have objects, such as gemstones, embedded in them. Resin can also be used as a bonding agent to hold elements of a jewelry piece together, as well as a coating medium or cold enamel.

Epoxy resin is the most suitable type of resin for jewelry making, because it dries tack-free, has minimal shrinkage, and no odor. Certain types of epoxy resin are less viscous than others, which can lead to problems with air bubbles forming during mixing. Resin usually becomes more fluid at slightly higher temperatures, so gently warming the mixture with a hairdryer or portable heater (at a safe distance—and NEVER use a naked flame) will encourage bubbles to the surface, and also accelerate the curing process. Pot life and curing times are dependent on the brand of resin used and the ambient temperature.

HEALTH AND SAFETY WHEN WORKING WITH RESIN

When working with chemicals such as resin, always wear goggles, gloves, and a mask suitable for chemical fumes. Ideally, liquid resin should only be handled in a fume cupboard with extraction, but working outside and upwind of the resin should also minimize any risks. Dispose of unused resin and hardener, mixing pots, and any other contaminated equipment carefully in a sealed bag or container.

EMBEDDING STONES IN EPOXY RESIN

Gemstones can be trapped between layers of epoxy resin, so that they are suspended within a piece. Allow one layer of resin to cure before applying the next.

TOOLKIT
- Silver frame
- Soldering equipment
- Epoxy resin
- Stones for setting
- Melinex foil (Mylar)
- Polyboard, masking tape, plasticine
- Dye or metallic powder
- Wet-and-dry papers
- Polishing materials

1 Construct a silver frame to hold the resin. The frame must be large enough to hold stones of the desired shape and size, and deep enough to take at least two layers of resin which will hole the stones. Solder on a hanging loop or other fitting, depending on the piece. Clean up the silver.

2 Tack a piece of Melinex foil (Mylar) onto a piece of polyboard with masking tape, and place the frame on top. Roll out a length of plasticine, and use it to seal the frame to the Melinex, pushing down on the frame so that the plasticine cannot get in underneath the frame. Mix up a small amount of epoxy resin and pour it into the frame. Allow the resin to cure before positioning the stones, table side down.

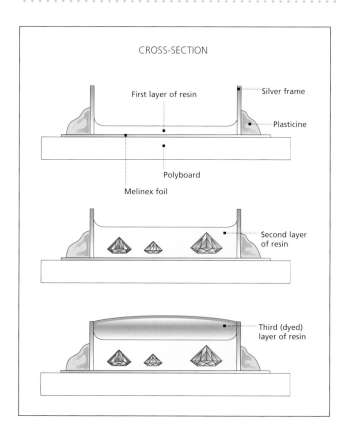

CROSS-SECTION

First layer of resin

Silver frame

Plasticine

Polyboard

Melinex foil

Second layer of resin

Third (dyed) layer of resin

Construction Details

Any constructed metal container or open frame could form a setting, with the stone held in place with resin. Open-backed frames must be well sealed to a base using modeling clay before the resin is poured in. The base may be acrylic or polyboard, but should be lined with Melinex foil (Mylar), a type of acetate sheet that the resin will not adhere to.

Weigh out the liquid resin and its hardener accurately, in the correct proportions, and stir them slowly until they are well mixed, taking care not to incorporate air bubbles. Once the resin is mixed, you can add transparent dyes or other additives such as fine metallic powders, but they should not make up more than 2 percent of the total mixture, otherwise curing will be inhibited.

Stones usually sink in the resin, so use a minimum of two layers of resin to trap stones internally. The first layer forms a barrier so that the stones will not break the surface, and the second contains the stones, which would be damaged during cleaning up and polishing if they protruded through the resin. Once the first layer has cured, you can position the stones, and pour in the second layer of resin. Slightly overfill the frame to counter shrinkage of the resin, and remove bubbles on the surface by dragging them out with a pin.

If you are using brilliant-cut stones, they need to be set upside-down on their tables, so that they sit straight. This means filling the piece with resin back-to-front, so that the base of the piece will face up.

3 Pour a second layer of resin over the stones, to fill the frame. You can add a dye or metallic powder to the resin once it has been mixed with the hardener to give a background color. Fill the frame with resin until the dome starts to form—the resin will shrink as it sets. Allow to cure for at least 24 hours.

4 Peel the frame away from the Melinex and clean off the plasticine. Rub the front and back surfaces of the resin down to the level of the frame using wet-and-dry paper with water. Start with 600 grade, and work up to 1200. The layer of transparent resin in front of the stones will protect them.

5 Polish the surface of the resin with a plastic polish such as Vonax or a cream polish on a piece of suede—the resin will look cloudy until it has been polished.

LA BELLEZZA DELLA LOTTA
Another aspect of using mixed, or nonprecious, materials is the ways in which they can be treated. In this brooch by Dauvit Alexander CAM-milled ebony has been claw set onto a pierced silver frame, combined with claw-set pear-shaped stones and an iron gear.

OTHER METALS

Choosing Stones
The choice of stones will very much depend on the piece being made and the metals being used. Hard stones (8–10 Mohs) that are not brittle should be used if they are being set into titanium or steel because these metals require more force to move them.

Metals
The refractory metals are named after the range of colors produced when they are oxidized. As a group of metals, they are relatively hard and cannot be annealed or soldered under normal conditions. This means that the range of techniques they are suitable for is limited to cold-joining methods, and a restricted range of forming and texturing processes. Aluminum and steel are somewhat more workable. A limited range of products including sheet, rod, tube, and mesh is available.
Niobium: The softest and most malleable of the refractory metals, it is possible to flush set, texture, and lightly form Niobium. This metal work-hardens slowly, but is not very strong. It gives the best range of refractory colors when anodized.
Tantalum: This metal has similar working properties to gold, and is therefore the most suitable for stone settings, but because of the fabrication limitations the most appropriate type of setting to use is rub-over. Tantalum can also be anodized.
Titanium: The hardest and lightest of the refractory metals, titanium cannot be annealed under normal circumstances, so techniques are limited to cutting and subtractive texturing. Use plenty of lubricant when working titanium so that tools do not blunt too quickly. Titanium is most suitable for tension setting (see page 142), and can be vibrantly colored using a torch flame or an anodizing bath.

A PIERCED SETTING IN TANTALUM SHEET
22-gauge (0.6-mm thick) tantalum sheet was used to make this pair of ear pendants. The metal was anodized before being shaped, but could also be anodized afterward. Tantalum is a light metal, similar in properties to titanium, but not as hard to work.

TOOLKIT
- 22-gauge (0.6-mm) tantalum sheet
- Dividers, scribe, steel ruler
- Center punch, drill, burr
- Jeweler's saw
- Hardwood
- Stone for setting
- Burnisher

1 Mark out the design on a piece of tantalum using dividers, a scribe, and a steel ruler. The central hole in which the stone sits needs to be ⁵⁄₃₂ in (4.5 mm) for a ³⁄₈ in (5 mm) stone; divide the circle into six—the lines radiating from this central point will form the tabs that hold the stone.

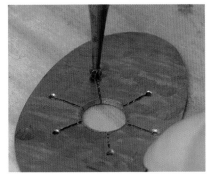

2 Draw a circle that intersects the six lines, and center punch for the seven drill holes. Drill the large hole and the six smaller holes surrounding it, using plenty of lubricant. Burr the central hole with a ³⁄₈ in (5 mm) ball burr, and use a small burr to remove the sharp edges from the small holes. Pierce the radiating lines with a saw.

Aluminum: This metal can be formed, textured, polished, and anodized to color the surface. The anodizing of aluminum is a commercial process, which creates a hard skin of oxides receptive to dyes. You can also buy pre-anodized metal, which can be colored with dyes or printed by hand. Because aluminum is so light, a thicker gauge of metal can be used for larger pieces, but it cannot be soldered. Aluminum is a contaminant to other metals because it has such a low melting point, so use separate tools to work it.

Steel: Stainless steel is the hardest steel alloy, making it useful for applications that require strength with a thinner piece of metal. It is commonly found in jewelry mechanisms, such as springs, catches, clasps, pins, and store-bought cufflink backs. It is easiest to form while red-hot, possible to solder with silver solder and a high temperature flux, and polishes well. Steel can be annealed, but not pickled—remove oxides with emery paper—and can also be spot, TIG, or laser welded. Complex wire forms which are durable and may contain trapped stones, can be welded.

Construction Details

It is possible to set stones in the traditional way with some of these metals, but the harder metals may pose a problem, and aluminum is too soft to offer enough security for valuable stones.

Any of these metals can be riveted with silver, gold, or brass wire or tubing, allowing stones to be trapped or "set" between layers of sheet metal. Use plenty of lubricant, either machine oil or cutting fluid, when drilling or burring these metals to improve the efficiency of the tools. Screw threads, folded tabs, handmade staples, and other cold-joining methods can all be used to design stone mounts with these metals.

CLUSTER BROOCH
A vivid cubic zirconia, bezel-set in sterling silver, nestles in the center of the fronds of anodized aluminum, titanium, and niobium that make up this brooch by Meghan O'Rourke.

PEACOCK VESSEL
Tabbed prong settings have been used to secure lampworked glass components into the titanium panels of this beautifully colored object.

3 Use a tapered piece of hardwood to prize up three of the cut tabs, because the wood will not damage the anodized surface of the metal. Lift up the tabs from the front, just enough to slip the stone into position.

4 Push the three tabs back down with the piece of wood so that they close over the edge of the stone and hold it securely in position. While setting the stone, support piece on a wooden surface with a hole for the culet of the stone to sit in so that it is set in the correct position.

5 Carefully burnish the edges of the tantalum to add a finishing touch to the pieces.

Pearls and Gem Beads

The fragile nature of pearls means that they cannot be set in the same manner as many harder gemstones, and they are often strung or adhered onto pegs. Gemstone beads are more versatile and can also be combined with wire in a large number of ways.

Traditional pearl-strung necklaces are made using silk that is knotted between each pearl to prevent them from rubbing together. Semiprecious gemstone beads are strung in the same manner but are much heavier, so a synthetic thread provides greater strength. Part-drilled pearls or gems can be secured on a short post with a suitable adhesive, often with a small cap to ensure that the hole is fully concealed. Beads may also be strung on wires and woven into complex designs, allowing color to dominate a piece.

CUP-AND-PEG SETTING FOR A BOUTON PEARL

(see page 182)   skill level 💍💍

Elegant cast white-gold caps have been used to secure the Southsea pearl drops to this pair of earrings by Lilly Hastedt. The caps conceal the top of the half-drilled hole in the pearls, which are secured in place on a twisted wire with a strong adhesive, euphemistically referred to as "jeweler's cement." Many variations of cup-and-peg settings are possible, but the design should be sympathetic to the piece as a whole so that the pearls do not look like an afterthought.

STRINGING PEARLS

(see page 184)   skill level 💍💍

The pearls that support this pendant by Peter Page have been traditionally strung on silk, and knotted between each pearl to protect them; this also means that if the silk breaks no pearls will be lost. The pendant forms the catch for this necklace—it slides into two parts, and is set with diamonds, sapphires, and pearls. The pearls used for necklaces should be well matched in terms of color and size to give the best results.

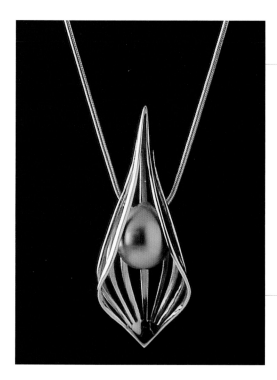

ILLUSION CAGE SETTING

(see page 182)   skill level

The Tahitian pearl in this pendant by Zoe Marie is actually suspended by the snake chain, rather than set in the cage, which creates a deceptively simple solution. Beads and pearls can be combined with metalwork in cleverly conceived ways, to add color or a contrasting surface to a piece.

WIRED BEADS

(see page 188)   skill level

Strands of rough pearl beads have been threaded onto thin gold-headed pins in this piece by Nicholas Yiannarkis. The wires are wrapped at the tops of the strands to form a loop. The beads are attached to the 18-kt gold earrings with a gold bar that was laser welded onto the backs of the forms, through the wire loops. Cold-joining methods such as wrapping or laser welding can be invaluable for combining beads with metal components.

RIVETED BEADS

(see page 188)   skill level

Antique coral beads have been combined with carved coral and cast gold flowers to create the focus of this bold two-finger ring by Ming. The coral elements have been riveted to attach them to the main body of the 18-kt yellow-gold ring. Take care when riveting beads, especially soft or fragile stones such as coral.

Working with Pearls

Applying pearls to metalwork can add a touch of classical elegance and subtle luster, whether they are contrasted with hard polished surfaces, brushed metal, or other colored gemstones.

skill level

ORGANIC GEMS
This large, sculptural ring by Ornella Iannuzzi displays coral and a Tahitian pearl held by rhodium-plated cast silver branches, evoking a feeling that the piece has grown organically into its final form.

PEARL PENDANT
An Akoya pearl nestles in the curved drop of this elegant pendant by Aleksandra Vali. The method of attachment is perfectly concealed, creating a contrast of both color and texture with the prong-set blue topaz.

Choosing stones

It is easy to source pearls to suit any budget or project. Inexpensive pearls are likely to be cultivated and dyed, but provide good scope for experimentation.

Cultivated pearls are available in many shapes, sizes, and colors. High-quality pearls with a good color and luster are expensive, but for fine jewelry these are a necessity.

Metals

When working with pearls, your choice of metal will depend largely on design or technique. Standard alloys of precious metals are best for constructed pieces, including posts for cementing pearls into position, which do need to be strong.

CUP-AND-PEG SETTING FOR A BOUTON PEARL
Twisted wires are used to secure half-drilled pearls in position. Curved caps will cover the area around the drill hole, making the mount look neater; this project combines a cup-and-peg mount with a fused wire silver pendant.

TOOLKIT
- Round silver wire
- Bouton pearl
- Drill
- File
- Sheet silver
- Dapping block and punches
- Soldering equipment
- Pickle
- Flat-nose pliers
- Jeweler's saw
- Epoxy resin
- Thin stick

1 Find a gauge of round wire that will fit snugly into the drilled hole in the pearl. The hole in the pearl can be enlarged carefully with a drill bit if necessary. File the wire to make it flat, but do not reduce the width.

2 Dap a silver disk enough to fit the base of the pearl, and drill part way into the inside center of the dome. Solder the flat wire into the drill hole with hard silver solder. Pickle, clean up, and then solder the dome into position on the final piece using easy solder.

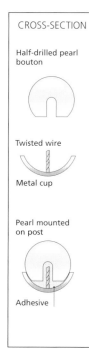

CROSS-SECTION

Half-drilled pearl
bouton

Twisted wire

Metal cup

Pearl mounted
on post

Adhesive

Construction details

In order to mount pearls on posts, it is often necessary to drill a hole, or to enlarge an existing hole to fit the post. High-speed twist drills may be used, but they must be sharp to avoid chipping the nacre around the hole. Special pearl drills are available; these clear the dust as they drill, are less liable to chip the nacre, and will help prevent the pearl from overheating. Drill large holes by working through incrementally larger drill bits until you reach the desired size. The dust created when drilling pearls is incredibly fine, so wear a mask.

Pearl clamps, used for holding pearls while drilling, allow greater accuracy, but alligator tape wrapped around the fingers will grip pearls adequately.

Wire posts for mounting pearls usually have a flat or cup-shaped base designed to cover the drilled hole and any damage caused during drilling, but these can be oversized as a design feature. The wires should be around 20-gauge (0.7–0.8 mm), flattened and twisted—this gives the adhesive more purchase. Carefully apply adhesive to the wire before inserting it into the hole; the wire should fit tightly into the pearl. Epoxy resin adhesive is the most appropriate because it allows for repositioning before it hardens. Wipe away any excess glue once the pearl is in position. Pegged settings are also suitable for mounting pearls.

TYPES OF PEARL

Round	Fully round with no drilled holes, sold individually or in matching pairs.
Three-quarters	Round with a small flat base; half-drilled or undrilled.
Bouton	Button-shaped, being domed on top and flat underneath; usually half-drilled.
Half-cut	This is a hemispherical pearl with a flat base.
Half-drilled	Drilled partway in, allowing for mounting on a post.
Fully drilled	Drilled right through to allow stringing, usually sold loosely strung.

3 Twist the flat portion of the wire with flat-nose pliers, and cut the wire to length so that the base of the pearl sits snugly against the dome. Ensure that the whole piece is cleaned up at this stage, and apply the final surface finish.

4 Mix equal parts of the resin and hardener of a suitable epoxy adhesive. Apply a small amount of the adhesive to the twisted peg, using a thin stick. The twist in the wire gives the adhesive more purchase.

5 Place the pearl on the peg and push it into place with gentle pressure until it sits down into the dome. Carefully wipe away any excess adhesive, and leave the piece to cure for the recommended length of time.

Stringing Pearls and Gemstone Beads

Pearls and gemstone beads are traditionally strung on silk, which is knotted between each pearl or bead to separate and protect them. Colored silks may be used to create contrast.

skill level

Choosing Stones

The choice of beads will most likely depend on budget, as well as the color, cut, or type of beads. The size of the drilled hole is also a consideration, but as holes can be enlarged this does not have to be a limiting factor.

The type of pearl or gem bead and its quality will affect price: it is common for low-quality gem material to be used for beads rather than cut stones, so better quality beads are likely to carry a premium.

Metals and Stringing Materials

A vast range of stringing materials is available, far too many to mention here. The most simple method of stringing uses tigertail (nylon-coated steel cable) which is secured at either end around the catch fittings using crimps and special crimping pliers. The ends of the wire are fixed into the hole of the first and last bead with adhesive. This

KNOTTED NECKLACE
The close-up detail of this necklace by Guen Palmer clearly shows the knotting between the pearls and the French wire used over the silk where it attaches to the handmade, diamond-set gold clasp.

PEARL STRINGING
This project describes the stages in producing a traditionally knotted string of pearls, using silk thread, French wire, and a knotting tool to create perfect knots between each pearl. Ensure that the silk is the correct thickness for the pearls that are being used.

TOOLKIT
- Pearls for stringing
- Silk thread
- Reamer
- Needle
- Gimp
- Clasp or metal fitting
- Knotting tool
- Superglue or clear nail polish

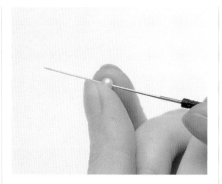

1 The first three and last three pearls of the string will have a double thickness of thread passed through them, so their holes need to be enlarged with a reamer. Check that the holes are large enough, and keep these six pearls separate from the rest.

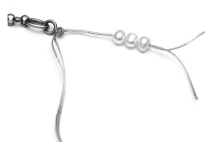

2 Cut a double-up length of silk three times the length of the finished string. Thread a wire needle onto it and move the needle up to the center of the strand. Thread the first three pearls onto the silk, down to the far end. Leave enough silk to hold in your hand, then thread on a short length of gimp, followed by the clasp or metal fitting.

technique is often used for less valuable stones, and can support heavier beads because tigertail is incredibly strong.

Traditionally, pearls and gem beads are strung on silk thread, which is knotted between each bead. This is so that they do not abrade one another, and if the string breaks, fewer beads will be lost. Silk threads are available in a range of thicknesses and colors, and you can find plenty of synthetic alternatives. To protect the silk from raveling where it is attached to the catch, use French wire (also called gimp or purl wire). This is a spiral tube of very fine wire which is very flexible and is threaded over the silk where it passes through the metal fitting; it is available in a range of gauges and is usually gold or silver plated.

Knotting tools greatly increase the speed at which a string of beads can be completed, and help keep the knots evenly sized—the device pulls the knot tight against the last bead as it closes the knot and is very easily operated. Twisted wire beading needles are available in a range of sizes and styles. Some are already attached to the silk and some have collapsible eyes, and so can be used more than once.

Many kinds of adhesive can be used to seal knots or secure stringing materials inside beads—cyanoacrylates are useful, but some brands of adhesive have a very fine applicator nozzle that is perfect for getting between beads. Clear nail polish also works well.

Any precious metal can be used for clasps—whether bought or handmade—though fine metal is not as suitable. It is important that the clasp complements the piece, whether it is a focal point or a discreet fastening.

MIXED GEMSTONE NECKLACE
Swiss granite and coral beads have been used in this necklace by Barbara Christie, creating a balance of color and contrasting textures, with the focal point of the piece being a cut and polished river stone.

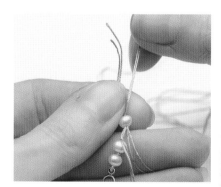

3 Thread the needle back through the pearl closest to the gimp, and pull the silk thread tight so that the gimp sits over the clasp and against the pearl. Tie a knot and pass the needle through the second pearl, then pull the silk tight and tie a knot. Pass the silk through the third pearl, but this time do not tie a knot or cut the end of the silk.

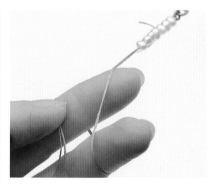

4 All the pearls, except the last three, should now be threaded onto the silk and moved to the needle end. Hold the end with the first three pearls with your right hand and wrap the silk once around your left-hand index and middle fingers.

5 Turn your left hand over and pass the pearls between the fingers and over and through the loop of silk.

Continued over

Construction Details

Before starting, ensure that the diameter of the holes in the pearls is compatible with the thickness of the silk, gimp, and beading needles you will be using. Thinner silks can be used as a double strand to increase the thickness and ensure that the beads will not slip over the knots. Make up a sample with a short length of silk and a few beads to check that the knots will be the correct size for the beads being used—this can save a lot of frustration! It takes many hours of practice to achieve speed, accuracy, and uniformity of knots, so it is always worth doing a trial run.

The silk should be cut to three times the length of the final string and stretched to remove any kinks. The holes in the first and last three beads must be enlarged so that they can take double the thread (see diagram).

Thread the first three beads onto the silk with the use of a suitably sized beading needle, followed by the gimp and then the clasp—pull them along to the far end of the silk, leaving a few inches to hold onto. Pass the needle through the third bead, taking care to ensure that the gimp pulls tightly around the jump ring or catch and neatly up against the bead. Tie a knot at this point, and pass the needle through the second bead, tying a knot after that. Pass the needle through the remaining bead, but do not tie a knot or cut the excess silk yet—use the knotting tool to make the knot after the third bead using the long end of the silk. The remaining beads (except for the last three) are then threaded onto the silk and the knotting tool is used to aid the stringing process. Slide the beads down into position one at a time before using the knotting tool to make a tight, neat knot after each one; take care to keep the sequence of beads and knots correct, as two knots together will mean starting over!

The process for finishing the string of beads is the same as for starting: thread on three beads with enlarged holes, then the gimp and the other end of the clasp. It is important to leave just enough space between the three beads for the knots when threading the needle through the last bead to tighten the gimp around the clasp fitting. Use a small amount of adhesive to seal the knots between the second and third beads, before carefully trimming away the ends of the excess silk as closely as possible.

PEARL NECKLACES
Small, off-white pearls and seed pearls have been strung on crimson silk for contrast in this pair of necklaces by Anastasia Young, with 18-kt yellow-gold clasps that have been prong and bezel set with rose-cut garnets.

6 Use the needle of the knotting tool to pick the silk loop up off your fingers. Be careful to keep the tension in the thread so that it does not tangle.

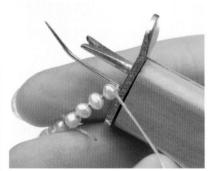

7 Pull the long end of the silk so that the pearl is tight up against the needle of the knotting tool.

8 Place the silk in the fork of the tool, and lift the knot off the needle by raising the tab at the front of the knotting tool with your right thumb. Pull the silk to keep the knot tight and flush up against the pearl. Slide the next pearl down and repeat the sequence for making a knot.

CROSS-SECTION

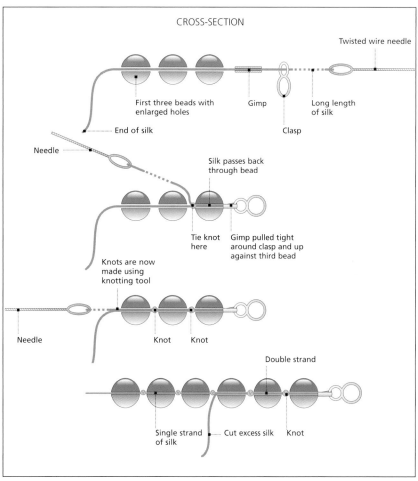

First three beads with enlarged holes

Gimp

Twisted wire needle

Long length of silk

Clasp

End of silk

Needle

Silk passes back through bead

Tie knot here

Gimp pulled tight around clasp and up against third bead

Knots are now made using knotting tool

Needle

Knot

Knot

Double strand

Single strand of silk

Cut excess silk

Knot

9 Once all the pearls have been knotted into position, thread on the last three pearls, a second piece of gimp, and the other side of the catch. Repeat the same sequence as for starting the string (Steps 1–3), making sure that the gimp is pulled tight, but leaving enough space between the last two pearls to make knots.

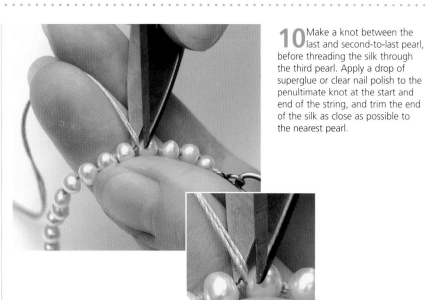

10 Make a knot between the last and second-to-last pearl, before threading the silk through the third pearl. Apply a drop of superglue or clear nail polish to the penultimate knot at the start and end of the string, and trim the end of the silk as close as possible to the nearest pearl.

Wired Beads

From simple head and eye pins to complex three-dimensional forms, wire can be used to attach pearls and gemstone beads to jewelry, adding both color and movement.

skill level

Choosing Stones

Most types of gemstone beads and pearls are suitable for this technique, but take care if you are using very valuable stones because they could be damaged by the wire through wear and tear. Similarly, very inexpensive beads may be made from more brittle gem material with fractures or faults that could cause the bead to crack. The size of the hole in the bead may also be a factor—if drilled holes are very small, then only very thin wire can be used, which could compromise the strength of the piece. Holes may be drilled larger or enlarged with a diamond reamer.

Metals

Gold, silver, platinum, and palladium are all suitable. Standard alloys of metals work best for constructed pieces, such as a framework to support beads—particularly half-hard wire as it will not be easily bent out of shape, and it is not possible to solder the wire once the beads are in position. Fine silver or gold wire is often used for wrapping beads because it is very malleable and easy to manipulate.

Construction Details

The wire forms used to support the beads and attach them to each other or larger pieces of metalwork can be very simple, such as straight wires with a hanging loop at

WIRED BEAD BROOCH
Wired beads are used to great effect in this Orchid Brooch by Sophia Mann. Two main wires running down the brooch allow the beads to be woven into position, and include ruby, sapphire, and yellow diamond cube beads.

USING HEADPINS AND EYEPINS WITH GEMSTONE BEADS

Wire for making unsoldered eyepins should be half-hard, and the thickest gauge possible for the holes in the beads so that it does not lose its shape easily. Thin-gauge fine silver wire can be used for balled headpins, and if thin enough, the end can be tucked back inside the drilled hole of the bead.

TOOLKIT

- Sterling silver wire
- Pliers
- Gemstone beads
- Fine silver wire
- Gas torch
- Jump ring
- Ring shank
- Soldering equipment

1 To make a beaded chain with eyepins—having previously calculated the length required—cut the same number of lengths of sterling silver wire as there are beads. Use the thickest gauge of wire it's possible to fit through the beads. Fold a right angle at one end of each wire using flat-nose or parallel pliers, then curl the end to form a loop using round-nose pliers.

2 Thread one bead onto each wire, and bend the protruding wire to a right angle. Use round-nose pliers to form a loop very close to the bead. The two loops can face in the same or opposing directions, as desired.

STRUCTURAL SUPPORT
Alternate links of this necklace by Chris and Joy Poupazis are set with amethyst beads held in position with balled wire. The surrounding silver protects the beads and also allows them to rotate within each frame.

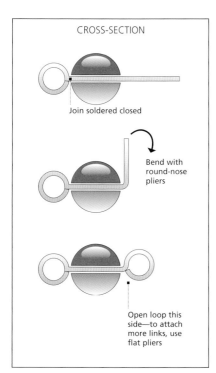

CROSS-SECTION

Join soldered closed

Bend with round-nose pliers

Open loop this side—to attach more links, use flat pliers

one or both ends, or more complex fabricated elements. Whatever the structure, use solder closures wherever possible to increase strength—if a loop at one end of a link can be soldered before the bead is put on, the structure will have greater strength. Soldered wires can be barrel polished to work-harden them before the beads are applied.

The correct use of pliers is crucial for accurate and neat wirework. Familiarize yourself with the different types of pliers and which processes they are most suited to (see page 66). Steel rods in a range of diameters are also useful—wire can be wrapped around these formers to make individual or multiple loops, and a coiled spiral of wire can be cut into jump rings.

Judging the correct length of wire for a piece can be tricky. Make up models in brass or copper wire, in the same gauge as the final piece so that you can calculate the lengths. When making repeating units, such as chain, it is always a good idea to perform each step on each component part in order to keep the elements uniform. Work out the sequence for the piece and plan ahead.

Very complex structures can be built up in this way, with the wires cross-linking through drilled holes, or around one another. Articulated forms will mean that the jewelry will be more versatile and comfortable to wear.

3 Open the loops one at a time to begin linking the chain links together—use flat-nose pliers and open the loops sideways so as not to distort the shape of the loop. Continue until all the links have been joined.

4 To make a cluster of gem beads using headpins, heat one end of a piece of narrow-gauge fine silver wire until it melts and forms a ball—no flux is required. You can then thread the beads onto the wire. Make an open loop on the protruding wire using round-nose pliers and leaving some space above the bead.

5 Thread the loop through a jump ring that has been soldered onto a ring shank, and wrap the wire around itself in the space above the bead. The coil of wire should continue right up to the top of the bead, and be cut to length if necessary. Use chain-nose pliers to tuck the end of the wire neatly in above the bead.

Jewelry designing and making usually requires a large amount of behind-the-scenes information, from knowing which suppliers to go to, to how to calculate and draw out a template for a stone mount, or convert a measurement. This reference section aims to provide a wealth of useful tables, charts, and resources. It is a good idea to keep your own notebook for information that you regularly use to form your own technical journal for projects. This will save you time and provide reference if you repeat projects.

CHAPTER *4*

Reference

Conversions

Temperatures			
°F	°C	°F	°C
32	0	1100	593
100	38	1200	649
150	66	1300	704
200	93	1400	760
250	121	1500	816
300	149	1600	871
350	177	1700	927
400	204	1800	982
450	232	1900	1038
500	260	2000	1093
550	288	2250	1232
600	216	2500	1371
650	343	2750	1510
700	371	3000	1649
800	427	3250	1788
900	482	3500	1927
1000	538	4000	2204

B&S gauge	Inches		Millimeters
	Thou.	Fractions	
-	0.787	$^{51}/_{64}$	20.0
-	0.591	$^{19}/_{32}$	15.0
1	0.394	$^{13}/_{32}$	10.0
4	0.204	$^{13}/_{64}$	5.2
6	0.162	$^{5}/_{32}$	4.1
8	0.129	$^{1}/_{8}$	3.2
10	0.102	$^{3}/_{32}$	2.6
12	0.080	$^{5}/_{64}$	2.1
14	0.064	$^{1}/_{16}$	1.6
16	0.050	–	1.3
18	0.040	$^{3}/_{64}$	1.0
20	0.032	$^{1}/_{32}$	0.8
22	0.025	–	0.6
24	0.020	–	0.5
26	0.016	$^{1}/_{64}$	0.4
28	0.013	–	0.3
30	0.010	–	0.25

Mohs' scale of hardness

1 Talc (softest)	6 Feldspar
2 Gypsum	7 Quartz
3 Calcite	8 Topaz
4 Fluorite	9 Corundum
5 Apatite	10 Diamond (hardest)

Stone	Mohs' scale value	Specific gravity
Amber	2.5	1
Amethyst	7	2.6
Aquamarine	7.5–8	2.7–2.8
Coral	3.5	2.7
Diamond	10	3.4–3.6
Emerald	7.5–8	2.75
Garnet	6.5–7.5	3.5–4.1
Jadeite	6.5–7	3.3
Lapis lazuli	5.5	2.3–3
Malachite	3.5	3.8
Moonstone	6–6.5	2.6
Opal	5–6.5	2–2.5
Pearl	2.5–4	2.7–2.8
Peridot	6.5–7	3.3
Ruby/sapphire	9	4
Topaz	8	3.5
Tourmaline	7–7.5	3–3.2
Turquoise	6	2.8
Zircon	6.5	3.9–4.7

USING RING BLANK MEASUREMENTS

Always add the thickness of the metal you are using to the length of blank required for a particular size, to ensure accurate results. When measuring a finger, use a measuring gauge that is a similar width to the ring you are making—a wide-band ring will need to be a larger size to fit over the knuckle than a thin band.

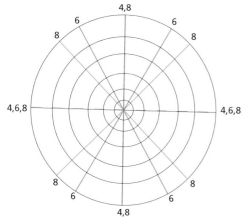

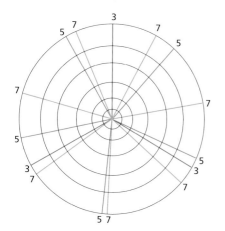

CIRCLE DIVIDER

Forms can be quickly divided up into equal parts when placed centrally on a circle divider. A polished ring will reflect the lines, making it easier to mark accurately.

Table of ring sizes

U.K.	U.S.	Europe	Ring blank length* (mm)	Ring blank length* (inches)	Inside diameter (mm)	Inside diameter (inches)
A	½	38	40.8	1.61	12.1	0.47
B	1	39	42.0	1.65	12.4	0.49
C	1½	40.5	43.2	1.70	12.8	0.50
D	2	42.5	44.5	1.75	13.2	0.52
E	2½	43	45.8	1.80	13.6	0.54
F	3	44	47.2	1.85	14.0	0.55
G	3¼	45	48.3	1.90	14.2	0.56
H	3¾	46.5	49.5	1.95	14.6	0.57
I	4¼	48	50.8	2.00	15.0	0.59
J	4¾	49	52.7	2.05	15.4	0.61
K	5¼	50	53.4	2.10	15.8	0.62
L	5¾	51.5	54.6	2.15	16.2	0.64
M	6¼	53	56.0	2.20	16.6	0.65
N	6¾	54	57.8	2.25	17.0	0.67
O	7	55.5	58.4	2.30	17.2	0.68
P	7½	56.5	59.5	2.35	17.6	0.69
Q	8	58	60.9	2.40	18.0	0.71
R	8½	59	62.3	2.45	18.4	0.72
S	9	60	63.4	2.50	18.8	0.74
T	9½	61	64.8	2.55	19.2	0.76
U	10	62.5	65.9	2.60	19.6	0.77
V	10½	64	67.4	2.65	20.0	0.79
W	11	65	68.6	2.70	20.4	0.80
X	11½	66	69.9	2.75	20.8	0.82
Y	12	68	71.2	2.80	21.2	0.83
Z	12½	69	72.4	2.85	21.6	0.85

Stone Shapes

The way in which a gemstone is cut determines its beauty, value, and the ways in which it can be mounted or set into a piece of jewelry. The crystal structure of certain gems means that specific cuts are more likely to be used, depending on their planes of fracture. Many stones are calibrated, meaning they are cut by a machine that produces very regular proportions and facets, but the range of cuts produced by this method is limited. Many more cuts exist than are described here, and vintage or antique stones in unusual cuts can be sourced.

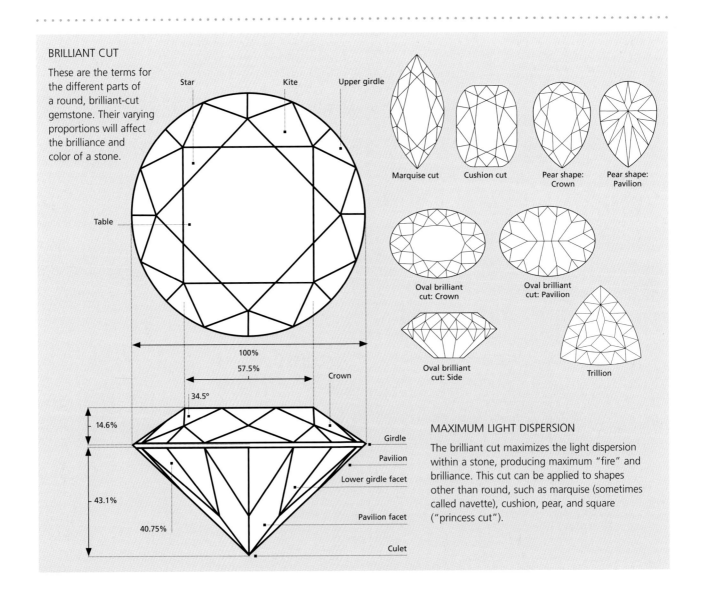

BRILLIANT CUT

These are the terms for the different parts of a round, brilliant-cut gemstone. Their varying proportions will affect the brilliance and color of a stone.

Star   Kite   Upper girdle

Table

100%

57.5%

Crown

34.5°

14.6%

Girdle

Pavilion

Lower girdle facet

43.1%

40.75%

Pavilion facet

Culet

Marquise cut   Cushion cut   Pear shape: Crown   Pear shape: Pavilion

Oval brilliant cut: Crown   Oval brilliant cut: Pavilion

Oval brilliant cut: Side   Trillion

MAXIMUM LIGHT DISPERSION

The brilliant cut maximizes the light dispersion within a stone, producing maximum "fire" and brilliance. This cut can be applied to shapes other than round, such as marquise (sometimes called navette), cushion, pear, and square ("princess cut").

STRAIGHT-SIDED CUTS

The step cut is used to show off the color of a stone, but does not produce the same sparkle as a brilliant cut. A modification of the step cut is the French cut, which is usually found on small stones with rectangular, square, and triangular shapes.

ROSE CUT

The rose cut is a historic cut; it was used as far back as the early 1600s and was still popular in Victorian jewelry. Its principal feature is the flat back, which allows it to be set like a cabochon. It can be simple, with three or six facets, or more complex with facets radiating in multiples of six.

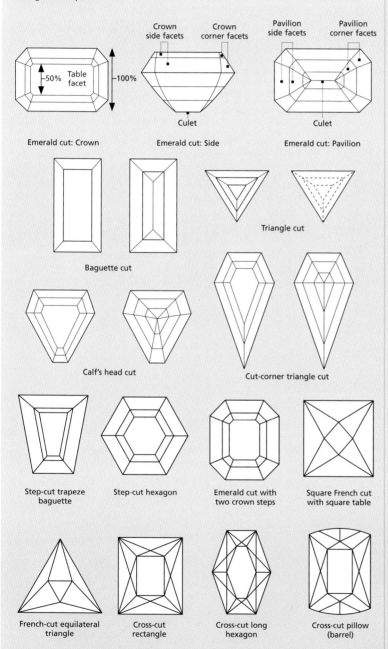

Crown side facets · Crown corner facets

Pavilion side facets · Pavilion corner facets

50% — Table facet — 100%

Culet

Culet

Emerald cut: Crown

Emerald cut: Side

Emerald cut: Pavilion

Baguette cut

Triangle cut

Calf's head cut

Cut-corner triangle cut

Step-cut trapeze baguette

Step-cut hexagon

Emerald cut with two crown steps

Square French cut with square table

French-cut equilateral triangle

Cross-cut rectangle

Cross-cut long hexagon

Cross-cut pillow (barrel)

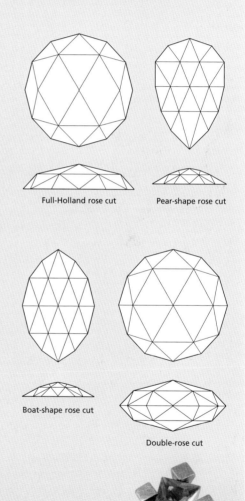

Full-Holland rose cut

Pear-shape rose cut

Boat-shape rose cut

Double-rose cut

An orange princess-cut sapphire is set in a hand-forged stainless steel prong setting, in this ring by Kara Daniel.

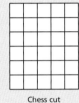

This incredibly clean Ukranian beryl was cut to leave some of its natural form intact—the rough edge makes an interesting design feature in this necklace by David Fowkes, complemented by the tube-set white and champagne diamonds.

The ring below, by Henn of London, features a stunning 20.8-ct green tourmaline. Pavé-set diamonds and green basse-taille enamel adorn the white-gold shank.

The tension-set ring below center by Natasha Heaslip features a faceted beryl in a contemporary cut.

Prongs hold a 7.36-ct uncut natural diamond in the 22-kt gold ring below right by Leo Pieroni.

FANCY CUTS

Fancy cuts, such as mirror and prism cuts, can be used to create optical effects in stones. Variations of existing cuts may be used to retain the maximum weight in irregularly shaped crystals.

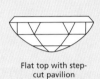

Flat top with step-cut pavilion

Buff top with brilliant-cut pavilion

Chess cut

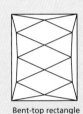

Bent-top rectangle triangle cut

Rondelle

Step-cut bead

CABOCHON CUTS

Cabochon cuts can vary in both outer girdle shape and the convex curve of the surface, which can range from a flat slab to a high-domed bullet. The base can be flat, or rounded as a double cabochon to increase color density in light-colored stones.

Low dome

High dome

Cone

Bullet

Double-beveled

Hollow/carbuncle

Double

Flat cut/slab

Buff top

Buff top (cross-vaulted)

Approximate carat weights for brilliant-cut stones

Stone (diameter in mm)	2	3	4	5	6	7	8	10
Diamond	0.03	0.10	0.25	0.50	0.75	1.25	2.00	3.50
Blue topaz	0.04	0.11	0.30	0.56	1.00	1.55	2.50	5.75
Ruby/sapphire	0.05	0.15	0.34	0.65	1.05	1.60	2.25	4.50
Garnet	0.05	0.13	0.30	0.60	1.00	1.60	2.50	5.75
Aquamarine/emerald	0.04	0.12	0.27	0.48	0.80	1.70	2.50	6.10
Quartz	0.04	0.10	0.20	0.40	0.70	1.30	1.80	3.30

Approximate carat weights for emerald-cut stones

Stone (diameter in mm)	5 x 3	6 x 4	7 x 5	8 x 6	9 x 7	10 x 8	11 x 9	12 x 10
Diamond	0.25	0.50	1.00	1.50	3.00	4.00	5.00	7.80
Blue topaz	0.40	0.65	1.25	2.40	3.40	4.00	5.75	8.00
Ruby/sapphire	0.55	0.75	1.15	1.75	2.30	2.75	4.00	6.25
Garnet	0.40	0.80	1.20	1.70	2.50	3.50	4.30	6.35
Aquamarine/emerald	0.30	0.60	0.90	1.80	2.30	3.15	4.50	5.25
Quartz	0.35	0.55	1.00	1.60	2.25	2.90	4.20	5.60

Approximate carat weights for oval stones

Stone (diameter in mm)	5 x 3	6 x 4	7 x 5	8 x 6	9 x 7	10 x 8	11 x 9	12 x 10
Diamond	0.25	0.50	0.75	1.40	2.00	3.00	4.00	5.00
Blue topaz	0.25	0.55	1.10	1.60	2.50	3.50	4.50	6.00
Ruby/sapphire	0.35	0.60	1.00	1.55	2.20	3.15	3.80	6.00
Garnet	0.25	0.55	1.00	1.40	2.10	2.80	3.75	5.00
Aquamarine/emerald	0.30	0.50	0.85	1.00	1.60	2.25	3.75	5.00
Quartz	0.25	0.45	0.85	1.25	1.75	2.40	3.20	4.50

1 metric carat = 200 mg
5 metric carats = 1 gram
4 grains = 1 metric carat
1 grain = ¼ carat = 50 mg

Birth stone

Month	Stone
January	Garnet
February	Amethyst
March	Aquamarine
April	Diamond, rock crystal
May	Emerald
June	Pearl, alexandrite
July	Ruby
August	Peridot
September	Sapphire
October	Opal, tourmaline
November	Topaz, citrine
December	Turquoise, tanzanite

Reflection Brooch by Lauren Tidd features a 22-ct pear-shaped checkerboard amethyst set in white and yellow gold.

A prong-set 17.14-ct faceted marquise-cut green tourmaline is the focal point of this ring by Henn of London.

Templates for Settings

MAKING A TAPERED BEZEL TEMPLATE

Traditionally, tapered bezels are made from sheet metal, and a template must be made in order to construct a cone that has the correct proportions for a particular stone.

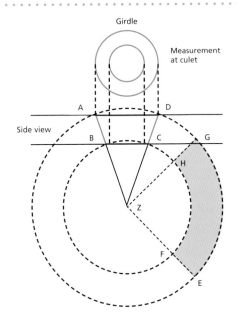

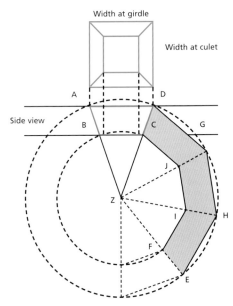

For a round stone:
1 Measure the diameter of the stone at the girdle. Use this measurement to draw AD.
2 Measure the vertical distance from the girdle to the culet, allowing extra if you are making prongs as part of the cone = AB–DC.
3 Use these measurements to draw lines, continuing AB and DC to meet at Z.
4 Draw a circle, center Z, with a radius DZ.
5 Draw a second circle, center Z, with a radius CZ.
6 Use dividers to measure the distance AD, and mark this dimension on the outer circle starting at point G. Mark the distance three and one-seventh times (π), and mark this point E.
7 Draw in line GZ.
8 Draw in line EZ.
9 Make points H and F on the inner arc.
The shape bounded by GEFH is the template for the cone. Transfer this to metal and pierce it out, then form and solder the join closed. The cone can then be trued in a bezel block—the taper of the cone will dictate whether a 17° or a 28° bezel block and punch should be used.

For straight-sided stones:
1 Measure the square stone along one side = AD.
2 Measure the height from girdle to culet (allow extra if you are making prongs or a rub-over setting) = AB and DC.
3 Extend lines AB and DC to meet at Z.
4 Draw a circle, center Z, with a radius DZ.
5 Draw a circle, center Z, with a radius CZ, and draw an arc, CF.
6 For a square stone: Measure the side of the stone (i.e. AD) with dividers and mark this measurement three times on the outer circle finishing at E.
For a rectangular stone: Work as for the square stone but measure both the long and short sides of the rectangle. The measurement AD and GH will be the long side; the measurement DG and HE will be the short sides.
The shaded area within these letters is the flat pattern that can be transferred to the metal. The lines DC, GJ, and HI are scored and bent up so that AB can be soldered to EF.

GEOMETRY FORMULAS

To find the circumference of a circle from the diameter:
Circumference = 3.142 x diameter

To find the area of a circle:
Area = 3.142 x (radius²)

To find the diameter of a circle used to make a dome:
Outside diameter of sphere minus thickness of metal x 1.43
e.g. 18 mm o. d., 0.6 thickness: 18 - 0.6 = 17.4 ; 17.4 x 1.43 = 25 mm
If less accuracy is required, add the diameter of the dome to its height to find the approximate diameter of circle needed.

Glossary

The black opal in this ring by Joanne Gowan has been set in a deep 18-kt yellow-gold bezel.

Acetone A flammable liquid solvent, used for dissolving setter's wax, stop-out varnish, and permanent marker-pen ink.

Adamantine The highest possible luster, which is displayed by a diamond.

Alloy A mixture of metals; sterling silver is an alloy of fine silver and copper.

Annealing The process of heating and then cooling metal to make it softer and thus easier to work with. The required temperature for annealing, the duration of heating, and the rate of cooling vary according to the metal used.

Arkansas stone A fine abrasive stone, used for sharpening steel tools such as gravers.

Assaying The process of determining the proportion of precious metal contained in an alloy. Most jewelry is assayed at an official Assay Office and given a hallmark that indicates the type and fineness of the precious metal.

Baguette A gemstone cut so that the shape of the top (table) is narrow and rectangular. It takes its name from the long French baguette loaf.

Base metal Nonprecious metal, such as aluminum, copper, iron, and nickel.

Beveled On a slant or inclination.

Bezel The rim of metal that is used to secure a stone in a rub-over setting.

Birefringence The difference between the highest and lowest possible refractive indices of a material.

Blanks Flat shapes cut from sheet metal.

Borax A flux commonly used when soldering jewelry. A special form of borax is produced for use by jewelers that is easier to dissolve and melt than ordinary borax.

Brilliance The reflection effect from the front and back facets of a polished stone.

Brilliant cut A round ideal cut created especially for a diamond, designed to give maximum brilliance and fire.

Burnish To polish by rubbing, usually with a polished steel tool.

Cabochon A stone that has been cut to have a domed top and a flat back.

Cameo A gemstone with a design cut in low relief.

Carat A unit of weight, now standardized as being equal to one-fifth of a gram; one carat consists of 100 "points." The weight of gemstones is usually expressed in carats.

Cat's eye effect A streak of light effect, best visible with a point light source that seems to hover just below or above the surface of a material.

Chasing The process of punching a relief design in metal from the front.

Chenier Thin metal tubing, often used for making hinges in jewelry. It can also form other parts of a piece.

Chips See pallions.

Clarity The relative amount of freedom from inclusions in a gemstone.

Cleavage A plane direction of breakage in a material. This is defined by a material's internal structure. Some materials may have cleavage, others may not. Ease of cleavage can range from very hard to easy.

Countersink The enlargement of the entry to a hole.

Culet The small facet on the base of some brilliant-cut stones.

Curing The process of liquid components turning solid—resin, for example.

Die Tool used for shaping by stamping or press forming, or a cutting tool used for making screw threads.

Dispersion The splitting of light into its component spectral colors by two non-parallel facets (see also fire).

Double refraction A visible doubling effect that can be seen through some gemstones.

Doublet A stone made of two materials joined together to give the appearance of one gemstone.

Draw plate A hardened steel plate with a series of holes of various sizes. Wire is drawn through the plate to reduce its thickness, or to change its shape. Draw plates are commonly available with round, square, or triangular holes.

Electroforming The process of forming metal objects by using an electric current to deposit the metal in a mold. The mold must be coated with a substance that conducts electricity. Electroforming is sometimes used to reproduce antique pieces; the process is also used for creating new individual pieces, and for mass production.

Electroplating The process of depositing a layer of metal on an object by means of an electric current. Jewelry made from base metal is often electroplated with silver or gold to enhance its appearance. Items made from plastic of other nonmetallic substances can be electroplated if they are first coated with a substance that conducts electricity.

Engraving The process of cutting away the surface of a substance, using a sharp steel tool called a graver. Lines are often engraved in a metal surface to form a decoration or inscription. Cameos and intaglios are made by engraving gemstones.

This white-gold ring by Lauren Elizabeth Tidd features a 7.5-ct fancy-cut citrine and a square-faceted pyrope garnet.

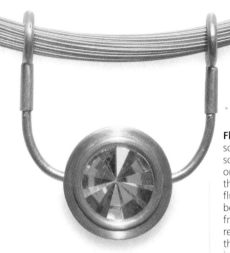

A mirror-cut yellow beryl is the centerpiece for this pendant by Roger Morris.

Etching The controlled corrosion of a surface with acid. In jewelry, the process is used to form surface decoration on metal—some parts of the surface are protected by an acid-resisting substance, while others are eaten away by the acid.

Facet A flat surface ground on a cut gemstone.

Ferrous Containing iron.

Findings Mass-produced jewelry components, such as catches, joints, and clips, which are commonly used, even on handmade jewelry. When such components are made by hand, they are sometimes called fittings.

Fire The colors visible when a faceted stone splits white light (see also dispersion).

Firestain (Firescale) The black coating that forms on silver when it is heated. The coating consists of copper oxide and is formed by the copper in the impure silver combining with oxygen in the air.

Fluorescence The emission of visible light by a material when excited by a higher-energy wavelength.

Flux A substance used in soldering to ensure that the solder flows. Any oxide present on the metal tends to prevent the solder from flowing. The flux is applied to the parts to be soldered and prevents air from reaching them. As a result, no oxide is formed, so the solder is able to flow and join the metal. Borax is the flux commonly used by jewelers.

Forging The process of hammering metal to change its shape.

Former See mandrel.

French wire A coil of very fine wire used to protect the ends of threads on which beads or pearls are strung. The ends are passed through gimps so that they cannot wear away by rubbing on the catch of the jewelry. Also called gimp.

Fretwork A sheet that has been pierced to make an ornamental pattern.

Fume cupboard A glass-fronted cupboard that has an extraction or air filtration system inside, in which chemical processes such as etching or resin are done.

Gallery (1) A wire fixed to the back of jewelry to raise the level of the metal so that there is sufficient clearance below for the stones.

Gallery (2) A mass-produced decorative metal strip, often with a series of elongated holes across the center, usually known as a closed gallery. Open galleries are made by cutting a closed gallery along the middle of the holes to produce a series of U-shapes on each piece. An open gallery can be used as a ready-made prong setting, the arms of the U-shapes forming the prongs.

Gauge A standard of measurement, such as the thickness of sheet or the diameter of wire.

Gilding metal A gold-colored alloy consisting mainly of copper and zinc. It is used to make inexpensive jewelry and is usually gilded.

Gimp See French wire.

Girdle The widest circumference of a gemstone. The girdle forms the boundary between the crown (top) and the pavilion (base).

Grain (1) A unit of weight, common to both the Troy and Avoirdupois systems. Four grains are equal to one carat, the unit of weight for precious stones and pearls.

Grain (2) A tiny ball of metal (see granulation).

Granulation The decoration or texturing of a surface by the application of tiny balls (grains) of gold or silver. Various techniques have been developed for making and attaching the grains.

Hallmark A series of impressions made in an item of gold, silver, or platinum. The hallmark is an official guarantee of the fineness of the metal.

Hardness The ability of a gemstone material to resist abrasion.

Host rock Original rock in which materials such as opal and turquoise may have been deposited.

Imitation A material that has the appearance of another but is not physically the same.

Inclusions Internal features of gemstones.

Intaglio An object with a hollowed-out design, the flat surround being the highest part. The opposite of a cameo, an intaglio is sometimes known as hollow relief. In jewelry, intaglio designs are usually made in gemstones and sometimes in metal.

Iridescence A rainbowlike play of color produced when internal structures interfere with paths of light.

Jeweler's saw A saw with a blade narrow enough to be threaded through a drilled hole so that a pattern can be cut out from sheet metal or other material.

Jig A tool used to form several items of identical shape.

Karat A measure of the fineness of gold or gold alloy. The number of karats is the number of parts by weight of pure gold in 24 parts of the metal. Pure gold is, therefore, described as 24 kt, and 14-kt gold is an alloy that contains 14 parts of pure gold in 24 parts of the alloy. In Britain, the legal standards for the fineness of gold are 9 kt, 14 kt, 18 kt, 22 kt, and 24 kt.

Loupe Magnification tool used by gemologists to view gemstones. A 10x lens is usually used.

Luster The degree of brightness reflected from the surface of a material. Luster is described based upon the appearance of a stone's surface reflection. For example, this reflection may look greasy, pearly, metallic, vitreous (glass-like), or adamantine (possessed by diamond).

Malleability The property, usually of a metal, of being easily hammered, rolled, or pressed to shape without fracturing.

Mandrel A steel shape for supporting metal while it is being hammered. Mandrels are also known as formers.

Marquise, also Navette Any gemstone with a boat-shaped girdle. The curved sides meet at a point at each end of the stone.

Melinex foil See Mylar.

Moh's scale A scale from 1 to 10 that indicates a gemstone's ability to resist scratches.

Mylar A nonreactive acetate film to which resin does not stick.

Outwork Processes or special professional services that are performed by someone else, for example engraving and electroplating.

Pallions Small pieces of solder, taken from the French word for "flake." Also known as chips.

Patina A surface finish that develops on metal or other material as a result of exposure to chemicals or handling.

Pickle A solution used during construction to clean flux and oxides from metal after heating, for example, after soldering. Pickle is also used to clean finished jewelry. Dilute sulfuric acid is often used as a pickle.

Planishing The process of hammering metal with a polished hammer to obtain an even surface.

Pleochroic A term used to describe a gemstone that appears to have two or more different colors when viewed from different directions.

Polycrystalline A material that is made up of many small crystals.

Refractive Index (RI) A value measuring the ability of a material to refract light. Most materials have a specific range of values that are helpful in identification.

Repoussé A relief design punched into thin metal from the back.

Rouge Jeweler's rouge is red iron oxide, a fine abrasive used for the final polishing stages of precious metals.

Schiller effect A sheen similar to iridescence, produced by the interference of light reflecting off internal layers within a gemstone.

Scintillation The sparkling effect of light seen across a diamond when it is moving.

Scorper A type of engraving tool—shapes include flat, square, and round.

Shank The part of a ring that passes around the finger.

Soldering The process of joining metal, using an alloy called solder. The solder is designed to melt at a temperature lower than the metal it is intended to join. The work and solder are heated until the solder melts. On cooling, it solidifies to form a firm joint. The terms easy, medium, and hard solder describe solders with progressively higher melting points. Thus, some joints can be made at a relatively low temperature without melting earlier joints made with a higher-melting-point solder.

Specific gravity The density of a material expressed as a ratio to the density of water. For example, sterling silver has a specific gravity of 10.4 and is therefore 10.4 times denser than water.

Sprue The unwanted piece of metal attached to a casting and formed by the access channel in the mold.

Stamping The process of forming a pattern in sheet metal, using a punch bearing the complete design. The pattern is formed by a single blow and the process is suitable for mass production.

Star effect Effect showing multiple intersecting streaks of light, best visible with a point light source that seems to hover just below or above the surface of a material.

Step cut A cut that consists primarily of rectangular facets in a stepped arrangement.

Soudé A gemstone containing a colored layer inserted between two colorless or near-colorless layers. The colored layer is usually near the girdle of a faceted stone, resulting in the stone appearing a single color.

Swaging The process of making metal U-shaped by hammering it into a U-shaped groove in a metal block.

Synthetic A material that is made by artificial processes but which has a natural counterpart.

Table The flat surface on top of a faceted stone. It is usually the largest facet.

Tap A tool used for cutting a screw thread inside a hole.

Tapered bezel A metal band that surrounds and supports a stone.

Tang The end of a file, graver, or tool that is fitted into a wooden handle.

Tempering The process of heating metal after hardening to reduce its brittleness.

Toughness The ability of a material to resist breakage.

Triblet A tapered steel rod on which rings are shaped.

Trillion Triangular-shaped stone with slightly rounded, bulging sides.

Bezel-set opals, sapphires, a garnet, and a pearl embellish these reticulated gold earrings by Irena Maria Varey.

Triplet A stone made of three materials joined together to give the appearance of one gemstone.

Tripoli An abrasive compound used in the first stages of polishing metal.

Vitreous A term to describe a gemstone's glassy luster.

Work-hardening The hardening of a metal caused by hammering or bending, which often makes the metal too hard to work with until it has been softened by annealing.

Graduated micro-pavé-set white diamonds retreat into the funnel of this ring by Jessica Poole.

Suppliers and Services

U.S.A.
Tools
Allcraft Tool and Supply
666 Pacific Street
Brooklyn
NY 11207
Tel. (718) 789 2800

Anchor Tool and Supply
Company
PO Box 265
Chatham, NJ
Tel. (201) 887 8888

Armstrong Tool & Supply
Company
31747 West Eight Mile Road
Livonia, MI 48152
Tel. (800) 446 9694
Fax (248) 474 2505
Web www.armstrongtool.com

Otto Frei Company
119 Third Street
Oakland
CA 94607
Tel. (800) 772 3456
Fax (800) 900 3734
Web www.ottofrei.com

Indian Jeweler's Supply Company
601 E Coal Ave
Box 1774
Gallup
NM 87305-1774
Tel. (505) 722 4451
Fax (505) 722 4172
Web www.ijsinc.com

Metalliferous
34 West 46th Street
New York
NY10036
Tel. (212) 944 0909
Fax (212) 944 0644
Web www.metalliferous.com

Myron Toback
25 West 47th Street
New York
NY 10036
Tel. (212) 398 8300
Fax (212) 869 0808
Web www.mjsa.polygon.
net/~10527

Paul Gesswein and Company, Inc.
255 Hancock Ave.
PO Box 3998
Bridgeport
CT 06605-0936
Tel. (203) 366 5400
Fax (203) 366 3953

Rio Grande
7500 Bluewater Road NW
Albuquerque
New Mexico
Tel. (800) 545 6566
Fax (800) 965 2329
Web www.riogrande.com
Also stock tools, gemstones,
and findings.

Swest Inc.
11090 N. Stemmons Freeway
PO Box 59389
Dallas
TX 75229-1389
Tel. (214) 247 7744
Fax (214) 247 3507
Web www.swestinc.com

Precious metals
David H. Fell & Company
6009 Bandini Blvd
City of Commerce
CA 90040
Tel./Fax (323) 722 6567
Web www.dhfco.com

T.B. Hagstoz and Son
709 Sansom Street
Philadelphia
PA 19106
Tel. (215) 922 1627
Fax (215) 922 7126
Web www.silversmithing.com/
hagstoz

Handy and Harman
1770 Kings Highway
Fairfield
CT 06430
Tel. (203) 259 8321
Fax (203) 259 8264
Web www.handyharmanproducts.
com

Hauser and Miller Company
10950 Lin-Valle Drive
St. Louis
MO 63123
Tel. (800) 462 7447
Fax (800) 535 3829
Web www.hauserandmiller.com

C.R. Hill Company
2734 West 11 Mile Road
Berkeley
MI 48072
Tel. (248) 543 1555
Fax (248) 543 9104
Web www.crhillcompany.com

Hoover and Strong
10700 Trade Road
Richmond
VA 23236
Fax (800) 616 9997
Web www.hooverandstrong.com

Belden Wire and Cable Company
PO Box 1327
350 NW N Street
Richmond
IN 47374
95352-3837
Tel. (765) 962 7561
Web www.belden.com

Base metals
NASCO
1524 Princeton Ave.
Modesto
CA 95352-3837
Tel. (209) 529 6957
Fax (209) 529 2239

Revere Copper Products
PO Box 300
Rome
NY 13442
Tel. (315) 338 2554
Fax (315) 338 2070
Web www.reverecopper.com

Gemstones
Boston Gems
333 Washington St # 646
Boston
MA 02108
Tel. (800) 225 2436
Web www.gemsboston.com
Wholesale gemstones.

JOSEPH P. STACHURA
435 Quaker Highway (Rt. 146A)
Uxbridge
MA 01569
Tel. (508) 278-6525
Web www.
stachurawholesalegemstones.com
Wholesale gemstones.

CANADA
Tools
Busy Bee Machine Tools
2251 Gladwin Crescent
Ottawa, ON
K1B 4K9
Tel. (613) 526 4695
or
1909 Oxford Street East
London, ON
N5V 2Z7
Tel. (519) 659 9868

Lacy and Co. Ltd
55 Queen Street East
Toronto, ON
M5C 1R6
Tel. (416) 365 1375
Fax (416) 365 9909
Web www.lacytools.com

Precious metals
Imperial Smelting & Refining
Co. Ltd.
451 Denison
Markham, ON
L3R 1B7
Tel. (905) 475 9566
Fax (905) 475 7479
Web www.imperialproducts.com

Johnson Matthey Ltd.
130 Gliddon Road
Brampton, ON
L6W 3M8
Tel. (905) 453 6120
Fax (905) 454 6869
Web www.matthey.com

UNITED KINGDOM
Tools
Buck & Ryan
Victoria House
Southampton Row
London WC1B 4AR
Tel. (020) 7430 9898
Web www.buckandryan.co.uk

H.S. Walsh
234 Beckenham Road
Beckenham
Kent BR3 4TS
Tel. (020) 8778 7061
or
44 Hatton Garden
London EC1N 8ER
Tel. (020) 7242 3711
Web www.hswalsh.com

Precious metals
Cookson Precious Metals Ltd
49 Hatton Garden
London EC1N 8YS
Tel. (0845) 100 1122
Web www.cooksongold.com
Also stock tools, gemstones,
and findings.

Rashbel UK Ltd
24–28 Hatton Wall
London EC1N 8JH
Tel. (020) 7831 5646
Web www.rashbel.com
Also stock tools, gemstones,
and findings.

Johnson Matthey Metals Ltd
40–42 Hatton Garden
London EC1N 8EE
Tel. (020) 7269 8400
Web www.matthey.com

Base metals
FAYS Metals
Unit 3, 37 Colville Road
London W3 8BL
Tel. (020) 8993 8883

Scientific Wire Company
18 Raven Road
London E18 8HW
Web http://wires.co.uk

Gemstones
A E Ward & Sons
8 Albemarle Way
London EC1V 4JB
Tel. (020) 7608 2703
Web www.aewgems.co.uk

R. Holt & Co.
98 Hatton Garden
London EC1N 8NX
Tel. (020) 7405 5284
Web www.holtsgems.com

Levy Gems
Minerva House 26–27
Hatton Garden
London EC1N 8BR
Tel. (020) 7242 4547
Web www.levygems.com

Marcia Lanyon
PO Box 370
London W6 7NJ
Tel. (020) 7602 2446
Web www.marcialanyon.co.uk

Casting
West One Castings
24 Hatton Garden
London EC1N 8BQ
Tel. (020) 7831 0542

Weston Beamor
3–8 Vyse Street
Birmingham B18 6LT
Tel. (0121) 236 3688
Web www.westonbeamor.co.uk
Full range of precious metals, also
offers complete manufacturing
service including stone setting.

Morflin Precision Castings Ltd
21 Northampton Street
Birmingham B18 6DU
Tel. (0121) 233 9361
Web www.morflin.com

BAC Castings (Clerkenwell Silver)
62 Britton Street,
London EC1M 5UY
Tel. (020) 7253 3858
Web www.clerkenwell-silver.co.uk

Electroplating and polishing
F. Sinclair Ltd
23 Hatton Garden
London EC1N 8BQ
Tel. (020) 7404 3352
Gold, silver, rhodium, and
ruthenium plating; polishing,
and sandblasting.

Cheyne & Close Ltd
Unit 3
14–16 Meredith Street
London EC1R 0AE
Tel. (020) 7837 5957
Web www.silverpolishing.co.uk
Gold, silver plating, and polishing.

Electroforming
Richard Fox
8–28 Milton Avenue
Croydon
Surrey CR0 2BP
Tel. (020) 8683 3331
Web www.foxsilver.net
Electroforming, plating,
and polishing.

CAD/CAM
Jewellery Innovations
98 Hatton Garden
London EC1N 8NX
Tel. (020) 7242 5535
Web www.jewelleryinnovation.com
Also offers complete manufacturing
service including stone setting.

CAD-MAN
Unit 8, 3rd Floor
11–13 Hatton Wall
London EC1N 8HX
Tel. (020) 7430 1317
Web www.cad-man.co.uk

Other materials
Hamar Acrylic Fabrications Ltd.
238 Bethnal Green Road
London E2 0AA
Tel. (020) 7739 2907
Web www.hamaracrylic.co.uk
Acrylic stockist, laser-cutting service.

Alec Tiranti
27 Warren Street
London W1T 5NB
Tel. (020) 7380 0808
Web www.tiranti.co.uk
Sculptors' supplies including
resin, silicone, ceramic clays,
and patination chemicals.

E-Magnets UK Ltd
Samson Works
Blagden Street
Sheffield, S2 5QT
Tel. (0114) 276 2264
Web http://e-magnetsuk.com/

AUSTRALIA
Precious metals
A & E Metal Merchants
104 Bathurst Street, 5th Floor
Sydney, NSW 2000
Tel. (029) 264 5211
Fax (029) 264 7370

Johnson Matthey (Australia) Ltd
339 Settlement Road
Thomastown, VC 3074
Tel. (039) 465 2111
Web www.matthey.com

Further Reading

Books
Jewelry Concepts and Technology
Untracht, Oppi
Doubleday, 1982

Complete Metalsmith
McCreight, Tim
Brynmorgen Press, 2004

Metals Technic: A Collection of
Techniques for Metalsmiths
McCreight, Tim (Ed.)
Brynmorgen Press, 1997

The Workbench Guide to Jewelry
Techniques
Young, Anastasia
Interweave, 2010

Jeweler's Directory of Gemstones
Crowe, Judith
Firefly, 2006

500 Gemstone Jewels
Lark Books, 2010

Diamonds
Dundek, Marijan
Noble Gems Publications, 2009

Gemstones: Properties,
Identification and Use
Thomas, Arthur
New Holland Publishers Ltd, 2009

Adorn
Mansell, Amanda
Laurence King Publishing, 2008

Jewellery in Europe and America
Turner, Ralph
Thames and Hudson, 1996

New Directions in Jewellery
Astfalck, J. and Derrez, P.
Black Dog Publishing, 2005

New Directions in Jewellery II
Clarke, Beccy
Black Dog Publishing, 2006

Ornament and Object: Canadian
Jewellery and Metal Art
Barros, A
Boston Mills Press, 1998

Jewels and Jewellery
Phillips, Clare
V & A Publications, 2008

A World of Rings: Africa, Asia,
America
Cutsem, Anne van
Skira Editore S.p.A, 2000

Traditional Jewellery of India
Untracht, Oppi
Thames and Hudson, 2008

Art Nouveau Jewellery
Becker, Vivian
Thames and Hudson, 1998

Rings: Jewelry of Power, Love
and Loyalty
Scarisbrick, Diana and
Fenton, James
Thames and Hudson, 2007

Magazines
Jewelry Artist
www.jewelryartistmagazine.com

Metalsmith (Society of North
American Goldsmiths)
www.snagmetalsmith.org

Schmuck Magazin
www.schmuckmagazin.de

Crafts
www.craftscouncil.org.uk/crafts/

Retail Jeweller
www.retail-jeweller.com

Web sites
Klimt02: International
community for art jewelry
and jewelry design
www.klimt02.net

Metalcyberspace: Information
and resources
http://www.metalcyberspace.com

The Ganoksin Project: Archive
of technical articles, and
much more
www.ganoksin.com

The Goldsmiths' Company
Directory
www.whoswhoingoldandsilver.com

Galleries, Fairs, and Organizations

Galleries

Velvet Da Vinci Gallery, San Francisco, USA
www.velvetdavinci.com

Ornamentum Gallery, Hudson, NY, USA
www.ornamentumgallery.com

Contemporary Applied Arts Gallery, London, UK
www.caa.org.uk

Lesley Craze Gallery, London, UK
www.lesleycrazegallery.co.uk

The British Museum, London, UK
www.britishmuseum.org

William and Judith Bollinger
Jewellery Gallery, Victoria and Albert Museum, London, UK
www.vam.ac.uk

The Scottish Gallery,
Edinburgh, UK
www.scottish-gallery.co.uk

Galerie Rob Koudijs, Amsterdam, Netherlands
www.galerierobkoudijs.nl

Galerie Marzee, Nijmegen, Netherlands
www.marzee.nl

Alternatives Gallery, Rome, Italy
www.alternatives.it

Oona, Berlin, Germany
www.oona-galerie.de

LOD, Stockholm, Sweden
www.lod.nu

Deux Poissons, Tokyo, Japan
www.deuxpoissons.com

e.g.etal Gallery, Melbourne, Australia
www.egetal.com.au

Fingers, Auckland, New Zealand
www.fingers.co.nz

Fairs

SOFA (Sculptural Objects & Functional Art), Chicago, New York, Santa Fe, USA
www.sofaexpo.com

International Gem & Jewelry Show Inc., USA
www.intergem.com

Collect, Saatchi Gallery, London
www.craftscouncil.org.uk/collect/

Origin, Somerset House, London
www.craftscouncil.org.uk/origin/

Goldsmith's Fair, Goldsmith's Hall, London
www.thegoldsmiths.co.uk/events/

Rock 'n' Gem Shows, UK
www.rockngem.co.uk

Inhorgenta, Munich, Germany
www.inhorgenta.com

BaselWorld, Basel, Switzerland
www.baselworld.com/

SIERRAD, Holland
www.platformsieraad.nl

Organizations

Society of North American Goldsmiths
www.snagmetalsmith.org

Gemological Institute of America
www.gia.edu

The Gemmological Association of Great Britain
www.gem-a.com

Hand Engravers Association of Great Britain
www.handengravers.co.uk

Association For Contemporary Jewellery
www.acj.org.uk

Crafts Council
www.craftscouncil.org.uk

Craft Central
www.craftcentral.org.uk

Ethical Metalsmiths
www.ethicalmetalsmiths.org

Goldsmiths' Company
www.thegoldsmiths.co.uk

Benchpeg newsletter
www.benchpeg.com

Jewellery Association of Australia Ltd
www.jaa.com.au

Society of Jewellery Historians
www.societyofjewelleryhistorians.ac.uk

Guild of Enamellers
www.guildofenamellers.org

The Institute of Professional Goldsmiths
www.ipgold.org.uk

Responsible Jewellery Council
www.responsiblejewellery.com

No Dirty Gold
www.nodirtygold.org

Fairtrade & Fairmined Gold
www.fairtrade.net/gold/

Index

Acknowledgments

Publisher acknowledgments

Alex Clamp www.alexclamp.com p.86cr; Alexandra Vali http://aleksandravali.com p.3br, p.91tr, p.182tl; Alidra Alic www.alidraalic.com p.174tr; Annie Cracknell www.anniecracknell.com p.25t, p.135tl; Annoushka www.annoushka.com p.121br, p.128tl, p.133tl, p.156tr, p.168-169t, p.204bl; Barbara Christie www.barbarachristie. com (Photo: Graham Harris) p.135tr, p.168tl, p.185cr; Ben Day www.benday.co.uk (Photo: Nigel Haynes) p.21bl, p.124tl Cameramannz p.18tc; Catherine Thomas www.ctsilver.co.uk p.89tr; Cathy Stephens www.cathystephens.co.uk p.24tl/r; Chris and Joy Poupazis www.cjpoupazis.com (Photo: Chris Poupazis and Rob Popper) p.19t (all), p.28bl/r, p.29bl/r, p.30, p.56b, p.114tl, p.126tl, p. 147t, p.189tr; Daphney Krinos www.daphnekrinos.com p.77tr; Dauvit Alexander, The Justified Sinner, http://www.justified.sinner.com p.1, p.14tr, p.109tr, p.178tl; David Fawkes www.dfjewellery.co.uk p.22, p.87tr, p.196tl; Donna Russell p.166tl; Elias Jaguar p.18tl; Elizaveta Gnatcenko evgjewellery@yahoo.com p.5tr, p.15b, p.68tr, p.99tl; Emma Baird www.emmabaird.wordpress.com p.159t; Fiona McCulloch www.fionamcculloch.co.uk (Photo: Nelson Photography) p.127tr, p.205br; Francis Levis www.franceslevis.com, (Photo: Keith Leighton), p.3t, p.96tl; Guen Palmer www.guenpalmer.com (Photo: Full Focus Photography) p.10br, p.30bl/r, p.184tl; Guntis Lauders, courtesy of Art gallery PUTTI www.putti.iv (Photo: Sergei Didyk) p.73tr; Gwyneth Harris p.16; Henn of London Ltd www.hennoflondon.co.uk p.76tl, p.125tl, p.196bl, p.197bl; Huan Pham p.171tl; Images Jewelers www.imagesjewelers. com p.28tl; Ingrid Prats p.18tr; Irena Maria Varey irena@ irenamariavarey.co.uk (Photo: Clarissa Bruce) p.75tr, p.86cl, p.201tr; Ishabel Watson p.121; J nis Vilks courtesy of Art gallery PUTTI www.putti.iv (Photo: Imants Gross) p.115t; Jayce Wong www.jaycewong.com p.21br, p.112tl, p.129t; Jeanette-Marie Lund Buer www.jeanettebuer.com (Photo: Knut Buer) p.4tr, p.87br; Jessica Poole www.jessicapoole. co.uk p.125tr, p.201br; Joanne Gowan www.joannegowan.

co.uk p.98tr, p.120tl, p.122tr, p.199tl; Julie Hiltbrunner www.silversmyth.com p.31bl; kara | daniel JEWELRY www.karadanieljewelry.com p.74tr, p.87bl, p.134br, p.195br; Karl Karter www.karlkarter.com, p.3bl, p.110tr; Katherine Agnew www.katherineagnew.co.uk p.111tl; Kelvin J Birk www.kelvinbirk.com p.135bl, p.163tl; Kika Alvarenga www.kikaalvarenga.com p.171cr, p.176tl; Ko Park www.kodesigns.ca, p.2br, p.92tl, p.105; Lauren Tidd www.lauren-elizabeth.co.uk p.107tr, p.197br, p.199br; Leo Pieroni www.pieronistudio.co.uk p.90tl, p.107br, 164tl, p.196br; Lilian Ginebra www.lilianginebra.com p.93tr; Lilly Hastedt www.lillyhastedt.com p.102tl, p.180bl; Liz Hancock www.lizhancock.com p.73tl; Liz Oliver p.10t; Lucy Sylvester www.lucysylvester.com p.155tr; Mabel Hansell www.mabelhansell.com p.160tr; Marianne Anderson www.marianneanderson.co.uk p.97tr, p.203tl; Meghan O'Rouke www.meghanorourkejewellery.com p.179tr/cr; Melissa Hunt www.melissahuntjewellery.co.uk p.167tr; Ming Lampson www.mingjewellery.com p.20t, p.104tr, p.108tl, p.120tr, p130tl, p.132tl, p.134bl, p.181br, p.302br; Natasha heaslip www.natashaheaslip.com p.120bl, p.196bc; Nicholas Yiannarakis www.nicholasyiannarakis.com p.100tl, p.157tr, p.181cr; Ornella Iannuzzi www.ornella-iannuzzi.com p.20br, p.78tl, p.154tl, p.182tr; Pat Waddington paw@pajed.co.uk p.158tl; Paul Battes, www.paulbattes.com, p.2t, p.103tl, p.131t; Paul Leathers www.alluvium.com p.5tl, p.79tl; Peter Page www.peterpage.co.uk (Photo: Nigel Wilson) p.180br; Philip Sajet www.philipsajet.com p.14, p.106cr, p.110tl; Regine Schwarzer www.regineschwarzer.com (Photo: Steve Wilson) p.107tl, p.119tl; Roger Morris www.rogermorris.eu p.23, p.200tl; Sian Huges www.sianelizabethhuges.co.uk p.87tl; Sophia Mamm www.sophiamann.com p.188tr; Tanja Ufer www.tanja-ufer.co.uk p.31t, p.88tl; Teena Ramsay t.k.ramsay@dundee.ac.uk, p.10bl; Thomas Smith www.tmjewellery.co.uk p.112tr; V&A Images p.12t/b, p.13tr; Whitney Abrams www.whitneyabramsjewelry.com p.118tl, p.135br; William Vinicombe www.williamvinicombe.com

p.172tr; Xin Ran Lu www.xinranlu.com p.175tl; Zoe Marie www.zoemarie.com (Photo: Michael Davies) p.71, p.117t, p.181tl.

Special thanks to Chris and Joy Poupazis for assistance with images.

All other images are the copyright of Quarto Publishing plc. While every effort has been made to credit contributors, Quarto would like to apologize should there have been any errors—and would be pleased to make the appropriate correction for future editions of the book.

Author acknowledgments

Gemstone consultant: Lizzie Gleave FGA, DGA.

A E Ward & Sons whose superb range of stones feature on pages 16–17 and in the Gemstone Directory, pages 30–51. For more information, check out their website: www.aewgems.co.uk

Cooksongold www.cooksongold.com

Niall Paisley for demonstrating grain, five grain, box, pavé, and micro-pavé setting.

Jack Meyer for the text and images so expertly explaining CAD/CAM, pages 80-85. www.h3-d.com

Paul Wells for helping out behind the scenes and on the photo shoots, for making the crown setting and the tantalum tab setting used in demonstrations, for being the voice of reason, and for making me more cups of tea than I probably deserved.

Vicky Forrester at Flux Studios www.fluxstudios.org

Central Saint Martins College of Art and Design

Phil WIlkins • Heather Wang • Hannah Terry • Sally Leonard • Jolan Kozak • David Valle • Scott Millar

Author's website: www.anastasiayoung.co.uk

EXPLORE MORE GEMSTONE SETTING
inspiration & techniques
WITH THESE JEWELRY-MAKING RESOURCES FROM INTERWEAVE

Jewelry Making Daily is the ultimate online community for anyone interested in creating handmade jewelry. Get tips from industry experts; download free step-by-step projects; check out video demos; discover sources for supplies, and more! Sign up at **Jewelrymakingdaily.com**

shop.jewelrymaking.com

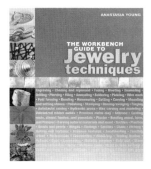

The Workbench Guide to Jewelry Techniques

Anastasia Young

ISBN 978-1-59668-169-9
$34.95